The Men Stood Like Iron

INDIANA UNIVERSITY PRESS   BLOOMINGTON & INDIANAPOLIS

The Men Stood Like Iron

How the Iron Brigade Won Its Name

Lance J. Herdegen

The paper used in this publication meets the minimum requirements of American National Standard for Information Sciences— Permanence of Paper for Printed Library Materials, ANSI Z39.48–1984.

Manufactured in the United States of America

Library of Congress Cataloging-in-Publication Data

Herdegen, Lance J.

The men stood like iron : how the Iron Brigade won its name / Lance J. Herdegen.

p.   cm.

Includes bibliographical references and index.

ISBN 0-253-33221-4 (cl : alk. paper)

1. United States. Army. Iron Brigade (1861–1865)—Name.

2. United States—History—Civil War, 1861–1865—Regimental histories.   I. Title.

E493.7.I72 1997

973.7'475—dc20   96-31095

4 5 02 01 00 99

For Shirley

IN LINE OF BATTLE, NEAR SHARPSBURG, MARYLAND
SEPTEMBER 18, 1862

My Dear Mother:—I have come safely through two more terrible engagements with the enemy, that at South Mountain and the great battle of yesterday [Antietam]. Our splendid regiment is almost destroyed. We have had nearly four hundred men killed and wounded in the battles. Seven of our officers were shot and three killed in yesterday's battle and nearly one hundred and fifty men killed and wounded. All from less than three hundred engaged. The men have stood like iron. . . .

—MAJ. RUFUS DAWES
Sixth Wisconsin Volunteers

Contents

Maps and Illustrations

Maps

Photographs

INTRODUCTION

Rufus Dawes of Juneau County put his name on a muster roll in 1861 because of his family's long tradition of service to the Republic. Edwin Brown of Fond du Lac left his wife and three children to purge the land of "the great curse of secession." John Cook of Hartford signed on "for the sake of seeing the sunny south and to be considered brave." Circus boy George Chamberlain enlisted to escape a hard life. Immigrant Werner Von Bachelle left Milwaukee seeking adventure and advancement. When they reached the great mustering place at Camp Randall at Madison all were assigned to the new Sixth Wisconsin Volunteer Infantry.

In the excitement following Bull Run in July 1861, the new regiment of 1,000 men was sent by rail to the war front at Washington, where it was placed with the Second and Seventh Wisconsin, Nineteenth Indiana Infantry, and Battery B of the Fourth U.S. Artillery. The new organization (the only all-Western brigade in Federal army gathered at Washington) was attached to the city defenses, and for a year the volunteers saw no action; officers and privates alike worried the war would be over before they could play a role.

When the fighting did come in late 1862, it was almost more than they could handle. In four battles in less than three weeks—Brawner Farm, Second Bull Run, South Mountain and Antietam—the Sixth Wisconsin and the other regiments became the famed "Iron Brigade of the West." But it was a reputation won at terrible cost. "My dear mother," Rufus Dawes wrote from Sharpsburg, Maryland, the day after Antietam, "Our splendid regiment is almost destroyed. . . ."

This is the story of how the frontier boys were forged into the soldiers who "stood like iron." Although only part of a larger record, their chronicles provide insight into such figures as George McClellan, John Pope, and Abraham Lincoln and the larger issues of slavery, the conduct of the war, and the beginnings of modern American military tradition.

So often the view from the ranks never makes the history books. It is, after all, one reality for a general to proclaim a shortage of supplies and quite another for a hungry soldier boy chasing a stray cow to get a canteen of milk.

Old Town of Granville
Milwaukee

The Men Stood Like Iron

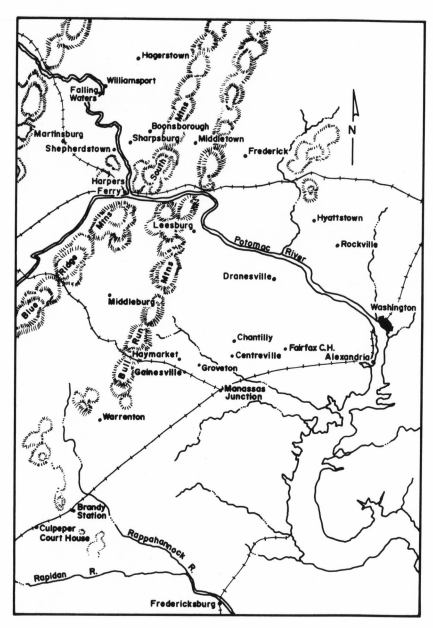

Overview of the Maryland Campaign of 1862. Drawn by John Heiser.
Used by permission.

1.
Gettysburg: July 4, 1863

For three days it had been all shouting soldiers, cannon fire, and long rips of musketry. Then the terrible clamor finally gave way to uneasy quiet and a long and somber night. In the faint light just before dawn, a drenching rain woke Lt. Col. Rufus Dawes of the Sixth Wisconsin Volunteer Infantry from what he called the "troubled and dreamy sleep of the battlefield." It was Independence Day, 1863—his 25th birthday—and, still half awake, he wondered if the great battle would be resumed. In his pocket was a letter, and during the night, as he waited behind the makeshift breastworks of his regiment, he had added: "I am entirely safe through the first three of these terrible days of this bloody struggle. The fighting was the most desperate I ever saw. O, Mary, it is sad to look now at our shattered band of devoted men. Tell mother I am safe. . . ."

The Sixth Wisconsin of the celebrated "Iron Brigade of the West" had been involved in the fighting around Gettysburg, Pennsylvania, from the very first. Of the regiment's 340 soldiers marched to Pennsylvania, fewer than 200 were still in ranks, many of those banged up or wounded.[1] But no regiment in the army had done better service. On the morning of July 1, the Sixth Wisconsin had come up on the run from south of Gettysburg to be thrown into the very opening of the infantry fighting northwest of the town. As the other four regiments of the Iron Brigade drove into a woods to repulse an advancing Confederate line, the Sixth Wisconsin (at first held back as a reserve with 100 men of the brigade guard) was ordered to the north ("Go like hell!" a staff officer had shouted at Dawes) to an unfinished railroad cut where a Federal brigade of Pennsylvanians and New Yorkers was giving way. The Wisconsin men made a quick charge into the flank of the advancing Confederate brigade and there was a sharp, brief, and bloody fight before the

Johnnies fled, leaving behind 232 prisoners and the red battle flag of the Second Mississippi.[2]

The early Union success, however, was short-lived. That afternoon the Confederates came again in thick lines and with loud yells. In the smoke, heat, and noise, the Federal line came apart with a suddenness bordering on panic, and soon the whole position was gone, most of the soldiers running for the town just ahead of the pursuing Confederates. In the press and confusion only a few units (the shattered regiments of the Iron Brigade among them) kept together, moving through the streets of Gettysburg until, finally, they came to a Federal line being put together near the tombstones of a cemetery on a low hill south of town. The Confederate pursuit sputtered to a halt in the deepening darkness as newly arriving Union regiments tramped in to take places along the growing Federal line. The delaying fight of the Iron Brigade and other units, as well as the hesitation of the enemy generals to press their advantage, proved decisive, and what some regarded as the bright Confederate opportunity of afternoon faded with the sun.

The Federal cost had been frightful. Dawes was shaken to discover he was one of four field officers in his brigade to escape uninjured.[3] In his own unit sergeants and corporals were in charge of broken companies; two company commanders were shot dead and six others wounded. Dozens of Wisconsin men had been killed outright and scores more injured or missing. The other regiments were in even worse shape. In the Second Wisconsin Infantry, oldest in service, the toll was three of four; the Seventh Wisconsin, one of every two; the Nineteenth Indiana, almost three of four. The largest and newest regiment—the Twenty-fourth Michigan—lost 399 of 496 men, finally winning the long with-held respect of the tough veterans of their brigade.[4] The losses in the Michigan unit were the highest of any Federal regiment in the three days of Gettysburg.[5] Indeed, the celebrated "Iron Brigade of the West" had been shot to pieces. Within a few hours, of 1,883 men taken into the battle, only 671 were still in ranks.[6]

The Union position south of Gettysburg proved the key to the Federal victory. For the next two days the brigades of the Confederate Army of Northern Virginia hammered the Federal lines in an unsuccessful attempt to dislodge the Union soldiers. In the Union breastworks on Culp's Hill, the soldiers of the Iron Brigade escaped most of the heavy fighting of July 2 and 3, although at one point the Sixth Wisconsin was rushed to the far right (the men stumbling in the dark) to resist an attack. "This remarkable encounter did not last a minute," said Dawes. "We lost two men, killed, both burned with the powder of the guns fired at them. The darkness and the suddenness of our arrival caused the enemy to fire wildly."

The next day, during the great cannonade before a massed Confederate assault on the center of the Union line, the men of the Iron Brigade hugged the ground and were spectators to the most fabled charge in American military history. The "air seemed full of missiles fired by the enemy," Dawes said, but "no man was touched, and we were devotedly thankful that such immunity was granted us."[7]

The division commander, Gen. James Wadsworth, and his staff were sitting nearby "at a cracker-box table" when the first Confederate projectiles arrived. A "dozen shells burst at once in our vicinity, covering our dinner with dirt," said John Kress of Wadsworth's staff. The old general and his officers moved a few yards to a place where they "had a fine view of the whole field of battle." They could see, Kress said, "the lines over a mile long of gray coats forming on the opposite ridge, saw them move across the valley and the low ground under the terrible fire of our artillery, posted as thickly along our lines as the ground permitted, blowing great gaps in their ranks." It was an irresistible sight: "On they came, banners waving in the battle smoke, cannon roaring, men shouting, horses neighing, small arms crashing in volleys! Still they come on . . . nothing stops them. . . . They almost reach our main line of battle with a fairly well-filled line of their own, as it seemed from our location."

Finally, Wadsworth, whose two small brigades were all but wrecked on July 1, could "keep quiet no longer" and he sent Kress off at the gallop to Army Commander George Gordon Meade to "ask him if he did not want our division." The aide found the general "close in rear of our main line where the enemy had but a moment before pierced it, and a large body of the brave fellows who had charged so recklessly, were just surrendering by individuals and detachments." Meade received the offer from Wadsworth "with evident pleasure," but said, "Tell the general I am much obliged for this tender of service, but we are all right and do not need his troops here."[8] Thereby, the Iron Brigade, which fought in the very opening of Gettysburg, missed a role in the final climax.

With the lull the next day, Saturday, July 4, parties of soldiers began moving over the fields and into woods searching for missing friends and comrades. One Badger wrote in his diary: "There was no firing today. I was out on the battlefield and there they layed in piles. One man got $30.60 and a watch out of a man's pocket."[9] The stench, another wrote home, "was so strong that it would drive a dog out of the tanyard," and third grumbled: "It was the poorest 4th of July that I ever saw for we had nothing to eat of any account until night and it was not half enough."[10]

In the retreat, the Western men left their dead and wounded to the Confederates and now, the immediate danger over, they were troubled. As soldiers from far away, they had been singled out as backwoods rustics in an army of Easterners. Early on they learned to rely on each other, and those left behind were classmates, relatives, and neighbors—the very boys they had grown up with in farming communities and small towns hundreds of miles from Gettysburg. "Our dead lay unburied and beyond our sight or reach," said Dawes. "Our wounded were in the hands of the enemy. Our bravest and best were numbered with them."[11]

At 8 o'clock the morning mist turned into a "constant rain" that made the ground "very muddy."[12] Behind his regiment's low breastworks of branches, stones, and dirt, Rufus Dawes was about used up. Steady and serious, he was one of the best volunteer officers produced by the war, although other soldiers did less and got more fame.[13] His horse shot from under him, on foot and waving his sword, he had led the Sixth Wisconsin in the charge on the railroad cut, shouting, "Align on the colors! Align on the colors!" The successful and sudden attack restored the line and set up the ultimate Union victory at Gettysburg, but Dawes's role was always overshadowed by the widely circulated claim of New Yorkers that an officer of the Fourteenth Brooklyn had ordered the charge.

By midmorning it was apparent there would be no resumption of the battle. But to Dawes and the weary soldiers of both sides it seemed little had been resolved despite the thousands of deaths. The three days of fighting had not produced the stunning victory needed to win recognition for Robert E. Lee's Confederacy, and the Federal Army of the Potomac—itself battered and disorganized—had been unable to respond with the decisive blow.

One of the Sixth Wisconsin men moving on the quiet battlefield was Sgt. Jerome Watrous, assigned to the ordnance wagons of Wadsworth's First Division. He found the "fields covered with unburied dead; hospitals, homes, sheds and barns were crowded with bleeding, dying men."[14] In the stream of Union wounded leaving the makeshift hospitals were a number of Wisconsin men. Pvt. James Sullivan, three days a prisoner in Gettysburg after being wounded, found the Sixth Wisconsin "about the size of a decent company supporting a battery in the center of the horseshoe in which our line was formed." His own Company K was down to "seven or eight men" with a sergeant in command; it had marched to Gettysburg with 34.[15] Another Wisconsin soldier brought in a bouquet of flowers (the bright petals strangely out of place on the grim hill), and Dawes took special care to note in his war memoir 25 years later that the flowers were "with the compliments of Miss Sallie Paxton. The lady had seen our charge upon the railroad cut."

At 6 P.M., Dawes added to his letter. "What a solemn birthday," he wrote. "My little band, now only two hundred men, have all been out burying the bloody corpses of friend and foe. No fighting to-day. Both armies need rest from the exhaustion of the desperate struggle. My boys until just now have had nothing to eat since yesterday morning. No regiment in this army or in another army in the world did better service than ours."

The letter was addressed to Mary Beman Gates of Marietta, Ohio, and Dawes always insisted her initials stood for "My Best Girl." The two had met the year before at her home, and the introduction had culminated in a surprisingly heated discussion on George McClellan, who proved a failure as a general but enjoyed the support of many of the young officers of the Army of the Potomac. Happily, those differences, and indeed all others (including a hometown suitor), were resolved. Dawes wrote later: "She was twenty years of age and of her charming qualities of mind and person it is not for my partial pen to write."[16]

From the very beginning, the romance was touched by the war. If the letters and all too short visits seemed directed by an urgency, it was because of the uncertainty of those days. The parents of the young lady seemed to understand and approve. With his record of service, prominent ancestry, and promising prospects, Dawes was welcomed by the parents of Mary Beman Gates with smiles, and she was acceptable to the Dawes family as well.

Mary Gates had attended schools in Marietta until, at age 18, she was sent to the Female Seminary at Ipswich, Massachusetts. Photographs of the time show a pretty woman with dark hair parted and bunched in the fashion of the day. Her eyes look confidently into the camera, and a close observer would see a friendly, if independent, glint. Her intelligence and outspoken manner (her father, an old newspaper man, admired and encouraged a bright mind) were attractive, and the tall and slight Dawes, always a bit stiff and proper, was beguiled from the very first. His attention was returned, and soon Mary Beman Gates found herself caught up in the war. A daughter said later that her mother

*Mary Beman Gates. From
the Collection of the
Author.*

"could seldom bring herself to speak of those months when she waited and watched for news from the front."[17]

The story behind the remark occurred during the Chancellorsville campaign in May 1863. Mary Gates had received two letters from the young officer and, going to the post office, found a third. No suspicion of harm was aroused as the letter was plainly in Dawes's own hand, but the first sentences chilled the young woman: "We are advancing upon the enemy. I doubt not that we must have a bloody battle. I leave this package where I have perfect confidence it will be sent to you in case I am killed, and only in that event." The scenes that ensued, Dawes wrote, "are not the business of the public, and will not be described." In the fear and tears and confusion, there was one comfort—Mother Dawes told the young woman to "take Rufus' word for anything but the fact that he was killed."

Four days of "painful apprehension" were relieved with a letter to Dawes's sister from Dr. A. W. Preston: "Your brother, Lieutenant Colonel Dawes of the sixth Wisconsin Volunteers, is alive and well." The doctor explained Dawes left him a letter to be sent "in case he should fall in the then coming engagement,—and although he came out safe, and is now in good health, yet I have either lost the letter with some other papers or sent it . . . by accident when mailing other letters for the North." So it came to be that Mary Beman Gates, in the quiet of her home, followed "with mental anguish the varying fortunes" of an officer at the front.[18]

As Dawes spent a grim Fourth of July at Gettysburg, Mary Gates was writing her own letter: "Your birthday, and I have been all the time anticipating so much pleasure in writing to you to-day, but it is only tonight that I have felt that I could write at all. It has seemed utterly impossible for me to write to you, not knowing you were where my letters could ever reach you or my prayers ever available to you. . . . When will they ever let you rest? From the papers tonight, I conclude you came safely through Wednesday (July 1) but your corps commander killed and your brigade commander wounded. I shall watch, oh so anxiously, for tidings this week, praying that God in His mercy may spare you."

Three days later, she wrote again: "I am beginning to feel as if I could write to you again, not quite sure you are safe yet but taking heart from the fact that we have had no bad news and we have the list of killed and wounded in the sixth Wisconsin up to Thursday evening. . . . If you are only safe how we shall rejoice! Of all times to think that you should have commanded the regiment in this great victory. . . . There has been greater rejoicing over your victory in Pennsylvania than I have ever known. . . . I do not know how as a Nation we are going to bear our success, but I know as an individual I can't bear much more of any thing."[19]

In six months, Rufus Dawes and Mary Beman Gates would be married, a union that proved long and happy, but her patience and kind manner were severely tested until August 1864, when her new husband left the Army of the Potomac for good and came home.

On the battlefield of Gettysburg, July 4, 1863, was "chiefly a day of gloom," said one Wisconsin man. "Nearly every survivor had lost from one to a dozen of his company comrades. It was a day like a funeral, a quiet day, save the labor called for in burying the dead and caring for the wounded." It was about sunset, he said, when the army commander "ordered all of the bands to move up close to the men who had fought and won one of the greatest victories that any army had ever won and play the patriotic airs. At first the music had but little effect upon the victorious army, but when the bands came to 'America' and the 'Star-spangled Banner' hearts were touched; men were thrilled and instead of sitting and looking at the ground and mourning for the loss of comrades, they stood up and came to attention and by and by a cheer started. It was taken up and went along the five mile line of battle and was repeated several times, and the old army had come to itself again and the next day was ready to start in pursuit of Gen. Lee and his brave army in gray."[20]

2.
Marching Day and Night

The next day, Sunday, July 5, 1863, the small regiments of the Iron Brigade moved from their earthworks on Culp's Hill to nearby Cemetery Ridge, where the great Confederate charge failed two days earlier. The scarred and shell-ripped ground was strewn with broken and discarded accouterments, wrecked artillery caissons, dead horses, and mounds of fresh dirt marking the graves of Union dead. Here and there, details of grim soldiers pulled dead Confederates into piles for mass burials. Among all this, under the gray skies, moved small groups of civilians on foot or in wagons and buggies, some curious, others red-eyed and grieving—one or two carrying shovels to open the fresh graves in a somber search for missing sons, husbands, and loved ones. "There is an unusual stillness everywhere," one Badger wrote in his diary.[1]

It was a dreadful place. The weary soldiers waited a time and, no new orders forthcoming, put up what small tents they had and rested through a "rainy night."[2] Around the cook fires, the talk was the Confederate army was withdrawing, but there was uncertainty whether the rebels were making a run for the Potomac River and safety. As Gen. George Gordon Meade organized his pursuit, he seemed to find more obstacles than opportunities. Meade, a steady and capable officer, had been thrust into command of a scattered army less than a week before Gettysburg and somehow had avoided disaster; he was not about to allow haste to lose what he had gained. If Lee's army was hurt and bleeding, the long march to Gettysburg and the three days of fighting had left the Federal soldiers exhausted and disorganized as well. The casualties in officer ranks alone were disabling, with regimental, brigade, and division command structures tangled. Steady rains had turned all roads but major turnpikes to mud, and also not at hand were stocks of rations, ammunition, and shoes.

By the second day after the fighting, there were reports Lee appeared to be returning to Virginia, but at army headquarters there was hesitancy as officers began preparations to follow the strung-out Confederate columns and prevent their escape. The general had fresh brigades at hand (soldiers in the Sixth Corps, for example, had hardly pulled a trigger in the three days of fighting), but Meade was careful committing his regiments. To Washington he reported that he was having "great difficulty in getting reliable information" but believed "the enemy is retreating, very much crippled and hampered with his trains."

Finally, "very early" the next day, the Army of the Potomac took to the road amid delays and frantic orders for haste as Meade tried to cover Washington and catch the rear guard of the Confederate army. It was raining again, and to one of the tired soldiers of the Twenty-fourth Michigan the "very heavens seemed to weep at the dreadful carnage just past."[3] The brigade camped that night near Emmitsburg, Maryland, with the men short of coffee and rations and many without shelter halves or blankets. "The experience of the past few days seems more like a horrible dream than the reality," Rufus Dawes wrote home. "May God save me and my men from any more such trials. Our bravest and best are cold in the ground or suffering on beds of anguish. . . ."[4]

By nightfall July 7, the brigade was at Bellville, where the column halted. Pvt. George Fairfield of the Sixth Wisconsin wrote in his diary: "It rained hard all night." The next day (with the telegraph lines from Washington urging pursuit), the Western regiments (marching in knee-deep mud in places) moved through Middletown, Maryland, to the west slope of South Mountain, where they bivouacked. The soldiers, without orders, piled "up rails as a defense," Fairfield recorded. "We lay still all day and never was a day of rest more welcome." There was good news as well—word had reached the column that the Confederate stronghold at Vicksburg, Mississippi, had finally fallen. But if Vicksburg was gobbled and a great success, Meade and his brigades were still on the march and Lee's army in flight. The general telegraphed Washington his army was "assembling slowly" and rain "made all roads but pikes almost impassable. Artillery and wagons are stalled. It will take time to collect them together."[5]

Rufus Dawes left a brighter picture. "Our pursuit of the retreating enemy has been rapid. We have marched night and day and we have beaten the rebel army. At last the Army of the Potomac has done what, well-handled, it might have done long ago, out-marched, outmaneuvered and defeated the great rebel army of General Lee," he wrote July 9 from Boonsborough, Maryland. "Our men have toiled and suffered as never before. Almost half of our men have marched barefooted for a week. Such energy as is now exhibited would have crushed the rebellion long ago. . . . We have had severe rains since the battle. I have not slept in a dry blanket or had on dry clothing since crossing the Potomac before the battle. If we can end this war right here, I will cheerfully abide the terrible risk of another battle."[6]

Later that day, in a postscript from South Mountain, he wrote: "We are again near the rebel army and unless they escape over the river, we may expect a battle. . . . Our army is worn out with toil and suffering, and looks hopefully for a season of rest after the enemy is driven from our soil. General Meade has shown himself equal to the emergency." There was one sad observation—the Second Wisconsin, oldest regiment in the brigade, "can not muster fifty muskets" but "this little representative remnant has been with the advance since the battle, and will probably open the next fight as it did the last."[7]

Finally, Sunday, July 12, a week after leaving Gettysburg, the Union columns caught Lee's retreating army at a Potomac crossing near Williamsport, Maryland. For a time it appeared the army might have its chance at trapping Lee against a river flooded by recent rains. But the Confederates threw up breastworks and reacted aggressively to Federal skirmishers trying to ascertain the strength and depth of the defensive line. The hours passed without serious fighting, the Union commands shifted here and there for one more final push (Meade and his generals worried their victory might be lost by an ill-planned offensive thrust), and soon the daylight was gone. In his diary a Wisconsin man wrote, "Rebels are retreating; we followed them almost to Williamsport, but we arrived too late. In a barn we found a Negro branded with hot irons because he refused to flee with the retreating rebels." Dawes wrote home: "We are again confronting the rebel army which is strongly entrenched in position near the Potomac river and another deadly struggle seems certain. I can not write more than that. I am to-night alive and well."[8]

In the end it all came to nothing, and one of the great Union opportunities of the war passed. That day, while the Sixth Wisconsin and the brigade lay in line of battle ("quietly roasting in the hot sun," Dawes said), the Potomac River fell and Lee's columns quickly were across fords and a hammered-together pontoon bridge to safety. On July 14, Meade telegraphed Washington the Confederates had escaped, and President Lincoln, in bitter disappointment, told a secretary, "We had them within our grasp. We had only to stretch forth our hands and they were ours."[9]

In reality, it was not that simple, and in the celebration over the victories at Gettysburg and Vicksburg, there was sour criticism of Meade for allowing Lee to escape. But it was easy for a citizen far from the action, sitting in a soft chair after a good dinner, or even a concerned president in Washington, to proclaim Meade and his soldiers should have done this or that and Lee's army would have been wrecked. Certainly Dawes, who with his regiment waited all day to attack the strong Confederate works, gave no indication he was dissatisfied with what he called Meade's "proper caution."

In a letter July 14 he told of the army's condition: "We may now reasonably hope for rest. The incessant and toilsome marching from Fredericksburgh to Gettysburg, the terrible battle, and the hurried pursuit of the enemy to this point has been the most trying campaign of this army. Our men have become ragged and shoeless, thousands have marched for days barefooted over the flinty turnpikes. The army has shown a willingness and alacrity under its toils, sufferings and privations, that entitle it to the gratitude of the Nation and I think for once it will receive it." A week later, after examining the rebel breastworks and finding them "strong and well-constructed," Dawes wrote: "I think General Meade would have certainly failed to carry them by direct assault. Both flanks of the works were on the Potomac river. We had no other alternative than direct assault. I take no stock in the stuff printed in the newspapers about demoralization of the rebel army after Gettysburg. They were worn out and tired as we were, but their cartridge boxes had plenty of ammunition, and they would have quietly lain in their rifle pits and shot us down with the same coolness and desperation they showed at Gettysburg."[10]

One of the Federal prisoners with the rebel column was Robert Beecham of Second Wisconsin. He wrote three decades later of the curious admiration of many Union soldiers for Robert E. Lee. The "superb Confederate chieftain," he said, was pointed out to him as he marched in a column of prisoners. "His long, grizzled beard was neatly arranged; his clothing was clean and faultless; his horse had been groomed and saddled with care; there was nothing about his personal appearance to indicate haste, uneasiness or even weariness; he bestrode his steed apparently cool and confident, not as one who had suffered defeat, but rather as a conqueror. Then I looked from him to his shattered battalions, and read the evidence of his terrible conflict and humiliating defeat, and it was plain to see that Lee himself must have full recognized the fact that the glorious dream of his ambition could never be realized. . . . Lee was the only man of that defeated army, so far as I saw it on the retreat from Gettysburg, who did not reveal the marks of defeat; but it is fair to presume that beneath this outward show of pride and unyielding courage there was an ambitious heart that was very sore."

There was a bitter addition: "We [the prisoners] reached the Potomac near Williamsport. The river was booming high, and for lack of pontoon facilities Lee was unable to cross over for several days. If Gen. Meade really intended to recapture the prisoners, here was a God-given opportunity; but, alas! it was not improved. If a single gun was fired by Meade's army it was not within my hearing. The prisoners were ferried across the river in pontoon boats during the forenoon of July 10 . . . and we were pushed forward toward our destination."[11]

Whatever the might-have-beens, Iron Brigade veterans came to believe Gettysburg was a turning point, and they were always proud of what they had accomplished. The Pennsylvania fighting, they felt, summed up their soldier service to the Union and, somehow, linked them to the myth and reality of the American story. If they were at a loss how to put that into words, they were convinced in some fundamental way that the war changed at Gettysburg and that the victory forged in noise and death finally vindicated the hard-luck Army of the Potomac. Within days of the battle a Wisconsin private wrote home: "I think the backbone of the rebellion is broken, or soon will be. They have played their hand long enough."[12]

The Wisconsin men never overlooked the price for the Pennsylvania victory. Each July, Jerome Watrous wrote, trying to explain it 30 years later, the "Gettysburg anniversaries come with an almost boundless grist of memories; and they are not such memories as make us gleeful; not such as set us to cheering; not such as smooth wrinkles and add greater freedom to our heart beats."[13]

In many ways Gettysburg was the last grand battle for the "Boys of '61," those volunteers who flocked to the flag with the firing on Fort Sumter. The war was changing, and later it would become clear that the time of stand-up battle lines had passed. The long march they had started in 1861, the soldiers were beginning to understand, had taken a sharp turn at a small town in Pennsylvania. But if there was now a glimmer of hope with Gettysburg and Vicksburg, the road ahead was still unsure, and a soldier just had to consider the faces missing from his campfire as rebel bullets claimed the bravest and sickness, injury, and fatigue took others.

There were other matters being noted in the letters and diaries—the throwing up of makeshift fortifications. The fighting at Gettysburg marked the first time the Westerners fought from behind breastworks, and Dawes, in writing of waiting "to charge on the enemy's entrenchments" at Williamsport, noted it was "no pleasant prospect to one who saw the awfully murderous repulse of the rebel charging columns from Gettysburg." After the Pennsylvania fighting, the Wisconsin, Indiana, and Michigan men—without orders, no matter how wearying the march—would gather logs and brush and pile up ground using shovels, canteen halves, tin plates, bayonets, even their hands. The action marked a change, and the protective shelters were both emotional and practicable, the survivors instinctively understanding that by conserving themselves their small regiments might continue to exist.

The other factor was a technical innovation—the new rifle-musket which had become standard in both armies. Rifles had long been used in war, but they were slow to load and the basic infantry arm until the mid–19th century was the muzzle-loading smoothbore musket. The smoothbore was easy to load, but its range was limited. The new rifle-musket had grooves in the barrel to spin and stabilize a hollow-based bullet the soldiers called the "minnie-ball" (after the French officer who designed it); that increased accuracy and velocity.

Accepted tactics of the day, however, were based on massed formations that could deliver dense swarms of bullets. The training was designed to bring soldiers quickly and in good order to a place where they could fire to best advantage. The regiments fought with companies abreast, forming a long, double line of men. An organization that was broken or disorganized was unable to deliver fire effectively, and, as a result, the regiments were drilled over and over again and there was much organizational pride in being able to fire a crisp volley—that is, the whole company, two companies or regiment delivering massed fire at the same instant. It was all based on the accepted theory that a regiment was able to advance to within 100 yards of an enemy position without taking significant casualties (given the limited range of smoothbores), then make a quick dash to close with bayonets.

The backwoods boys of the Western regiments understood the value of hitting a mark, but they were exceptions, and in the armies of both sides the training emphasized drill, quick-loading, bayonet training, and not aimed fire. While the new rifle-musket made much of such training obsolete, it would be easy to overstate the importance of improved accuracy and point to it as the reason for the terrible casualty rates of 1861–65. The technology did not increase the rate of fire by individual soldiers (about two to three shots per minute) and, in fact, there was a drawback. If a soldier under ideal conditions was able to hit a man-sized target at 500 yards, the lobbing arc of the minnie-ball (about 12 feet above the point of aim at midrange) made it easy to over- or undershoot a target at the longer distances. Even clear-eyed frontier boys would find it difficult to consistently strike a moving line of infantry at distances of more than 300 yards.

The tragic significance of the rifle-musket came at ranges under 200 yards—it was here the massed fire knocked apart battle lines with brutal efficiency. The point-blank killing range became 200 yards (not 50 or 75) and all the previous experience was based on the shorter distances of the smoothbores. This was especially critical making an assault on earthworks where the defenders could simply shoot advancing soldiers at longer distances while taking limited casualties. It also meant a smaller number of soldiers could hold an entrenched position against a larger force (an advantage Lee would use in the coming months), as had been shown in the failed massed Federal attacks at Fredericksburg. Certainly the men of the Western brigade, who fought behind breastworks on Culp's Hill and who watched the collapse of Longstreet's massed assault at Gettysburg, recognized the advantage.

But the most disturbing topic of campfire discussion in the Western camps those days was what would become of the old Iron Brigade. In 1861 the four regiments brought 4,000 men to Washington. The Twenty-fourth Michigan added 1,000 more a year later, but now less than 700 of the 5,000 remained. A soldier only had to look around his own company to see the regiments were used up. "It is awful to a soldier in this kind of way, only five or six men to a Company," a Second Wisconsin man wrote home, "and were we N.Y. troops, we would be taken home, or at least relieved from the *front*. But we have no friends at home to speak for us, and as our Generals know very well that the Wis. boys will fight and not run, they just shove them ahead like a lot of cattle going to the slaughter. Well, it will take but one more shove to the Second, and then the 'jig is up.' Then, some man who *saw* us fight will be promoted to Brigadier General as a reward for our gallantry."[14]

So there was discussion of the uncertain weeks ahead, memories of those left behind, and grim recognition of the cost of their hard service. The road on which the men of the Sixth Wisconsin had started so long ago in 1861 had not been anything at all as they had expected.

3.
Greenhorn Patriots

He was born Independence Day, 1838, in Morgan County, Ohio, the fifth child and second son of Henry Dawes and Sarah Cutler Dawes. The event was greeted with high expectations by relatives, friends, and neighbors. The families of the mother and father, after all, were prominent and had been part of the American story from the very first days. The infant's great-grandfather was William Dawes, Jr., a companion of Paul Revere on the night before Lexington, and his mother's grandfather was Dr. Manasseh Cutler, a Massachusetts churchman of wide reputation and accomplishments. The baby was given the single name "Rufus" after a distant cousin, a Boston poet, but family members (noting his birthday) took to calling him "Rufus Republic," which soon was shortened to "R. R." or "Railroad" Dawes. In time, the middle initial became part of his legal signature.[1]

Childhood was not always carefree. His parents obtained a legal separation the year after his birth, and his father, who operated a warehouse and general store at Malta, Ohio, was gone much of the time dealing in grains and real estate. The senior Dawes, restless in the American fashion, moved to Wisconsin in 1855 and recorded extensive land purchases near Mauston in Juneau County. He enrolled his two sons at the state university at Madison for the fall term in 1856. During the summer of 1857, the brothers returned to Ohio to spend time with their mother and to complete their education. Rufus Dawes graduated from Marietta College in Ohio in 1860, then returned to Wisconsin, where he and his father opened a general store and began to clear their land outside Mauston.

It was hard work and a hard frontier. "This is a tremendous job of 'log rolling' or to use the dialect of the country 'bush whacking,'" Dawes wrote his sister in Ohio. "Father is . . . devoting his whole time, energy

*Rufus Dawes. Courtesy
of the State Historical
Society of Wisconsin.
[WHi (X3) 27940]*

and business talents to the sole object of making a productive and profitable estate, to which he looks forward for a home and sustenance." There was much to do those days in frontier Wisconsin, and the nation's deepening sectional dispute was far removed. In fact, the prevailing opinion was that the secession crisis would soon blow over.

It was the election of Abraham Lincoln as president in 1860 that set off the political storm. Within weeks, South Carolina voted itself out of the Union, and the states of Mississippi, Florida, Alabama, Georgia, Louisiana, and Texas soon followed. By February, delegates of the seceding states met to establish the Confederate States of America. Jefferson Davis, a Mississippi planter and former U.S. secretary of war (who himself had spent time in Wisconsin during his soldier days), was elected president, and he called for 100,000 volunteers to defend the new Confederacy.

In the following weeks, sensation seemed to pile on sensation, and there was hot talk of war. Military organizations, North and South, were quickly organized and began drilling. In the seceded states, officials began seizing Federal property. Soon public attention was centered on

Charleston, South Carolina, where a small Federal garrison was holding Fort Sumter in the harbor despite demands it be surrendered. Abraham Lincoln, in office just weeks and grimly determined to maintain the Union, announced April 10 (some said later it was a clever ploy to force the Confederates to make the first move) that he would attempt to resupply the garrison. Two days later, the Secessionists responded by opening fire with their harbor batteries. Fort Sumter was quickly surrendered, and within the week Lincoln issued a call for 75,000 volunteers to put down the rebellion. The call for Federal troops, as expected, sent North Carolina, Tennessee, Arkansas, and Virginia into the new Confederacy, and a civil war, so often threatened, had finally started.

In Wisconsin, the mood changed almost at once. "'We must lick 'em.' 'Southern rights be damned.' 'No Southerner or any other has a right to fire on our flag.' 'Charleston must be destroyed.' 'Jeff Davis should be hung,' etc. etc., were the expressions used by even the most conservative men," said one Badger. "War, war, war, was the theme of every fireside and gathering; the people felt that the secessionists had forfeited all their rights under the constitution by treasonably making war against our government." Within days, the young men and boys were drilling at city parks and on vacant lots and in farm pastures. War rallies were held in Milwaukee, Baraboo, Fond du Lac, and dozens of smaller communities. The parades, the patriotic meetings, and the hot oratory would take on a golden glow afterward, but war fever was a raw emotion those days. Parents tried to hold them back, one volunteer said later, but "the enthusiasm in young America was too great."[2]

The would-be soldiers signed the muster rolls with light hearts and a painful innocence. "Patriotism was effervescent," said Michael Fitch, then a young man at the Mississippi River town of Prescott. He and a friend took a pair of horses and buggy on a recruiting swing. "Every rugged backwoodsman, whether American, German or Norwegian, was full of patriotism," he said. "Indignation at the firing on Fort Sumter was genuine and universal. . . . Wherever we stopped over night the host would refuse pay for our entertainment. The mother and daughters would look after our comfort, even drying our apparel when wet with rain. Everywhere we were bidden Godspeed in our patriotic efforts. . . . There were no better soldiers in the army than many of these backwoods farmer boys. A number of them never returned."[3]

One of those backwoods farmer boys was James Patrick Sullivan, a 17-year-old just then working as a hired man on a backwoods farm at Wonewoc in Juneau County. Brought to America as an infant, Sullivan was barely average height and had few prospects beyond his brash Irish

*Pvt. James P. Sullivan of
the Sixth Wisconsin. From
the Collection of the
Author.*

intelligence. He was one of the first to sign the muster roll to defend the Union. "I want to do what I can for my country," he said, enlisting in a military organization of "hardy lumbermen, rugged farmer boys and sturdy mechanics" from Mauston, New Lisbon, Wonewoc, Necedah, and surrounding farms and villages. Elected captain of the new organization was young Rufus Dawes, late of Ohio and now living on the frontier. The "company" of 100 volunteers gave itself the name "Lemonweir Minute Men" for the river flowing through the valley where the men resided. One of the recruits said the name would remind them of home, said Dawes, and "this argument carried the day." Called to the mustering place at Camp Randall in Madison, they were designated "Company K" of Wisconsin's new Sixth Regiment.[4]

Dawes had been caught up in the war from the first, and if some of the men in his new company (Sullivan among them) thought the new officer took himself too seriously, no one doubted his ability. The brightest moment of his soldier days would come two years later at

Gettysburg on July 1, 1863, where, acting without orders, Dawes led a charge on Confederates firing from an unfinished railroad cut.[5] In the end, however, Dawes's sense of duty and decency proved his undoing as a soldier. He expected himself to be good and brave in a war where goodness and courage brought death. What he called "the carnival of blood" finally wore him down. "About the worst demoralized man I have seen in the army was Dawes before he got his discharge," a soldier wrote in 1864. "With him the Government was every thing but what it should be. . . ." Dawes went home to Ohio, where his new wife waited. Before his death in 1899, he operated a lumber business, served one term in Congress, and wrote a thoughtful memoir of his days in a Wisconsin regiment of an "Iron Brigade." One of his four sons, Charles G. Dawes, became vice president of the United States (1925–1929), but Rufus did not live to see it.[6]

But all that was still ahead in the summer of 1861, and if the companies of the Sixth Wisconsin were slower to organize than those in the state's first regiments (some created around existing militia units), they were led by steady men of ability. The captains and lieutenants, in many cases, came forward after tending family and business responsibilities. Their decision to go was not made in the first flush of patriotism, and when they picked up the sword they did so with a determination to see the matter to its conclusion. The three field officers—Col. Lysander Cutler of Milwaukee, Lt. Col. Julius Atwood of Madison, and Maj. Benjamin Sweet of Chilton—were of New England origins and had little or no military experience. Several line officers, however, mostly in the German companies, such as John Hauser of Fountain City, who brought in Company H, and the courtly lieutenants of Company F, Frederick Schumacher and Werner Von Bachelle, had extensive European service. The regiment also contained veterans of the Mexican War—Thomas Kerr of Company D from Milwaukee, Adam Malloy of Sauk County's Company A, and John Marsh of Company B from Prescott, among others—and their ability added an expertise to the drill.[7]

Most of the volunteers were of rural origins, but there were companies from populated areas—the Irish "Montgomery Guard" and German "Citizens' Corps" from Milwaukee, "Bragg's Rifles" from Fond du Lac and Appleton, and the "Beloit Star Rifles" from the Illinois-Wisconsin state line. From towns on the Mississippi River came the "Prairie du Chien Volunteers," "Prescott Guards," and "Buffalo County Rifles," with the red-shirted river men remembered for their imaginative cursing. The soldiers of the "Sauk County Riflemen," "Anderson Guards" (named for Fort Sumter hero Robert Anderson), and Rufus Dawes's "Lemonweir Minute Men" were farmers and small-town boys. Native-born "Americans" made up the majority of the regiment, but there were Germans, Irish, Norwegians, Swedes, Welsh, and Scots as well.[8]

To James Patrick Sullivan, he and the others were always the "green-horn patriots" who "slept on the soft-side of a board" and marched to the music of hometown cornet bands and the cheers of friends, neighbors, and relatives, all puffed up by the great task at hand and the admiring looks of young women who came to wave flags and handkerchiefs. If the war fever stirred the men, the women—mothers, relatives, sisters, and sweethearts— would not be denied a role. They baked and cooked for "soldier banquets," sewed uniforms and flags, gathered pocket testaments, and prepared bandages and packets containing scissors, buttons, thread, pins, and needles.[9] They also added voices and enthusiasm to the recruiting. While it was easy to get caught up in the war speeches and the band music, the actual deed of signing the roll was a more serious matter, and it was at that moment a young man might need an extra shove.

Told long after (and variations can be found in the war records of other states) was one story how a "young girl" added her powers of persuasion in urging one fellow to sign the roll. "John, if you do not enlist," the patriotic young miss said loudly during one war meeting, "I'll never let you kiss me again as long as I live! Now you mind, sir, I mean what I say." The remark was greeted with "much merriment," and other young men, who had signed the muster roll, added their own exhortations: "John, if I were in your place I'd enlist, before I'd give up what you've got to." Alas, the record showed "John" stubbornly refused to sign the roll; not revealed was whether the patriotic miss kept her vow. Another woman accompanied her spouse to the place of enlistment. As he laid down the pen, she took it up, writing next to his name, "God Bless and protect you, my husband." In the final tally, one early historian concluded, "Wisconsin women were as patriotic and courageous in giving up their soldiers, as the latter were in marching away to fight for their country."[10]

Certainly Sixth Wisconsin men remembered the send-off celebration at Milwaukee. The "city of beer and pale bricks" was home to Col. Lysander Cutler and two of the regiment's companies, and the towns–folk turned out to cheer and admire when the Sixth Wisconsin arrived July 28, 1861, en route to Washington. Jerome Watrous of Appleton, then a 19-year-old private, wrote later that old Cutler commanded "a notoriously awkward lot of youngsters, but he was intensely proud of them and ambitious to show his neighbors the class of men he was to lead into battle."

It was a day not forgotten: "The regiment arrived at the old St. Paul station a little past noon, hurriedly disembarked and marched to a large storehouse on West Water street where a feast awaited. There were many long tables groaning with the best in the market, and lined up along those tables were Milwaukee ladies who had volunteered to wait upon the boys. . . . At the close of the feast, the men were called to attention and three rousing cheers were given for Wisconsin and the Nation, three for Milwaukee and three boisterous ones for the beautiful, patriotic women and girls who had kindly acted as waiters at the soldier banquet. That over, the companies filed to the street. . . . It was a hot, sultry day, and the heavy knapsacks, heavier then, than they were on any future march, were hard to bear, but Col. Cutler marched us along street after street for an hour and a half, then to the Northwestern station on the South side where more cheers were given for Milwaukee and her people. Then that band of a thousand youngsters left the city for the seat of the war, tired and reflecting upon the sudden changes of the past few weeks and what was in store for them."[11]

While awaiting departure, one "young lady, perhaps sixteen or seventeen years of age," was walking beside the rail cars filled with soldiers when one cheeky fellow leaned from a window with a bright smile. "Say, Miss, won't you kiss me for my mother?" he asked. To his surprise and the amusement of his friends, "with tears in her eyes, she reached up and clasping both arms around his neck, kissed him 'for his mother.'" The young volunteer drew back into the car as the young miss, one witness recalled, "continued on her way with the consciousness, apparently, of having done her duty."

The Milwaukee hospitality, another soldier said, "sustained many poor fellow . . . by reminding him that at home . . . he had many strong and warm friends, and nerving him with the thought that come what would, they should have no cause to be ashamed of him."[12]

Once the fathers, husbands, and sons were off to the war front, Wisconsin women turned to organizing fairs for the relief of soldier widows and orphans, nursing wounded and ill volunteers, and knitting wagonloads of socks and mittens to keep their menfolk warm and dry. What was little recognized was how mothers, wives, and sisters went into the farm fields, clerked the stores, and operated the businesses those war months. The sight of "women in the Wisconsin fields" at first displeased Mrs. Mary Livermore, who was active in the Soldier

Aid Societies, and she said she "turned away in aversion." But, after a time, she said, "I observed how skillfully they drove the horses round and round the wheat field. . . . Then I saw that where they followed the reapers, binding and shocking, although they did not keep up with the men, their work was done with more precision and nicety, and their sheaves had an artistic finish that those lacked made by men." It was a far-reaching development, and when the men came home nothing would ever quite be the same.[13]

4.

The Volunteer Army of 1861

The Sixth Wisconsin reached Washington on August 7, 1861, the new soldiers finding crowded sidewalks and magnificent, but unfinished, Federal structures of stone. The streets were marked by "deep, ugly squares of as unclean mud as ever fell in the way of man or beast," one said, and farther out were the city defenses and the tent camps of the regiments arriving in answer to President Lincoln's call for troops. The Wisconsin soldiers were marched to City Hall Park and later to Meridian Hill, where the Badgers (proud of their uniforms of militia gray) carefully laid out company streets and began learning—officer and enlisted man alike—to be soldiers. The drill calls, dress parades, and guard mounts were all new and exciting. "A thrill of joy passes through our being when we think we are in the great Volunteer army of 1861, and able to raise our hand in defense of this, the purest and best of Governments in existence," Jerome Watrous wrote home. "Rather would we be pierced with the bayonets and bullets of our wicked enemies or our bones to bleach in this Southern clime, than turn our face homeward before the victory shall have been won and peace reigns triumphant in these United States once more."

The pleasant camp occupied the heights at "a bend in Rock Creek, on the east side of the stream," a spot "deeply fringed with a forest of oaks, presenting a beautiful picture to the visitor." The weather, however, was "intensely hot and the water not good," and measles and other maladies swept the companies, the backwoods boys suffering the most. Melons freely sold in camp by peddlers produced a disorder the soldiers labeled "the Virginia quickstep" and a week after the regiment's arrival in Washington, Rufus Dawes reported that his Company K had 35 of 100 men "sick and unfit for duty." The other companies, he said, "were in like manner severely scourged." But one private painted a more optimistic picture in a letter to his hometown newspaper: "We can stand guard in the rain, and . . . have no difficulty in 'lopping' down on the wet ground, rolled up in a blanket sleep as sound as if our beds were made of down; can eat our rations ever time . . . ; can march thirty miles per day 'quick time,' fix up streets and pitch tents before going to rest. What do you think of that! Tell you what, soldier is a fine institution—if one is a mind to think so."[1]

One Washington attraction was the president. "Mr. Lincoln is very tall and very homely, but no one can look at him without being impressed with the serious earnestness of his face," Rufus Dawes wrote home. Another Badger left a slightly different view: "I have seen Lincoln and must say that the idea he is homely is erroneous, at least since he has allowed his beard to grow. He looks determined and physically fresh notwithstanding the fact he works almost unceasingly."

Jerome Watrous of the Sixth Wisconsin had the clearest memory. He had secured a pass to visit his brother, Henry, who was camped nearby with the Fourth Wisconsin Infantry, and the two, who had been Lincoln partisans in the 1860 campaign, went to the White House "hoping that our candidate of the year before would appear." As they watched a regiment passing on Pennsylvania Avenue, the two soldiers were surprised to find Lincoln standing behind them. "My boys, I see by your uniforms that you have come to help me save the Union, to be my partners in the enterprise," said Lincoln. He asked what state the two soldiers were from, said Wisconsin was "sending many good men," then shook each man's hand, expressing "the hope that our lives would be spared, and that we would never regret the partnership."

It was a chance meeting never forgotten. "To have looked into the Lincoln face, at close range, heard the Lincoln voice, had our hands enclosed in the ample Lincoln hand was glory enough for more than one August day," said Jerome Watrous. But the story of how two Wisconsin boys met the president and became "partners" in his effort to preserve the Union had a sad ending. Jerome Watrous survived the war, but his brother, Henry, was killed less than two years later in the fighting at Port Hudson when a rebel artillery shell took away part of his head.[2]

Just after that encounter with the president, Jerome Watrous said, there occurred an important event in the annals of the Sixth Wisconsin—the arrival of the Second Wisconsin Infantry, a unit famous as the first three-year regiment to reach Washington and for its service in the battle the boys were calling Bull's Run. Marching by fours, the regiment made its way up the hillside, and the men of the Sixth Wisconsin gathered to watch, taking in the field-worn gray Wisconsin uniforms and the way the arriving soldiers marched with a smooth and easy Western step. "They had been through the first battle of Bull Run," said Watrous. "They had fought for their country. We looked up to them, we regarded them as heroes, and they were." But if there was admiration for the arriving soldiers, there was also a realization there could be no peace between the two regiments. The new volunteers of Wisconsin's Sixth, as young men are wont to do, would not take a back seat to anyone, even tough fellows from their home state who had fought in the first battle of the war.

A few days later, the Fifth Wisconsin arrived on the heights amid loud shouts of welcome and a great helloing. It had been at Madison when the companies of the Sixth Wisconsin were called and in its ranks were friends and relatives. One main attraction was pretty Eliza Wilson, the "Daughter of the Regiment," who attracted a circle of soldier admirers. Her father was William Wilson of Dunn County, a mill owner and former member of the Wisconsin Legislature. Several of her relatives served in ranks with the Fifth Wisconsin as well as men lately in the employ of her father. One Badger, obviously smitten, reported the "quite pretty" *vivandière* wore a military dress patterned "after the most approved French style," while another soldier described her as "decidedly smart and intelligent, of medium size, amiable, twenty, and pretty."

Having a young woman in camp was disconcerting. "The boys have no sweetheart to see and therefore white shirts, standing collars, hair-oil, bosom-pine and tight boots have disappeared completely," said one volunteer. "We have not seen a woman for a fortnight . . . [and it] would do you good to see her trudging along, with or after the regiment, her dark brown frock buttoned tightly around her waist, her what-you-call-ems tucked into her well fitting gaiters, her hat and feather set jauntily on one side, her step firm and assured, for she knows that every arm in our ranks would protect her. . . . Were it not for her, when a woman would appear, we would be running after her, as children do after an organ and monkey."[3]

It was comforting for the three Badger regiments to be camped together in the great army being raised at Washington. Men in the various regiments were guests at other cook fires to talk of friends and relatives and of things back home. ". . . [O]ur men have got a good name," one Wisconsin volunteer said, "and if we get together when in battle we can do a huge amount of tall fighting." Of course, there were youthful rivalries—the Second Wisconsin men were arrogant in the manner of veterans—but all in all it was a pleasant bivouac, the backwoods boys, shy around strangers, laughing and taking in an easy Western fashion among themselves.[4]

At sundown less than a week later, the "rattle of a large drum corps" signaled the arrival of the Nineteenth Indiana. "Looking up, our boys saw, astride a black horse, what seemed to us the tallest man we had ever seen," said one Badger. The imposing figure was Col. Sol Meredith, a six-foot-seven North Carolina Quaker who had moved to Indiana in the 1840s. He was clerk of Wayne County at the outbreak of the war, and one of his cronies was Gov. Oliver Morton of Indiana, a political figure of national influence. Upon his appointment as colonel of the Nineteenth, some critics suggested, not completely in jest, that "Long Sol" Meredith be cut in two so his "lower and better half" could be appointed lieutenant colonel of the regiment. But James Sullivan of the Sixth Wisconsin always had a fondness for the Hoosier officer, saying that Meredith took double the risk because he was twice as big as most men. Another Badger explained: "Stray scraps of iron running at large over the heads of a regiment are apt to pick out the tall ones." In any event, it was generally agreed the Nineteenth was the Indiana governor's pet and, in the politically charged army of those days, it was a matter duly noted by the officers in other regiments, especially those with ambitions themselves.

The addition of the Nineteenth Indiana completed the brigade, and if three regiments were from Wisconsin, there was no dismay over the fourth. The Hoosiers, with their flat accents and quiet ways, were Westerners, after all, and the Badgers looked them over and came away with satisfied nods.[5]

The commander of the new brigade was General Rufus King, also a figure from back home. A native of New York and 1833 graduate of the U.S. Military Academy at West Point, King arrived in Wisconsin in 1845 to assume the editor's chair of *The Milwaukee Sentinel*. He soon became prominent in framing the Wisconsin Constitution and as superintendent of Milwaukee schools. At the outbreak of the war, King declined appointment as U.S. minister to the Papal States at Rome to accept a commission as brigadier general of volunteers. The general made a good first impression on his new soldiers. He is "a homely looking man" but "cultivated gentleman," said one Badger, while another volunteer described King as "a popular officer, as is proven by the efforts made to get regiments into his Brigade, and the fact that some of the best fighting material in the army has been and is under his command."[6]

In early September a picket post alarm along the Washington defenses sent the new regiments hurrying ("and what a long tiresome tramp it was," one soldier said) to the Chain Bridge over the Potomac River, where they were halted and, after a time, put into camp. Seen at the very head of the column was Charley King, the 17-year-old son of the general, "swinging along at a Zouave Gait" with his "buff leggings and a red fez cap, and a little 'Volcanic rifle.'. . ." Another soldier caught a glimpse of Eliza Wilson "in her tweed short skirt and trowsers, marching gaily with one of the companies." On that march, said John Marsh of the Sixth Wisconsin, a captain, "in the presence of his company, tore from his shoulder the insignia of his rank." When the company was again in camp, the officer was "invited to resign, which he did." The morale of the regiment, said Marsh, was so high that "no officer could hold his place who showed for a moment the white feather."

For Edwin Brown, a new lieutenant in the Sixth Wisconsin, there was a more disturbing matter. He had visited the Congress and wrote shortly afterward how disappointed he had been: "The majority of the Senators look like bald headed Methodist class leaders with just about brains enough to howl & blat without much substances to their speech. I don't wish to boast, but I think I know as much as the average of the Representatives of this Nation."

It was a conclusion not comforting to a new officer ready to risk life and limb on a battlefield to protect the national government.[7]

5.
Alas, It Was a Dream

The regiments were moved a few days later across the Potomac River to Arlington Heights near the columned home of Robert Lee of Virginia, an old army officer just then in rebellion. The mansion, which had been seized when Lee resigned to take a Confederate commission, was used by Rufus King as a brigade headquarters, and its historic ties to the nation's first president made an impression on the young volunteers. The house had been built by George Washington's stepson, John Parke Custis, and passed to Lee through George Washington Custis, his father-in-law. "We encountered a 69-year-old Negro," one Badger wrote home, "who had lived in Arlington House for more than 50 years. He told us that George Washington had often visited there for days at a time. Several of the listening soldiers cried." Julius Murray of the Sixth Wisconsin reported the "property contains over one thousand acres and has been in the family since before the revolution, and now for this act of treason he loses it all, and his head with it if they do not succeed. It is the same way with thousands of others in this state."[1]

It was at Arlington Heights that the Fifth Wisconsin was sent across the river to the brigade of Winfield Scott Hancock.[2] The general was a West Pointer whose star was just then rising in the army, and it was said that he took such a "fancy" to the Wisconsin unit that he "begged or stole it away from Rufus King. . . ." The general ("vexed at the loss of the Fifth," one soldier said) "insisted upon having another Wisconsin regiment in its place." About that time, the Seventh Wisconsin was dispatched from Madison, and when it reached Washington on October 1 it found orders attaching it to King's Brigade.[3]

The arriving regiment was given a joyous welcome. "Our boys and those of the 2d made extravagant demonstrations of delight when they saw the grey uniforms and blue flags coming up the road from towards

Washington," said a Sixth Wisconsin private, while another soldier observed that it "seemed kind of natural to see some one fresh from Badgerdom." The Seventh Wisconsin, the latter said, "makes a very good appearance in uniform, but they don't carry bronze enough on their cheeks to give them a real good soldierly appearance. . . ." One Wisconsin brigade officer said the new regiment was "said to be the finest body of soldiers yet sent from our State. . . . The men are not only of good size and hardy looking, but they have an intelligent and smart look, which is assurance that they bring brain as well as muscle to the work." Less taken was Edwin Brown of the Sixth Wisconsin: "The Seventh Wisconsin Reg. arrived here yesterday and are encamped just across the road from us. They are not so good looking Regt. as the Fifth and Sixth are and never will be."[4]

The colonel of the Seventh Wisconsin was an old Hungarian campaigner named Joseph Van Dor, who had been living in Milwaukee. He had been recommended to the governor for a colonelcy as "a brave man and thorough disciplinarian," but the old soldier was still trying to master English. One remembered mix-up came during a drill in firing by front and rear ranks. Van Dor, mounted and at his proper place behind the regiment, ordered, "Rear rank, about face! Ready, aim. . . ." This "sudden innovation brought the long line of file closers and officers to their knees, while the gallant lieutenant colonel and major were seen charging toward some friendly trees." The adjutant shouted, "Colonel, that is not correct; you will shoot the file closers." "I don't care a tam," said the stubborn Hungarian. "If your colonel ish te mark, fire anyway," and "a thousand muskets emptied their blank cartridges at the noble colonel." Van Dor, it was recalled, was soon "promoted to a foreign consulship, a polite way Mr. Lincoln had of banishing general officers not wanted in the field."[5]

King's organization was the only Western brigade at Washington; that singled out the Wisconsin and Indiana soldiers, and they wanted to prove themselves. "We are all anxious for a 'set to' with the Rebels," said Jerome Watrous of the Sixth Wisconsin. One Sauk County man explained: "we would have died rather than have dishonored the West. We felt that the eyes of the East were upon us, and that we were the test of the West." Edward Bragg of the Sixth Wisconsin said it was "the reputation of the Brigade and the Regiments they were fighting for, the reputation of themselves and of their brothers, and the reputation of their state. . . ."[6]

The organizations would soon become famous, but the volunteers were young—many away from home and on their own for the first

General Rufus King (without cap) and staff. Courtesy of the Milwaukee County Historical Society. Used by permission.

time—and the rivalry to be singled out as the crack regiment smoldered through guard mounts, brigade drills, and dress parades as they learned the dozens of things needed to make them soldiers. The "veterans" of the Second Wisconsin provoked the competition, making much of Bull Run, even if, in the end, they had to run for it with the rest of the Union army. The four regiments, one observer noted, "despite their pull-together way in battle, had, nevertheless, their individuality, their rivalry, their jealousies, if you will. The 2d had been through First Bull Run and swaggered a bit in consequence. They rather patronized the other regiments, put on veteran airs. They were superbly drilled, but decidedly given to sarcastic comment on the other commands. The 6th, 7th and 19th had not had the 2d's opportunities, but were cock sure that when the time came they could fight every bit as well, stay as long in a hot place or charge just as daringly into a hotter."[7]

The loud talk by Second Wisconsin men was more than just the boasting of young soldiers,[8] and Edwin Brown of the Sixth Wisconsin touched on it in a letter home: "The 2d Wis Regt joined our Brigade yesterday. They look as though they had been *'through the wars,'* ragged and saucy, and without discipline. The Regt is demoralized since the affair at Bulls Run, instead of drilling, they spend their time telling big stories about their exploits, and horrible scenes on the field of battle. Every sentence is embellished with some tall swearing. They are a hard nation, I will assure you, and their officers have very little control over them. I happened over to their camp ground this morning and *Capt. Bouck* [Gabriel Bouck of Oshkosh] was having some altercation with a private and both seemed to try who could *swear the worst and call each other the hardest names.*"[9] Another officer observed the soldiers of the Second "look dirty and more callus than ours. . . . The men are of good stuff, but . . . with little confidence in the officers & that they care little what they do." The men of the Second Regiment, a third officer observed, "did not have that exuberant, dashing, self-reliant manner which distinguishes the other Wisconsin men."[10]

In the Washington camps the Sixth Wisconsin became the "pet babies" (because of suspected favoritism from King) or the "Calico Sixth," a mean-spirited reference to the homespun shirts of some of the men in the back ranks.[11] The fellows in the Seventh Wisconsin tried to label themselves as the "Hungry Seventh," but others called them the "Huckleberries" because the soldiers "liked to talk about pies and things to eat." The "lean, lank" men of the Nineteenth Indiana, "a quiet set," were "old Posey County" or "Swamp Hogs No. 19," and "every man of them did not care a goll darn how he was dressed, but was all hell for a fight."

The Hoosiers were generally regarded in the camps as a slippery lot of fellows. It was "a common thing" among the Nineteenth Indiana men, a Sixth Wisconsin man claimed, that whenever in "a hungry mood raided a henroost, to remove the figure 1 from their hats and inverting the 9, and pass as the old Sixth and make themselves the terror of the country." Early on, the Second Wisconsin was the "bloody Second" (for Bull Run) or the "Hungry Second" (for talented foraging), but that gave way to the "Ragged Assed Second"—for the sad condition of their trousers. There was nothing, a comrade said, quite like the "view of their rear ranks when they attempted a dress parade," as the "lively boys . . . were more like Highlanders minus kilts than model infantry."[12]

There were, of course, a number of stories, and one involved the wife of a Wisconsin congressman visiting the army. She was seated in her carriage when the Sixth Wisconsin passed, and she asked a nearby lieutenant the name of the marching regiment. "The Baby Sixth, Ma'am," the officer replied. Not understanding the joke, the lady indignantly replied, "Sir! I am from Wisconsin, and allow me to inform you, that we send no infants to war from there."

The story made the rounds, and finally a frustrated Milwaukeean wrote home that some regiments "have the strange habit of christening their yet unborn reputation as for instance: 'The Bloody This,' or 'Invincible That,' or 'Ragged Other.' Please set us down as the plain 'Wisconsin Sixth' until we bring forth something for which history will have a name." Of course, all the protests were for nothing, and even a half century afterward the gray-haired veterans of the "Old Sixth" were always hailed as "the Calico boys" or "the babies of King's old brigade."[13]

The four regiments did not live "on the best of terms" and were "separate and distinct communities," one soldier recalled, while a second volunteer said it was with "great reluctance that we got up even a calling acquaintance with those other regiments, yet some of us had friends, cousins and even brothers in their ranks." And the tension was not just between the regiments. "Americans are a materialistic people, and are interested only in making money and raising hell," said a German immigrant of the Seventh Wisconsin in regard to his new comrades. "Exceptions, of course, are some well-bred and educated families and persons."

One Second Wisconsin soldier tried to explain it. The men in his regiment, he said, "are probably the hardest set of boys, but good natured and easy to get along with. They wear an air of fearless carelessness wherever found. The Sixth is more stately, and distant, and march to slower music than we do. The Seventh puts on the least style and crow the least . . . and is well drilled. It is the truest friend the 2d ever found. The 19th Indiana is an indifferent, don't care regiment. They pride themselves on their fighting pluck—which is undoubtedly good—more than their drill." He concluded, "As a brigade we get along finely together."[14]

So the young volunteers drilled and drilled some more; battled measles, smallpox, and lesser ailments along with boredom and homesickness. It was all rather slow for a new soldier expecting drums, brass buttons, and glory. "The prospects of a speedy & favorable close of this war at times looks gloomy enough," one Wisconsin officer wrote home. "I don't believe if the Army was disbanded, to be called voluntarily together again in a month, that one Enlisted man in twenty would reenlist in this vast army of ours. I don't believe that one third of Commissioned Officers would stay if their pride did keep them. The discipline is very strict. The hardships are many now, and most every one thinks of the cheerful faces & blazing fires of home with a very strong desire to be there." Julius Murray of the Sixth Wisconsin wrote the home folk: "I would not advise any one to enlist. It is irksome to be so closely confined and to have to implicitly obey all orders."[15]

One never-ending duty was drill call. "The Colonel took us up hill and down double quick and by the right flank, right face, double quick march, close column on the tenth company, left flank, left face, double quick march," wrote Stephen Vesper, a Patch Grove farmer now a private in the Sixth Wisconsin. "After the drill was over, we went back to camp, held dress parade, eat our supper; went to bed and slept till morning. Then we got up, washed up, combed our hair, ready for another days labor at drill."[16]

Adding to the general misery was the mud. "If the people of Virginia attempted to repel us with arms but didn't," one soldier said, "[it was because] the 'sacred soil' stuck to the Union cause on every available occasion. . . ." Another Badger reported that the "roads & Country everywhere in this vicinity is *terribly muddy*," and on one tramp to a sentry post, said Rufus Dawes, "the mud rolled down upon the men in a kind of avalanche. They waded up the hill through a moving stream of red clay mortar." A few days later, in his journal, Dawes confided: "I never saw mud before, equal to that I encountered." The entry the next day was one of exasperation—"Mud-mud-mud precludes drill, every-thing." The Sauk County boys recalled that they cut and carried wood for fires as "teams could not get around, it was so muddy." James Sullivan of the Sixth Wisconsin never forgot "that awful winter. The Potomac froze and during the January thaw we were compelled to split puncheons and plank our street in order to go from one end of the other, while the blood-thirsty editors at home were asking 'why don't the Army move?'"[17]

The soldiers bore all in a light fashion. One rainy day, confined to their tents, the "men beguiled the weary hours, by croaking like frogs, quacking like ducks and barking like dogs," said Dawes. While march-ing in miserable weather, a leader would shout, "When our army marched down to Bull Run, what did the big bull frog say?" Hundreds of men responded "in deep base, bull frog croaks, 'Big thing. Big thing.'" Then the leader would call, "When our army came back from Bull Run, what did the little frogs say?" "Run Yank. Run Yank" would be screeched in "an excellent imitation of a swamp full of frogs." Finally the leader would ask, "What does the bully Sixth say?" and the soldiers would answer in "bull frog bass voices"—"Hit 'em again! Hit 'em again!" Dawes concluded: "Brave boys, how they contended against adverse circumstances with their cheerful and courageous spirit."

Mud made for a hard soldier's life and danger loomed outside the Washington defenses, but there were other matters just as threatening. While out on a picket line Dawes discovered that his Juneau County boys had "fared sumptuously" despite orders against foraging. "They declared that even the pigs were secessionists and they burned them at the *steak* for their treason. Turkeys and chickens shared the same fate. It was impossible for me to restrain men who had been starved on salt-beef and hard tack, when they were scattered over four miles of territory and sneered at as Yankees by the people." And he added: "The fact is I ate some pig myself." Even Rufus King looked the other way, one soldier wrote in his diary, "requested us not to steal, but said, 'Boys, do not go hungry,' which in the English language, and in war time, means take what you want whenever you can get it."[18]

A more serious matter to Rufus Dawes was "that ever-present curse of camp life"—the playing of cards and other types of gambling. But "the strict orders of Colonel Cutler against this vice, and his vigorous discipline greatly restricted the evil," he said. "It was well the regiment had so resolute a commander. He gave almost no passes to the city. Thieves, speculators, gamblers and vile characters of all kind had flocked to Washington to prey upon the army. The enemy in the rear was now more dangerous than the enemy in front. . . . In spite of the constant marching of the armed patrols, our soldiers were constantly made victims by the Harpies. Washington was a very sink hole of iniquity in other ways of evil. The unfinished dome of the United States Capitol, and the half built Washington monument well typified the uncertainty of a continued national existence."[19]

The Wisconsin volunteers admired the firmness of the straight-backed New Englander. The 53-year-old Cutler had moved to Wisconsin before the war looking for a fresh start after several financial reverses. The colonel was, said one soldier, "stern, rugged, determined, yet kindly face, which, when a smile found place there, was rarely attractive; the gray, almost white hair and full but clipped beard; the slim, tall, erect thoroughly soldier figure, and the grave, calm dignity of every motion." Cutler, he said, was "nothing of the martinet. He imposed upon us severe duties—but only for our good as he told us, and we came to know this in time and thank him for it." Another soldier called Cutler "a strict disciplinarian, but courteous and kind to his men, and, I firmly believe, brave and true."

Old Cutler was just the man to root out sin, and if he and Dawes were unsettled by those giving in to temptations of the flesh, one who took a less serious view was John Cook of the Sixth Wisconsin. He was one of the "jumping Jesus Christers" of Company D, he said, "eighteen years of age, and a tough one." With the firing on Fort Sumter, Cook enlisted at Milwaukee in the "Montgomery Guard," an Irish militia company being readied for the war. He signed the roll, he said, "not for my country (being nothing but a boy did not know what that meant; did not know what my duty to country was), but for the sake of seeing the sunny south that I had heard so much about and to be considered brave."

On reaching Washington, Cook, who stood a half-inch short of five feet four, and some of the others ran the guard for a spree in the Washington saloons. "When I returned to camp I got what I deserved, and so did the rest; but we had a bully time." The result, he said, was "three days on short rations and clothing."[20]

Cook quickly took to the soldier life. "I had cheek, which was a very necessary article to have in the army," he said. "When plenty of the boys were dry, I was wet. Some are awful slow in getting around. I recollect when shoulder straps could get commissary [whiskey], and privates could not; but us, cheeky fellows could always find some way of doing it. I became a first lieutenant on short notice. I bought some shoulder-straps and my name was Lieut. Cook; but . . . [I] found myself in the guard house next morning. Well, I could not help it. When you see a man try to do a straight thing and nobody will let him, he will finally become careful who he associates with."[21]

In Washington, there were "whole platoons of liquor stores, and then more liquor stores, and then, travelling on, you just begin to come to the liquor stores," said a Wisconsin man. "Whiskey is contraband. It is not permitted to be taken over the river to the camps, and that is what makes it so astonishing where so much whiskey goes in. Perhaps now that Congress is here, much of that may be accounted for; but still the consumption of whiskey is wonderful even in view of the fact. As for the army, it gets its whiskey in a modest and demure way. Cans, labelled 'Oysters,' and 'Pickles' and 'Preserved meats,' are very popular with the army."[22]

One stop was the division of German soldiers commanded by Louis Blenker.[23] "German enthusiasm always ran high," a Wisconsin volunteer said. "They sell whiskey in quantities to suit; we do not, so our boys visit BLENKER frequently. Formerly they would go over in small squads, and some liberal German soldier would meet them with, 'Does you fight mit Blenker?' The reply would be, 'Yah.' 'Dat is good. Come and take some lager.' This was very well for a time, but matters now clash. Men drink the German whisky, and then pick a quarrel with the Germans. The result has been, so far, that German whips Yankee, and I hope it will be so just as long as the boys 'go over to fight mit Blenker.'"[24]

So there was a soldier or two who found a way to keep his haversack full and his canteen wet. It was troubling—how the army life changed a fellow. "I have forgotten many good things that I once knew, and even though I try to guard myself, or think I do, pretty well, I feel that when I return, if ever I do, it will be without improvement," a private wrote home. "We have had preaching but three times since last July and hardly knew when Sunday comes."

So whiskey was one danger to a soldier, gambling another; and there was a third just as serious temptation. Fifer Ludolph Longhenry of the Seventh Wisconsin touched on it in a diary entry: "This evening and during the night 30 soldiers were incarcerated. Some got drunk and others had run after the whores." It was illustrated in a letter from Edwin Brown, the Fond du Lac attorney then a new captain of the Sixth Wisconsin. He had gone to war leaving behind his wife, Ruth, and three children. In one of his first letters from the muster place at Camp Randall at Madison, Brown had written he was concerned she had gotten the wrong impression "because I did not show my feelings before the crowd at the time of parting that I did not feel very bad at going from you. But Ruth it was pride that kept me up. I did not want people to think that soldiers were baby's."[25]

The young officer, his serious face made old and sober by his mutton-chop whiskers, was also one of the regiment's singers. He and others ("all young, brave and handsome") had formed a musical society, and, it was later recalled, it had always been Brown who called in a cheery voice, "Now let's sing 'Benny,'" for "Benny Havens, O," the West Point drinking song, was a camp favorite.[26]

But he was finding it harder and harder to be away from home. His wife had written an unsettling letter asking if she might, on special occasion, go out socially while he was away. In his response, after husbandly cautions about proper circumstances, Brown gave his approval. But he added a few troubled lines: "There are plenty of things called women in and around Washington whom I might have visited for a consideration in hand paid. . . . But I determined when I came into the army to steer clear of those vices which cast a shade over the character of so many military men. It is a fact that Washington the capitol of our much loved Country abounds in women of easy virtue, some of whom I have had pointed out to me on its streets, were fair to look upon and beautifully dressed. Gambling and visiting houses of ill fame is the great curse of an Army that is lying inactive and is near a city like Washington." As for himself, he said, "Thus far I have shunned these things, desiring to live as not be a reproach upon family and friends and thinking too that the less sins one had to answer for the better, *when one might have to meet the 'King of terrors' at any hour.*"[27]

In the end, it was not hardship or the dangers or the bad food but simple loneliness that was most troubling to the soldiers. "Tell Emily to write. Tell them all to write a family letter. You don't know how much good it does a soldier to hear from the loved ones at home," pleaded one Badger. Edwin Brown, in the quiet of his tent, wrote: "Give my love to all, especially our parents. I often think of them all—My dear children— give them all a kiss and god bless them from their pa. And Ruth, my love in this and the other world are yours and may God watch over and protect you All. *I wear your miniatures in my breast pocket. . . .*"[28]

Another example was in the diary of Ludolph Longhenry, the quiet German immigrant serving as a fifer in the Seventh Wisconsin:

> Thursday, Jan. 16 [1862]—Last night I saw in my dreams my sweet-heart. She smiled so sweetly, as she did on the last evening we were together. With the thought and the hope that I would see this fine and thoughtful girl again, I fell asleep. I hoped that reality would not produce just the opposite.
>
> Jan. 24—[in the margin] The old proverb, Dreams are like bubbles, has again become true. I have just received a letter that my sweetheart got married on January 19.[29]

The same theme was voiced by Stephen Vesper of the Sixth Wisconsin. When the soldiers retire to their hard beds, he wrote to a sister, "[they indulge] in one of the sweetest pleasures that ever was bestowed on the heart of man. . . . We dreamed of our homes and those fond souls which our bosom holds dearer than any else on the earth. We clasped them to our bosom, but alas it was a dream."[30]

6.
Little Mac

A rebel army stood in front of a troubled Washington that late summer of 1861 following the Union defeat at Bull Run. Not for a half century had the capital been so threatened. But if rebel brigades camped within sight of the city, there were national regiments on hand as well, with more tramping in every day, and they had a bright, new hero to lead them—George Brinton McClellan.

The man looked and acted the general, with his well-fashioned uniform and fancy horse. Called to Washington a week after Bull Run, he found the city and government in near panic, streets and saloons full of wandering soldiers and everywhere talk of doom. McClellan moved decisively to restore order. Within hours, the general's provost squads began to sweep off-duty soldiers back to their camps.[1]

McClellan's earlier success against a Confederate force in northwest Virginia (looking so much better against the bungling of Bull Run) was discussed and hailed, the newspapers filling their columns with praise and descriptions of the young general. From his headquarters on Jackson Square, the young officer moved through army camps, political meetings, and social circles with studied dash. He seemed to be everywhere, and to his new regiments and brigades he gave a name to ring down through the decades—the Army of the Potomac.[2]

Within weeks, or so it seemed to the general's new soldiers, chaos was replaced by order and confusion by discipline. The new camps were policed, sentry posts established, and schedules posted for drills and other training. Under McClellan's direction, the sprawling defensive works ringing the city were strengthened and expanded, and it sometimes seemed the general was always on hand to personally lay out an extension of this fort or that new line of earthworks. "McClellan

*General George McClellan.
Courtesy of the Wisconsin
Veterans Museum. Used
by permission.*

is very active, and is in his saddle a large portion of the time," a Wisconsin officer wrote home. "It is said that he even visits the camps incog., in citizen's dress—so determined is he to know that everything goes right, and that his soldiers are properly cared for. Such conduct on his part is certainly well calculated to win the confidence of his men. His youthful appearance causes very many to distrust his abilities. He looks, however, as though he knew his business."[3]

Under McClellan's order the volunteers drilled and drilled some more and attended schools of instruction, guard mounts, parades, and reviews. Always in the foreground of the tents and camps and marching columns was the general on his big black horse, "Dan Webster," watching with a nod of approval and a jaunty twirl of his cap. In the newspapers he was the "young Napoleon," but his soldiers called him "Little Mac," and he galloped along the lines of his new army to cheers he accepted with a tight, pleased smile. The general, said Rufus Dawes of the Sixth Wisconsin, "is a splendid looking man, just in the prime of life. The boys are all carried away with enthusiasm for him."[4]

Lt. Edwin Brown of the same regiment, dazzled by the show of military pageantry, described one McClellan "Grand Review" as "a sight that no man this side of the Ocean has probably seen the like of." It included "90 Regts. of Infantry, 20 batteries of Artillery and upwards of 5,000 well appointed Cavalry moving at once all in sight with 'all of the pomp & circumstance of war'" and "is more of a sight than I ever expect to see again. The President, Cabinet and about twenty thousands spectators of all ranks & conditions of life were in attendance. . . ." He added: "The Sixth Wis. has a very good name for discipline, appearance to, and rec'd the especial [recognition] . . . of McClellan at the Review. T'was said by many that we marched like *regulars* and were a robust set of men."

It was certainly a day to remember. Capt. Edward Bragg of the Sixth Wisconsin wrote home: "Genl. McClellan and suite, splendidly mounted, with old Abe, alongside, rode at a dashing gait along the entire lines in front of each battalion—cheer after cheer filled the air as he passed, caps were flung high in the air. . . . He acknowledged the complements, and rode by uncovered, as did also Abraham. Our Brigade, of the whole number was the very one that was silent. I wonder what the Genl. thought. We have been taught and teach our men that perfect silence in the ranks is evidence of the true and well disciplined soldier. I was in command of this, and sat looking grimly to the front."[5]

As the regiments passed in review, the marching Wisconsin soldiers tried to catch a glimpse of President Lincoln. As one Badger said, "the line of our company was serious harmed by hurried glances at the tall man under a high hat. Many other companies fared no better."

But most remembered was the march back to camp. "The Lincoln carriage passed our regiment that evening while we were swinging back to camp singing 'John Brown,' a song just introduced to the army," said Jerome Watrous of the Sixth Wisconsin. "The thousand Western voices, giving forth the already popular air, seemed to please the President, for he lifted the high hat and gave us a smile and gracious bow. Still another carriage passed the regiment that evening—passed it several times. One of the occupants was Julia Ward Howe. Mrs. Howe seemed to like the song and the singers, for she, too, smiled and bowed her approval."[6] Rufus Dawes said it was John Ticknor who led the singing "with his strong, clear and beautiful tenor voice" as the regiment joined the chorus. "Julia Ward Howe . . . has said that the singing of the John Brown song by the soldiers on the march and the scenes of that day and evening inspired her to the composition of the Battle Hymn of the Republic. We at least helped to swell the chorus."[7]

Such "Grand shows" may impress new captains of infantry, but the tiring reviews were often staged by McClellan just to impress visitors. On one such display, the general was showing the army to "an English snob." The men "were disgusted as they had a right to be, with such exhibition," said Michael Fitch of the Sixth Wisconsin. "When noon came, the arms were stacked and the men ate lunch in groups on the ground, from their haversacks. While thus engaged, this Englishman in citizen's dress, on a bob tail horse, and an English saddle that brought his knees up to his waist, rode among the men inspecting them through his eye-glass. As a rebuke to his self-importance, a big burly infantry soldier held out to him a large piece of red corned beef saying, 'George, will you have a piece of dog?'"[8]

Lt. Edwin Brown's was the more thoughtful view. "Everything that patriotism could devise, everything that the almost unlimited resources of the North could provide, has been *lavishly poured at the feet of McClellan*," he wrote home. "President, Cabinet & people respond to his every wish, almost before it is expressed, and wo[e] to him if the vast power that he exercises is not wielded for the general good. Wo[e] to him, and the *administration that appointed him*, if in the hour of trial he proves incompetent, or insufficient for the emergency—An *enraged soldiery* and an *outraged people* would be difficult to control."[9]

It may have been that McClellan was a man whose keen intellect identified every danger and rarely an opportunity. His soldiers, during the war and afterward, loved and respected him—even while recognizing his limitations—and many puzzled over their lingering affection for the general they called "Little Mac." Whether McClellan was successful or not, one wrote afterward, "he had the confidence and admiration of the best soldiers in the army to a remarkable degree" and "with the rank and file of the army he was the idol, the one in whom our confidence remained unshaken."[10]

Long afterward it was realized that the days spent in the Washington camps had been a milestone. It was there the young men developed—under McClellan's hand—a view as to how soldiers looked and behaved. It was in those camps that tens of thousands of citizens began to think in terms of a nation rather than collection of states, and there was displayed the last innocence of a young United States. It was in the

Washington camps that the volunteers freely gave their loyalty to their new young commander—a blind trust that left Abraham Lincoln uncertain whether the army was more committed to McClellan or the nation's government. This loyalty to "Little Mac" was the innocent emotion of young men filled with their great cause and the strong bond of soldiers. To them, McClellan looked the grand general, acted the great soldier, and, in the final result, made the volunteers feel they were real soldiers. They never doubted his affection and understanding or backed away from the notion he was the only commander who protected them from the foolish whims of their own government. In his own manner, McClellan stamped the Army of the Potomac with a certain dash and identity that carried it through many wet camps and over many hard roads.

At the same time, however, by his own words and attitude, McClellan created a lingering mistrust that "the meddling politician and the bull-headed Senator," as one Wisconsin private described them, would try to use the army's fortunes for their own political ends. The unfortunate result of all this was that the general became too protective of what he had created. Emotionally he was unable to submit to hard use the grand army he had fashioned or accept the hard war that was required. His hesitation would reveal itself at the critical moment, and the very soldiers McClellan sought to shield would pay the price.

Edward Bragg of the Sixth Wisconsin, a man of intelligence who later used his war days to build a long and distinguished career in the Congress, admitted three decades afterward that he never escaped McClellan's spell. The Army of the Potomac, he said, trying to explain it, "was organized, equipped and drilled by one who, whatever else may be said of him, had no superior in that branch of the service, and in defense. He was a master of grand strategy, but he did not meet the requirements of popular demand by more rapid progress. . . . He blended the untutored enthusiasm of a nation unused to war, and taught it by bitter experience to yield itself to the cunning hand of discipline. . . . It was this drill and discipline that made the Army."[11]

While the Wisconsin and Indiana men cheered McClellan with youthful enthusiasm, they were less sure about the man named to command their new division, Irvin McDowell, who had led the national army in the defeat at Bull Run. He was an 1833 graduate of the U.S. Military Academy, where one of his classmates was Rufus King, now leading the Western brigade. McDowell's staff service in the Mexican War was distinguished, and in the years before secession he served in

the Adjutant General's Office, earning a reputation for steady compe-
tence and a certain ability in the social graces. In May 1861, in part
through the intervention of his patron Treasury Secretary Salmon
Chase, McDowell was appointed a brigadier general and named to
command the forces raised to defend Washington. In all his years of
military service, McDowell had never held a field command and, unable to resist the political pressure, he marched his untrained soldiers to
Bull Run and disaster.

Initial acceptance of McDowell by the Wisconsin men soon faded. A
typical reaction was that of Edwin Brown, who at first was willing to
dismiss as "beyond human control" what he called the general's "mis-
fortune at Bull's Run." But the new officer was soon convinced
McDowell was "headstrong" and "*too anxious to retrieve his defeat at Bull
Run.*"

The general's reputation "was peculiar," admitted another Wisconsin officer. "I have seen him attempt to handle a division . . . only to get
his brigades and regiments so divided and twisted that he completely
lost control of his command; his horse was always blundering over a
fence into a ditch until at least there was a general impression with the
men that couldn't be shaken, that this man who never tasted wines or
liquors or even tea and coffee was a drunkard. They also believed him
to be in some way in criminal communication with the confederates,
and it was current gossip in the ranks . . . he wore a peculiar light-
colored and conspicuous hat that the enemy might distinguish and not
hurt him. The charge of drunkenness and disloyalty was equally ab-
surd, but McDowell's greatest success, was as a society man in command of a department after the war."[12]

One of the best McDowell stories came before McClellan's "Grand
Review" at Bailey's Cross Roads. The task of preparing the field was
given to King's Western Brigade, and the regiments had been marching
out to work on the parade ground. When the Badgers and Hoosiers
complained of their full cartridge boxes, an agreement was struck to
leave behind the heavy cartridges. Then, late in the day, "McDowell had
the brigade marched in review before him, in order that he might
ascertain, as he alleged, whether the field was adapted for the review of
120,000 troops the next day," one veteran said. "After the brigade had
performed that service, and 'stacked arms,' the enemy's artillery attacked the picket line, perhaps a mile and a half away. General
McDowell ordered General King to take his brigade to the assistance of
the picket line at the front. Then came the 'tug of war.' There was no

dodging the fact that the brigade was without ammunition. General McDowell gave the order to General King in the presence of the troops. General King turned to the colonels and repeated the order. Lieut. Col. Lucius Fairchild studied a moment, then replied to General King, 'I am informed that the 2d Wisconsin is without ammunition.' Immediately the colonels of the 6th and 7th Wisconsin, and the 19th Indiana, made a similar report. General King appeared displeased, though I believe he knew it, but could not, of course, at the time confess it. General Mc-Dowell was in a great rage, and ordered the brigade to quarters with a sharp rebuke, and sent a staff officer post haste for Augur's brigade, which came forward at the double quick. We passed them not far from the crossroads. They were simply swearing mad at us, and did not hesitate to express themselves as they passed."[13]

But any excitement was an exception those days. From Arlington Heights, Dawes wrote his sister: "A military life in camp is the most monotonous in the world. It is the same routine over and over every day." Entertainments, the young captain said, included "whist, chess, and other games on wintry days, and, despite restrictions on political discussion . . . we discussed all questions of politics or religion, with the utmost freedom." In these far-ranging sessions, said Dawes, "Bragg was a Douglass or war Democrat, Brown and Kellogg, Republicans,[14] and I was called an Abolitionist. But the baleful shadow cast by slavery over the border, and the fierce and brutal insolence of the slave catcher, who was often seen on our free soil of Ohio, tended to make Abolitionists."

One Shawano County man, Julius Murray, reflected "on the sad crisis" facing the country. "I can come to no other conclusion that should the Gen. Government be overpowered there will be but one continued scene of anarchy and confusion for the future," he wrote home, "and that it is the duty for every one that can possibly do so to enlist willingly and crush out the traitors. Some must fall but all must take their chance."[15]

An officer of his company, Edwin Brown of Fond du Lac, was reaching the same conclusion. "Thousands of patriotic lives may be laid a sacrifice on the Altar of our Country's good," he wrote his wife, "but this Country will be purified of this blighting breath of treason and corruption, and history will record of the Republic, that in the year 1861 her patriotic children rallied around the emblem of the early fathers, and purged the land of the great curse of secession. . . . I wish that every man in the great North was animated by the same patriotic feeling that I think I have. This monstrous and unholy rebellion would be crushed. . . ."

The letter also carried a more personal plea from a man wondering about his future: "For God's sake, Ruth if the care of bringing up my children should descend wholly upon you, try to infuse something besides selfishness and the love of gain into their minds. Don't crush out the love of the good and the true in nature and in life and leave nothing in its stead but the love of the Almighty Dollar."[16]

7.
The Fair Miss Peters

Edwin Brown and other Wisconsin men were anxious to crush the "monstrous and unholy rebellion," but the most exciting duty, for officer and soldier, was to march to the sentry posts of the city defenses. Once out in front of the army, the officer of day instructed the pickets as to the "sign" and "countersign" (such as "Putnam" and "Norway" for October 8, 1861),[1] and it was there the new soldier faced his first test of courage. If danger of an attack was remote (as they later came to understand), it seemed very real to a volunteer in the line well forward of the army—especially in the quiet of a long night, as Jerome Watrous of the Sixth Wisconsin discovered.

"Dennis and I were posted on the extreme right and told to keep a close watch, as the rebels were expected to cross the river and try to capture Washington," said Watrous. "The probabilities are that there was not an armed rebel within a dozen miles of that post, but Dennis and I watched things very closely all day. . . ." At last night came, said Watrous, and he was soon nodding. "An hour later I came to myself by yelling 'halt.' I don't know how long I had slept, but surely I had sat by that scrub pine tree long enough to dream that Jeff Davis' minions were on the point of turning the right of the Union army.

"There are several reasons for my not telling the rest of the company about my sleeping on picket. . . . That was just at the time when they were shooting soldiers who while on picket indulged in sweet sleep. . . . Good 'Old Abe' Lincoln had got up quite early in the morning to ride six or seven miles to save the life of a sleeping picket who had been sentenced to be shot. It occurred to me that it would be my luck to have Mr. Lincoln oversleep, or take the wrong road, if it should get out that I had slept on picket, and a court should fix a morning for my shooting, hence, as I before remarked, I did not go to the trouble and expense of billing the camp announcing any slumbers on outpost duty. But that was the last time I ever slept on guard."[2]

The folks back home, said another Badger, know nothing of the experience. "You have never been startled half out of your boots by the jump of a squirrel, or the fall of a rotten limb," he wrote his hometown newspaper. "You have never seen a large, charred and blackened stump standing 'fornist' you, which in the bright moonlight is soon 'trans–mogrified' into a grey uniform Secesher, while one gnarled, knotty limb is pointed toward you on which the bright rays of the moon glitter and glance off, as they would from a gunbarrel. . . . You never have laughed at yourself for your folly in mistaking such a piece of wood for an armed opponent. Of course you haven't, you poor, benighted civilian. You don't know anything about it."[3]

One dark and stormy night the sentries of the Sixth Wisconsin fired on an old empty barn. When the weary "Calicos" came off the picket line they were jeered by the boys of the Seventh Wisconsin for their mistake. A few nights later, the Seventh Wisconsin was on picket (another dark and windy night) and fired on a rustling in the bushes which did not respond to challenge. They charged it only to find a stray calf. Upon returning to camp, they were pointedly asked about the calf that attacked them, to which the "Huckleberries" responded, "Don't worry about the calf; we put him in that barn that attacked you the other night."

Hugh Perkins of the Seventh Wisconsin wrote that it "snowed a little" during his turn on the picket line. "It made the night awful noisy; and as one sat listening for Rebels, he could imagine he heard them approaching him every few moments, especially if he was a little scairt. One of the boys ordered a bush to halt, and at the same time fired on it. He shot three times at it."[4] Another sentry from the Seventh Wisconsin was brought in with a leg wound. "He had probably shot himself, because he didn't know how to handle a revolver. The bullet penetrated the calf muscle," a comrade confided to his diary.[5]

One development was troubling to the Sixth Wisconsin. "The Seventh Wis. Regt. while out on picket last week got alarmed and fired a good deal at nothing but shadows, and alarmed several other Regts. who were going to their assistance," a soldier correspondent reported. "It was a great disgrace to them, but the worst of it is that the New York Tribune Correspondent in speaking of it says it was the Sixth Regt., which makes us all mad. . . . The matter will get set right in print this week."[6] The Second Wisconsin "takes considerable credit to itself for never starting an alarm," said one brigade officer. "On the other hand they say in the other regiments that the pickets of the Second are always so busily engaged in stealing fruit beyond the outposts that they never see what happens along the picket line. I cannot say what truth there is in this; but I can vouch that the Second will never dishonor its state by going hungry when eatables can be had for the taking."[7]

In early March 1862, there was excitement when McClellan, under pressure from Lincoln, gathered the Army of the Potomac for a move on Confederate fortifications at Centreville, Virginia. In the Seventh Wisconsin, the orders to "be held in readiness to march at a minute's warning with knapsacks packed, and three days' rations cooked ready at all time" were read to the assembled companies. Then an officer stepped forward and said, "Boys, if them orders exactly suit you, you may cheer," and one volunteer wrote home, "You had better believe that we roused him up three times good. . . . The boys seem to be in the best of spirits, and anxious to smell powder." The army carefully pushed out of the Washington defenses to Centreville only to discover the Confederates had withdrawn. "The men were greatly disappointed. They had made their wills, and written their farewell letters, and wanted to fight a battle," said Rufus Dawes.[8] The Confederate fortifications, of which McClellan made so much, proved a sham, with no rebel soldiers on the parapets and painted wooden logs for cannons. The newspapers were full of the embarrassment, and, a few days later, the army was back in the Washington camps—the great advance ordered by Lincoln and executed by McClellan was a bust.

The destruction troubled Julius Murray of the Sixth Wisconsin. "You can hardly form any idea of the terrible havoc and desolation this war has occasioned in old Virginia. Splendid houses deserted, some knocked partly to pieces, some burnt up and one large mill past still burning, fences all burnt up, excellent orchards entirely destroyed. It is a sorrowful sight, but they have brought it on themselves." As the column returned from Centreville, he said, "the road was strewn with gloves, socks, shoes, blankets and all kinds of clothing thrown away by our troops who were too tired to carry them. New 2.00 gloves and most of the rest of the clothing as new was tramped into the mud. No one wished to pick them up. My load getting heavy after going two miles I fell out under my knapsack, threw away my blanket, a pair of new shoes, two shirts, one pair of boots, and one pair drawers. Lute [Murray's son] threw away part of his clothing and one pair of 4.00 boots. The Major [Edward Bragg] came up to me whilst I was unloading and asked me what I was doing (he was wet through). I told him I was lighting up, well said he—hurry up for we all have a hard time of it."[9]

But McClellan's caution limited the army's activity to marching only. In the politically charged Washington of those days, that would not do. Lincoln grew impatient and decided if he was unable to get McClellan to move the army he would do so himself. One presidential order organized the Army of the Potomac into four corps; another directed McClellan's advance on Richmond via the Chesapeake Bay to begin no later than March 13, 1862, provided the capital was left "entirely secure" in the judgment of McClellan and the four corps commanders.[10] These developments were reported in the Washington newspapers and, after a time, carried South, where they could be studied by elements in armed rebellion against the government.

The news was greeted in the ranks with enthusiasm. Rufus King was promoted to one of the divisions in McDowell's new corps, and Lysander Cutler of the Sixth Wisconsin became temporary brigade commander. More important, it now appeared the Wisconsin and Indiana men might see action. "There is some prospect of this Corps joining McClellan before Richmond," Jerome Watrous wrote his hometown newspaper. "I only hope it may." And there was a line to ease the worry of the home folk: "With two or three exceptions, the Appleton Boys are well, and as tough as so many bears."[11]

McDowell's Corps tramped to Fairfax, then Bristoe Station, Catlett's Station, and finally Fredericksburg, Virginia, arriving April 23. The march was hard, and, wrote Dawes, "in accordance with our customary fate," the weather was very rainy. One night, camped in a muddy field (the men "wet, wood scarce and mud deep, air chilly and everything in a forlorn condition"), a "heavy whiskey" ration was issued. "It was the first experiment of the kind in the history of our regiment, and it proved a miserable failure," Dawes said. "There were many who would not drink their liquor at all, and others, as a result, obtained a double or triple portion." In his journal he wrote, "A thousand drunken men in the brigade, made a pandemonium of the camp all night."[12]

Recalled was one incident that was an example of the selective memory of the veterans. They would see sights so horrible not to be put to paper, yet write of their soldier days with moist eye over a seemingly insignificant matter. The remembered story involved the Crawford County boys and a gray squirrel named "Bunnie." "The little fellow was tamed in a day or so and was a great pet with the Badger boys," one said. The squirrel was taken with the company during the march, and was allowed to run free among the small trees while the men rested or prepared meals and it "never failed to join them when called especially

*General Irvin McDowell.
Courtesy of the Wisconsin
Veterans Museum. Used
by permission.*

if tempted by a lump of sugar." One day, the men sat about a log fire watching the squirrel run up a tree and jump "to the broad shoulders of some kind friend." On one leap, the pet sprang into the flames. "It was," the storyteller said, "a clear case of cremation. Bunnie did not know what a fire was."[13]

In telling the story, the veterans, it seemed, understood of those innocent days that they too would soon make a bold, trusting leap, and afterward nothing would quite be the same.

The halting of McDowell's Corps at Fredericksburg as the army pushed south for the grand "On to Richmond" campaign provoked sour frustration in the Western regiments. The war might soon be over without even a chance to strike a blow, and how could the boys ever explain that to the folks back home? "I cannot tell you how we all felt at being left behind when the Army went to the Peninsula and we were left out of the ranks of McClellan, the idol of all the army," Frank Haskell of the Sixth Wisconsin wrote. They would learn later that the order to hold McDowell's Corps at Fredericksburg had been President Lincoln's. He was concerned that the force left in front of Washington was insufficient to ensure its safety. McClellan, stunned by the president's decision, afterward complained bitterly that the loss of McDowell's force prevented his success outside Richmond.

But at Fredericksburg there was still a slim hope those days that the Western brigade might be called to assist the Army of the Potomac, and even the weather brightened. "The spring had been very backward," one Badger said. "It had been cold and raw, with alternating storms of rain and snow. But when we went into this pleasant camp . . . summer seemed to come suddenly; the sun shone bright and warm, the air was full of delightful fragrance, and it was, to us younger ones at least, a joy to merely live and breathe." Another Sixth Wisconsin soldier told the home folk: "You can hardly form an idea of how beautiful the country looks on the opposite side of the river. . . . You have a view of the country for miles in every direction, and how beautiful and green everything looks, at the same time how desolate. Deserted mansions and all kinds of property going to ruin, but the way they treat our men they are entitled to no pity. Government ought to confiscate their land and everything else. You have no idea of the animosity of these people, I mean the upper crust."[14]

The weather was warm, the country beautiful, and some of the "boys" were thinking of matters other than war or soldiering. "You must look out for the best looking gal for me," Lute Murray of Shawano County wrote his sister, "for you know I can't be there to see to it. There are any number of girls here, but they don't suit my style—too much Secesh to suit me." Another Badger closed a letter, "Give my respects to all the girls I used to know, *pretty ones you know, Sis*." George Downing of the Sixth Wisconsin confided to his diary: "There is plenty of girls here and good-looking too. The women thought the Yankees had not but one eye and that was on their forehead." Even Edward Bragg of the Sixth Wisconsin took note of a nearby farmer's "fat, greasy, dirty daughter." One officer, he reported, "went up to get some milk this morning, and describes her, with flowing sleeves, dirty arms, dirty frock & full breasted, but thinks that unless she was compelled to scrub first, close proximity to her person would be decidedly dangerous."[15]

Sauk County men hung a Union flag over a Caroline Street sidewalk in Fredericksburg. "A group of ladies coming down did not observe it until nearly under it when they went right out in the middle of the muddy street to escape going beneath it," it was reported. "The boys looked on and enjoyed the scene, but soon strung seven flags which covered the whole width of the street. After that the ladies did not walk on that street at all."

The inhabitants of Fredericksburg "are mostly colored, a few old hoary headed white men, rosy cheeked damsels (all in their sweet sixteenth)," Jerome Watrous wrote home. "They all think we are 'right smart looking fellows and wear right good clothes' but they can't become reconciled to that name 'Yankee.'" Fredericksburg is "rampantly rebellious," another Badger said. "But few inhabitants are left behind, and those entirely women and children. Some of the most zealous of the former amuse themselves by making mouths at the Union soldiers as they pass through the streets, in some cases even spitting at them and threw water upon them from the windows."[16]

The officers of the Sixth Wisconsin, said Loyd Harris, then a lieutenant, were left with a bittersweet memory of the "fair Miss Peters," a belle of 18 living with her mother in a mansion the regiment was assigned to guard. The picket post "was within stone thrown of their house, and some days, before it was my turn to go on picket duty," Harris said, "the officers who had served, came in with stories about visions of a pretty girl who was seldom seen out side of the garden gate, and how they had exhausted every strategic idea their heads ever contained in order to obtain an introduction to the Peters family, but in vain."

Two weeks passed, and then: "It was our good luck to be assigned to the reserve post, near the Peters' mansion. I had quietly determined to meet the fair Miss Peters. I marched boldly up the graveled walk, rang the bell, sent my name by the servant and in a few minutes was met by both mother and daughter in the parlor. As I gazed at the fair Miss Peters, after a few commonplace remarks, I realized that she was indeed a very pretty girl. Of course, I had to explain why they were honored by a visit from a distinguished subaltern of the Union army and with a smile and a voice calculated to convey the idea that I had moved in the very best circles in the most ancient city on the Mississippi above St. Louis [Prairie du Chien], I ventured: 'Ladies, I am in charge of the picket line for the next two days, and knowing how rough some of the eastern soldiers are (will they ever forgive me for such a fib), I thought it my duty to call in and assure you that the gentlemen who are with me are very quiet and orderly, in fact could not be otherwise as they are sons of some of the first families in Wisconsin, and I hasten to assure you that I wish you to feel safe, and that not the slightest thing on your place shall be disturbed.'"

Here Harris said he paused to see the "effect of my volley at the fair enemy." "May I ask the name of your company?" asked Miss Peters in a quiet voice. With a "feeling of pride," Harris replied, "Company C, Sixth Wisconsin Infantry."

Both ladies "gave a slight start, and the young lady, with heightened color on her cheeks and with an air of hauteur that only a Southern girl can perfectly assume slowly said: 'I regret to inform you that only two weeks ago all of our chickens were robbed by your Company C, whom I now learn are the sons of the first families of Wisconsin. Heaven save the first families if these are the sons!'"

Harris (who always made a good story a better one) said he "mumbled over some words of explanation and was only to glad to beat a hasty retreat to the camp-fire . . . and there [stood] in front of an old, deserted fishing hut" with a wind chilling him through. It was a desolate moment. "I gazed at the lamb like countenances of . . . 'Devil Jack' Bowman, innocent youth; Jesse Adams, who scorned to have a top on his hat and was never known to have the broad part of his pants in proper repair; Al Witherow, who might buy a few eggs now and then, but steal, never; they were among the leaders." He concluded: "As I watched them I wondered why they did not content themselves with the fat, generous pork and the hard and lively crackers provided by the great 'Uncle Sam,' and leave the Virginia hen roosts alone. Then I remembered that a couple of weeks back, Witherow had presented 'our mess' with a pair of chickens, and we had never thought to enquire if they were loyal or disloyal birds, whether he had borrowed or paid for them; perhaps they were the Peters' fowls."

Harris left a postscript: "The wind howled more than ever and as we chattered merrily over a midnight cup of coffee, we little thought that the order was then issued that on the following morning would remove us . . . and the fair Miss Peters would be only a tradition of the past."[17]

8.
Massa Linkum's Men

The Wisconsin men looked into the hard face of slavery those first months in uniform. The Union columns pushing out of the Washington defenses were met by thousands of fugitives bound for freedom. The runaways—men and women, young and old, in family groups and alone—stood along the roadways and at the fences and farm gates, sometimes silent as they watched the long lines of marching soldiers in blue, other times laughing and shouting in joy and excitement. "They came in clouds," one Wisconsin officer said. "The first party I ever saw was a family of some sixteen—an old couple with some children, a young married couple with one child, and some men and boys. They took possession of our camp fire without saying a word, and as composedly as if it had been built for them." They told the soldiers they had become fugitives because their master threatened to send them south.

"One of the little darkies" kept "the camp alive for an hour with plantation jigs," the officer said. "For the information of those who are interested in the great moral question as to the effect of freedom upon this oppressed race, I will state that this particular offshoot . . . is as graceless a vagabond as ever assisted in upheaving a nation and producing civil war."[1]

When the army moved, the crowds of fugitives followed, gathering in tatterdemalion camps near Lincoln's soldiers simply because they did not know where else to go. Senior army officers had no idea what to do about them—there was no official regulation for dealing with runaways, no plan to house and feed them; indeed, the army had never faced such a situation. In lower ranks that was not a problem. From the very first the ex-slaves cooked and washed for the soldiers, tended horses and mules, polished boots and harness, drove wagons, put up tents, and gathered firewood, all for food or coins.

The former slaves were soon a fundamental part of camp life—a fact witnessed in the photographs of the army bivouacs. In the background of hundreds of the dim images, the black cooks, teamsters, and strikers stood in twos or threes, looking into the camera from afar with solemn faces. The volunteers accepted them from the first and in hard soldier fashion took to calling them "contrabands"—from a statement by Union Gen. Benjamin Butler, who had described fugitives reaching his line as "contraband of war." The runaways, freedmen, and others would, in the months ahead, be in blue uniforms themselves and would attract attention. But often overlooked was the simple truth that from the earliest days the ex-slaves were as much a part of the fabric of the Union army as the soldiers themselves.

The initial reaction of the Western men ranged from cool ambivalence to friendly curiosity to outright hostility. "Had a regular negro dance . . . white inhabitants all left—negroes monarchs of all they survey—tell some curious tales. Negros more intelligent than their masters," one Badger reported. Another volunteer wrote his sister that the "more I see of them the more I hate them. I wish that the Nigger lovers in Boston were down here and had to take charge of them. I did once have more sympathy for them. Now I do not think they are no better than cattle and I will use them as such." Lt. Edwin Brown of the Sixth Wisconsin wrote his parents that he felt it "was a shame that the 'almighty Negro' should bring us into such a fix as this great nation is at present. Why more lives will be lost in the next big battle, more treasure expended than the necks of the whole Negro race are worth."[2]

A political proposal to arm freed slaves and put them into the Union army caused consternation on the company streets. "Great God!" one Wisconsin solider wrote his hometown newspaper, "is Congress going to . . . put the African on an equal footing, and beside the hundreds of thousands of true patriots, and self sacrificing men who have left all, that they may help to crush treason and restore peace to our Government. It was by the howlings of Northern fire-eaters that this great Rebellion was hurled upon us. . . . Better that the struggle continue for years than to end by such means. Then, we say, is it to be wondered at that the soldiers feel hurt; insulted. . . ."[3] A Badger officer upset over "this great national nigger question" grumbled that he had not come "from the grand west . . . to wrangle over Virginia niggers and South Carolina niggers and other niggers. . . ."[4]

But there was sympathy in the camps as well. One private told of a "colored boy" who came to the camp, "bare-footed and ragged" and the volunteers took the "little fellow in their charge, intending to clothe and feed him until he could be otherwise cared for." Then two officers sharply "ordered him out of the company at once, and threatened with severe punishment the man who should attempt to shelter him." It was an "atrocious act," the writer said, this "turning out a child of ten years in a place where, if caught by his unnatural master, nothing could save from a brutal and barbarous flogging—such as a Western farmer would be ashamed of."[5]

One of the two officers was Loyd Harris of Prairie du Chien. As a young lieutenant he ordered from camp a fugitive boy, but as a veteran 20 years later he had a different view, and it was revealed in a story. It was in early 1862, he recalled, and the officers of the company were without a cook. Brought to their campfire was a fugitive introduced as Matthew Bernard. "Old Matt must have been fifty years old the day he made his first bow," said Harris, "and in a quiet voice, said, 'Gemmen, I hopes I'll always suit you.' Bless his kind, old heart, he always suited us, never failed us, and even in the hour of danger . . . brave old Matt waited for his orders to seek safety."

Bernard "in his quiet way" told his early history and Harris took care in recording it some 20 years later: "Over the river, just below Fredericksburg on Massa Arthur Bernard place, was born. It was dar I grew up as a slave, and with the consent of Massa Bernard I married one who was raised on de same place. We was very happy, sah; had a little baby girl who is now almost grown. Just before de war, I heered that my wife was to be sold. I went to Massa Bernard wid tears in my eyes, and begged him not to sell her. He would do it; and he sold her to go far south. When she was gone I went to him and said Massa Bernard, I's always been your faithful slave, but you have dun sold my wife and the first chance I get I will leave you, and de old place. Soon after dat, de federal soldiers come along and I went in to see him and said Massa Bernard, good bye, and den I jined de old Sixth."

It was not six months later, Harris said, that the Sixth Wisconsin found itself camped "in the yard in front of Arthur Bernard's fine dwelling." Landowner Bernard had coldly refused to recognize his old slave and was "completely demoralized" by the turn of events that had Federal soldiers scattered in groups on his front yard. "The night was bitter, cold and our men experienced difficulty in securing wood to keep the fires replenished," said Harris. "And here there happened an incident that many others remember well. The 'Jay-Hawkers'—Co. C, were shivering around the poor campfires, occasionally looking at the rows of noble, old chestnut trees that lined the roadway that led to the main road, and at dark, requesting that they could cut a few straggling dead limbs for their fire. The scanty supply was soon exhausted and the cold . . . night was pinching them worse than ever."

Permission was requested to "fell one of the grand old trees," said Harris. "Two stalwart men who had often felled the mighty pines in northern Wisconsin, seized their axes, but before they could strike a blow, old Matt stood before them, filled with alarm and wonder and consternation clearly depicted on his sable face. 'Mr. Russell, are you gwine to cut down dat tree.' 'Yes, Matt, we have permission and must do it or freeze,' answered Russell. With a big tear starting from each eye, and with hands raised in a most imploring manner, the old slave, forgetting how his master had treated him, slowly said: 'Please, sah, don't cut down dat tree; Massa Bernard's fader planted it dar when Massa was a little boy, and if you cut id down you will break the old man's heart. . . .' Old Matt's appeal was listened to, and for a while the tree was spared, but as the night grew colder, the order was given and the grand old tree fell to the ground. It was by the fire from that tree I listened to the band that played the 'Star Spangled Banner,' near the first line; it was by that fire we passed a very uncomfortable night, awaiting for dawn. . . ."

When the Sixth returned to Wisconsin in early 1864 on 30-day veteran furlough, Bernard was with the regiment as it marched along the "streets of Milwaukee in at least a foot of snow." A few days later, however, Bernard was stricken by smallpox. "Human skill and good treatment were of no avail," said Harris, "and in a retired spot in the outskirts of beautiful Milwaukee lies buried a poor old slave—who, freed by the pen of Lincoln and the sword of McClellan, proved his gratitude in more than one way by faithful service to his country."[6]

The farmers, pinery workers, and frontier mechanics were confronting that "peculiar institution" they had read so much about in the newspapers back home and it was unsettling. The war, which most of them started on as an adventure and a defense of the Old Flag, was becoming something deeper and more complex, and the common soldier wondered how it was all going to come out. Back home there were so few blacks and here there were so many. In Wisconsin, a frontier where a man was pretty much judged on his energy and ability rather than his class, blacks could travel, own property, serve on juries, and send their children to public schools. In a company in his own regiment, said Earl Rogers of the Sixth Wisconsin, were two enlistees from a "settlement of colored people" in the Town of Forest in Bad Ax County. The two volunteers, unnamed, "were faithful soldiers, each of them receiving wounds in battle." They had enlisted together after Fort

Sumter; one was killed in action in 1864, and the survivor was remembered for his "faithful service." In Company E was a black barber who accompanied the regiment from Fond du Lac and who was, said "Mickey" Sullivan of the Sixth Wisconsin, as "well known" in the regiments as the brigade commander.[7]

Others were less accepting. "I understand there is a Negro regiment in town, but . . . I have not had my nerves shocked, by seeing a 'wooly head and black face,' decked out in 'Uncle Sams' uniform," Edward Bragg wrote from Washington, where he was recovering from an injury. "I wish a white man was as good as a Negro, and elicited as much sympathy and attention. A man must be either 'a foreigner or a black' to receive early notice at the hands of our exceedingly discriminating public." In the same letter: "A little nigger just came to my room, with 'our Corps' badge on his hat which was given him by a Lieutenant. By the aid of a knife I soon destroyed the 'cuffies' plumage. What an ass a man must be, to put his uniform on a dirty nigger that don't belong to him." If the fugitives were "Government propity," said a Second Wisconsin man, the "best thing to do with them is to send them to Cuba to pay the expences of the war. Confiscate the Propity of the men of the South that are found in arms against us and to do the same with the Nigs Lovers North who are as much to blame as the Rebs. . . ."[8]

Rufus Dawes, who had come to oppose human bondage during his boyhood in Ohio, was curious about the whole matter and finally "cornered a very black, but quick witted little imp" called "Mink." "Mink," said Dawes, "where did you come from?" "Bides Hole sah!" (Boyd's Hole below Fredericksburg). "Where do you sleep?" "I sleeps under a leaf, sah!" "What do you do?" "I teaches school, sah!" Dawes added: "Sure enough, investigation proved that this little black 'Mink' was teaching a class of other contrabands their letters, which he had already quickly learned himself. As 'Mink' explained matters to me, our colored barber, who came with us from Wisconsin, 'done bossed the school,' but the colored barber himself could not read. He was only useful in keeping order."[9]

Also remembered by Dawes was a foraging raid to a plantation by his Sixth Wisconsin. The detail was about to depart by steamer when confronted by the plantation's field and house workers. "There were men, women and children, about seventy slaves, gathered up on the beach," Dawes said. "They were of every age and size from the old patriarch . . . to babes at the breast. They had their worldly all with them." The sister-in-law of the owner came down from the main house. The lady was a "remarkably handsome and manifestly superior wom–

an," and she "went among the slaves with tears in her eyes and implored them by every recollection and attachment of a life-time, and by the sacred memories of their dead, not to go away, and she painted in high colors the miseries that would be inflicted upon them when they became 'free niggers' up north."

The slaves, Dawes wrote, "regarded her with affection and the highest respect and they were deeply moved. But there were friends of freedom and fair play among the men who carried muskets. They warned the negroes that before our steamer was out of sight the chains would be on them, and they would be driven south. They told them that their liberty was here, to take it. I remember the squeaking tenor voice of private Edwin C. Jones of company 'E,' asking, 'Shall these babes be slaves? Almighty God forbid it.' The negroes all went on the boat. The lady's maid hung weeping upon her, but she went with her people to be free."[10]

Ohio-born Edward Kellogg of Boscobel, the newspaperman turned soldier in the Second Wisconsin, wrote an abolitionist friend in Wisconsin: "I really wish you could see as much of negro life as I have the past month. I never dreamed they were as a race so unique, so foreign to the soil in language and custom, so clearly distinguished from the ruling face in every habit and feeling." In another letter to the same friend: "How intense your interest is, in the cause of the Negro! Stronger than mine, I confess but I can have no controversy with you, or with any other sympathizer with the down-trodden. For, however good men may differ with regard to the policy which should be pursued in dealing with our great national evil, all who ever felt a single heart-beat for the good of humanity, are anxious that the great wrong should be righted, and the African placed upon his proper footing as a man and a brother." In a later letter: "It would have done your slavery hating heart good to have seen the contrabands pouring into our lines during the past four weeks. Thousands upon thousands have found refuge among us. . . . They were generally more intelligent than I expected to find them, some of them equal to some Northern voters, perhaps, though you must not imagine that I would make them such by any manner of means."[11]

The Sixth Wisconsin's Albert Young was one of those beginning to realize that the war was becoming more than just a defense of the Union. "I had never thought I had entered the army in the interest of the slave," he wrote later. "But here I came to feel that I wished the war might result in the freeing of the colored people of the South. I was glad I was in the army if it might that our battling would result in the doing away with what I then for the first time fully recognized as being a most gigantic wrong. . . ."

It began when a group of ex-slaves approached the regiment. "Among them I noticed a man of attractive appearance and good presence, not much darker in complexion than many in our regiment, and I wondered what he wanted," Young recalled. "I learned that he was a slave—owned, body and soul by a man he called master. Listening I found him to be intelligent, a man of ability, that he was a carpenter by trade and a skilled mechanic. . . . Looking at this man—this slave—I fervently thanked God that there were men—a few only, it is true—in our country who had set apart their lives to right this cruel wrong. I felt that we—the soldiers of the Union army—might be the power to place this mighty manacle upon the anvil of freedom and deal it herculean blows until the massive links were severed. . . . I was awakened at last; my soul raged within me. This finally became our work, and we were permitted to accomplish it—and it was granted me to see it. . . . Surely we were serving God in this, for He loves good and hates evil. . . . He hates slavery and loves freedom, He hates sin—what a monstrous evil, what a monstrous wrong, what a monstrous sin was this accursed institution."[12]

Rufus Dawes heard the thump of history's drum: "Our camps are now flooded with negroes, with packs on their backs, and bound for freedom. No system of abolition could have swept the system away more effectually than does the advance of our army. Behind us the slaves, if they choose, are free. All civil authority is gone. . . . Thus the great question of liberty is working its own solution. The right must, and surely will, triumph in the end. Let us thank God, and take courage."[13]

9.
The Boss Soldier

The Wisconsin and Indiana men were learning to be soldiers, even looking, marching, and, now and then—like soldiers—capturing a secessionist chicken. But there was one matter that still needed to be resolved. The volunteer regiments were composed of friends, relatives, neighbors, and schoolmates, and the relationship between enlisted man and officer was casual. Levi Raymond of the Sixth Wisconsin, for example, had been pitched onto a stump "scuffling and fooling" with an officer.[1] If the brigade was to be a disciplined organization, such free and easy "scuffling and fooling" between private and officer would have to end. The man to do just that arrived May 7, 1862.

His name was John Gibbon, and he had just been named to replace the promoted Rufus King as commander of the Western brigade. An intense professional, Gibbon had previously commanded Battery B of the Fourth U.S. Artillery (famous in the Old Army for its for service at Buena Vista) and served as chief of artillery for McDowell's Division.

But the Battery B officer who early on had caught the eye of the Westerners was James Stewart, a tough old regular promoted from ranks to be second lieutenant. He was, a comrade said, a "handsome man, of fine, soldierly presence, rather grave and taciturn in manner . . . , fond of 'creature comforts,' and sometimes indulged in them quite as much as was good for him. But he always realized when it was 'time to quit,' and . . . was always on hand in the morning when duty called." Pvt. John Cook of the Sixth Wisconsin, who spent time in the battery as an infantry volunteer, said later with admiration that "Old Jack was very strict with the rest of the battery, but would at the same time drink more than any one else." Stewart, Cook admitted, was the only soldier—Union or Confederate—he gave wide berth.[2]

General John Gibbon.
Courtesy of the Wisconsin
Veterans Museum.
Used by permission.

Cook's trouble with the regular officer began after he transferred into Battery B and, coming off guard duty, stopped at a sutler, where he purchased two bottles of whiskey. "I took them to my tent and left one of them out then went out before the fire and set down to enjoy a drink by myself. When almost at once, Miller, one of our squad (6 in number) called out from the tent 'What you got there?' I told him nothing, to lay down and go to sleep. He said, 'You can't fool me. You have whiskey,' and up he got. Making considerable noise, he woke the rest and they got up. I gave them all a smell of the bottle. They wanted to know where I got it and I told them. They said they were a going to get some. And went and got *seven* bottles, then got pretty noisy and I told them we would all be put into the Guard house." With that Cook went off to his blankets. "I had been there about one hour when I was jerked out of my tent by who I did not know until I found Lieut. Stewart lying on his back in front of me. I supposed I have knocked him down. I tried to apologize but he would not allow it, but took me and the rest and tied us to the Gun carriage."[3]

The battery had been associated with the Western brigade from the first days, and the new commander, Gibbon, was a familiar figure to the volunteers. In fact, when the artilleryman needed cannoneers, he had gone to the regiments, and in the Sixth Wisconsin it was recalled how Gibbon had trouble convincing the soldiers to join his battery. Following his opening appeal, only one man stepped forward. Finally, Col. Lysander Cutler explained a second time what was wanted, and then a "large number stepped forward" and Cutler cautioned, "There, there, that will do—you needn't all come out—they don't want the whole regiment for the battery."[4]

Gibbon came away from his recruiting impressed. "The first marked feature I noted with these men was their quick intelligence," he said. "It was only necessary to explain a thing but once or twice to enable them to catch the idea and then with a little practice they became perfect." His problem was "to take these active, intelligent young men, fresh from the walks of civil life and from every profession and station, and mold them into soldiers.... This was not a little complicated by the fact that in such a mass of raw material it not infrequently happened that brothers, fathers and sons were serving in the same company, the son, perhaps, being senior to his father!" Another Battery B man explained the "fearless, independent" Westerners were "splendid raw material" but were "'quick on the trigger' and would not take any nonsense from anybody, with or without shoulder-straps.... [They] were ready to fight anything on earth at any time or in any shape!"[5]

One example was the trouble that Capt. John Marsh of the Sixth Wisconsin had with Pvt. John Cook before Cook went off to serve in Battery B. "The men in the Co. despised him through out as much as I did and would like to see him sunk into the lowest pits of hell...," Cook said. "When he took the Co. he told a gentleman from Milwaukee that the Co. was dirty and lousy but since he took charge of the Co. he had made them clean and neat, which was a lie, for the Co. was alright before he took charge of it." Hamilcar McIntosh of Milwaukee and Josiah Fowler of Mazomanie soon added to the problem. "They would dam him and he would not do anything with them for he was afraid of them.... [One time] Capt. Marsh was put under arrest for 2 weeks by Col. Cutler, and Cook would holler from his tent, 'Bully for the brute. May he die under arrest,' and occasionally Mc. would say 'Amen.'"[6]

In the brigade there was at first little acceptance for Gibbon and his old army manner. "I recall," one soldier wrote, the "comical appearance he presented when mounted because of his height, his legs were abnormally long and he rode a small horse [and] that he issued an order instituting a daily review at what seemed to us an unwarrantably early hour in the morning—5 o'clock, I think—to be followed immediately at its close by the drinking of a cup of hot coffee by each member of the brigade whether he liked it or not."[7]

Born in Pennsylvania in 1827 into the family of a physician, Gibbon grew up in North Carolina and was appointed to the U.S. Military Academy from that state. He graduated from West Point in time for occupation service in Mexico and then was sent to Florida against the Seminoles. A competent, steady, and respected professional, Gibbon served from 1854 to 1859 as an artillery instructor at the U.S. Military Academy, winning recognition in 1860 for publication of his highly regarded *Artillerist's Manual*. At war's outbreak, Gibbon was a captain in command of Battery B, then stationed at Camp Floyd in the Utah Territory.

With the war and despite the decision of three of his brothers to join the Confederate army, he stayed with the Union. In manner and outlook, Gibbon, with his close-cropped hair and trim beard, was always the regular. Long after the war, his soldiers were surprised to discover the hard brigadier general who drilled them in the hot sun so many long hours opposite Fredericksburg, Virginia, secretly wrote sentimental poetry and enjoyed singing.

Gibbon also had a dark side. He was marked by a professional soldier's jealous ambition, and during his war days he was embroiled in lingering disputes with fellow officers over slights imagined and real. Portions of his war memoir were filled with long grumbling passages justifying his actions. But Gibbon proved to be one of the few West Pointers to adapt the rigid discipline of the regulars to volunteers. And, although he never complained, some in his brigade believed that Gibbon's advancement was slowed by his Southern background. In fact, when his promotion to brigadier general was delayed in Congress because he had no patron, Gibbon went to James Wadsworth, a New York State political general whose headquarters was nearby, to ask advice. Wadsworth immediately saw that the promotion was advanced and won Gibbon's friendship and gratitude.

Gibbon's appointment to the Western brigade began a long association (one that continued through the postwar reunions), but that May of 1862 he was puzzled how to turn his frisky volunteers into soldiers. One who caught his eye was the adjutant of the Sixth Wisconsin, Frank Haskell of Madison, whom he accepted on his staff. Haskell quickly won not only Gibbon's confidence but also his respect, and even Rufus Dawes, a one-time rival, wrote home that "Frank A. Haskell is one of the best Adjutants in the army." Another Wisconsin man claimed that "Haskell's soldierly bearing—I never saw a finer-appearing soldier— gave birth to ambition in the rank and file to become soldiers in the fullest sense of the word. Haskell's running fire of criticism and em- phatic, plain instructions to individuals and companies as a whole, on Sunday morning inspections, gave the men . . . information without which no regiment can become thoroughly competent in either war or peace. Though others became adjutants of the Sixth, Frank A. Haskell never had a successor."[8]

Over the passing decades Haskell would become Wisconsin's most widely known Civil War figure—not for his service with Gibbon's Brigade but as "Haskell of Gettysburg," the soldier who rallied the Union line on the third day of July 1863, and who sent a lengthy description of the battle to a brother in Portage, Wisconsin. The account would be published and reprinted, and what Haskell saw, did, and wrote would be so important no subsequent historian writing of Gettysburg could ignore his words. The irony was not the fame—for he did a great deed and wrote well about a momentous battle—but that Haskell's role in shaping a Western regiment and the Iron Brigade would be overlooked.

He was already a man of reputation in Wisconsin when he accepted appointment as adjutant of the Sixth Wisconsin in 1861. A native of Vermont and grandson of a New Hampshire captain of the Revolution, Haskell was 33 and practicing law in Madison and had been active in a militia company, the Governor's Guards. As a result, his transition to a soldier was an easy one. But from the first days he was not well liked. The men in ranks feared and respected the cold and arrogant Haskell, but there was little affection. In one letter from those days, a Sixth man wrote a careful description to *The Milwaukee Sentinel:* "Frank Haskell, our efficient and active Adjutant, is liked better every day, although scrupulous exact in all that pertains to duty, and rigid as iron in disci- pline."

Haskell was always a man Dawes admired and respected as a soldier who "exercised at that time a marked influence upon the progress of the regiment in soldierly knowledge and quality . . . and had been drawn by natural tastes to some study of military tactics." Dawes added: "It was a good instruction in the school of a soldier to serve a tour of duty in the regimental guard. One especial and untiring effort of Adjutant Haskell was to exact cleanliness and neatness of personal appearance, an essential condition of the soldierly bearing. The cotton gloves, which he required the men to wear, were kept snow white, nor did he allow them to cover dirty hands. It was a dreaded ordeal for a man to step four paces in front and face the Adjutant before the assembled guard and in fear of this he went there clean at however great and unusual a sacrifice of customary habit. To see Haskell, 'About face' and salute the Colonel before the regiment when we were on dress parade was an object lesson in military bearing."

But there was tension in the relationship. Haskell's strong and unconcealed ambition, Dawes always felt, was more than a gentleman should display. The two would be rivals for promotion to major of the Sixth Wisconsin, a competition in which Dawes was successful, and in writing long afterward, the Ohioan left a statement that revealed lingering heat from those days when both were young officers in the Western regiment. "Haskell had been born with every quality that goes to make a model soldier. He took great interest and pride in the instruction of the regiment, and so elevated his office, that some men then thought the Adjutant must at least be next to the Colonel in authority and rank." Within a few months of Gettysburg, Haskell would be killed at Cold Harbor serving as the colonel of the Thirty-sixth Wisconsin.[9]

But all that was ahead, and if Gibbon was pleased with his new brigade, among the officers there was grumbling (mostly by ambitious Sol Meredith of Indiana) over the appointment of a regular to command volunteers. In ranks, the acceptance was mixed. Gibbon was, one veteran said, "a most thorough disciplinarian, and the manner in which he put the brigade through drill will never be forgotten by those who participated. There were early morning drills, before breakfast, forenoon drills, evening and night drills, besides guard mounting and dress parade. Probably no brigade commander was ever more cordially hated by his men. He was all soldier, both in looks and deeds. When Gibbon's brigade marched there was no straggling." The time, another soldier said, "was mostly spent in camp duties and drilling—company, battalion and brigade drill—under Gen. John Gibbon, and I do not believe any body of men could attain higher efficiency in drill and discipline that we had attained. Mornings at 5 o'clock, Gen. Gibbon and Adjt. Haskell would ride in and around the camp, taste coffee in the company cook kitchens, and look after all sanitary matters pertaining to the general well fare."[10]

In his six months commanding the brigade, Gibbon developed just

the right knack in shaping the volunteers into a cohesive fighting brigade. He found the boys and men to be intelligent, willing, and more
responsive to reward than punishment. "I was already impressed with
the conviction that all they needed was some discipline and drill to
make them first class soldiers, and my anticipations were more than
realized," Gibbon said. He also found the Second and Sixth Wisconsin
"had decidedly the advantage" over the two other regiments, and "each
strove to become the 'crack' regiment of the brigade."[11]

Gibbon immediately instituted schools of instruction. "[The boys] . . .
drilled before sunrise and had a dress parade after sundown. There
were company drills, reviews, excursions into the enemy's country, and
all sorts of work that was required in converting raw material into
fighting material," said Jerome Watrous of the Sixth Wisconsin. "My,
my, how the boys disliked John Gibbon in those days of hard work—
work which they thought was not necessary. They had enlisted to fight
for their country, not to wear themselves out in drilling and marching
around. Gibbon was a soldier. They were not when he took them. He
knew what was before them; he knew how much they needed the discipline he was giving them, and they learned to most keenly appreciate
it before they were a year older."[12]

The Westerners on occasion would knock down a rail fence for
firewood; Gibbon established a rule that when a fence was torn down
the regiment camped nearest was required to rebuild it. Soldierly appearance was encouraged with an order giving the well-turned-out
soldier a 24-hour pass to go "blackberrying." Officers were required to
attend morning roll call. A circular directed commanders to "see that
their men bathe regularly at least once a week."[13]

One problem persisted—getting the sentinels to walk their posts.
"Men who had been working hard all their lives for a purpose could see
no use in pacing up and down doing nothing," Gibbon said. "Hence
logs of wood, a convenient rock or campstool, were frequently resorted
to as resting places, and often I would ride by a sentinel without any
attention being paid to me whatever, the men on the post being entirely
too much occupied enjoying his ease, perhaps even smoking a cigar, to
notice my approach." Finally, Gibbon came upon a solution. One day,
"perhaps being in a less amiable frame of mind than usual," he ordered
a lax sentry relieved from his post, stripped of equipment, and placed
on the head of a barrel in front of the guard-tent. "He soon attracted
many observers and when it was known for what he was placed there,
he was most unmercifully ridiculed by his comrades. I never had any
more trouble after that about my sentinels, either saluting me or walk-

A Sixth Wisconsin man in full dress: Pvt. Charles Keeler. From the Collection of Alan T. Nolan. Used by permission.

ing their posts, and that is the only instance in which I ever resorted to arbitrary punishment in that command."[14]

One other thing needed to be done. The regiments had Federal uniforms, but remnants of the state-issued gray clothing remained. In October 1861, when the Wisconsin militia uniforms became tattered, the Second Wisconsin was issued the dark blue nine-button regulation frock, dark blue trousers and Model 1858 hat of the U.S. regulars. The hat was a showy black felt affair looped up on the side with a brass eagle crest, trimmed with an infantry-blue cord and black plume as well as the brass infantry bugle, company letter, and regimental numeral. The Sixth and Seventh Wisconsin had been issued the frock coats and sky-blue trousers earlier, but retained some state-issue clothing.[15] On May 5, 1862, Lysander Cutler, then the acting brigade commander, ordered the black hats for the Seventh Wisconsin. When Gibbon assumed command, he determined to make the Model 1858 hat a consistent item for his whole brigade. Accordingly, the Sixth Wisconsin was issued hats in mid-May and the Nineteenth Indiana about the same time.[16]

It was the hats that left a striking impression—making the rangy Westerners look taller and more distinctive—and soon other soldiers began talking of the "Black Hats." It was, as events proved, a significant step in transforming volunteers into an "Iron Brigade."

At the same time, under Gibbon's order, the soldiers were issued linen leggings and cotton gloves. In the Sixth Wisconsin, the hats and gaiters were "received with the greatest merriment" and some grumbling, for the additions depleted the clothing allowances. The displeasure was displayed one morning when Gibbon found his "pet horse" equipped with leggings; the general was never able to determine the soldiers responsible for the prank.[17] Rufus Dawes said the boys "all felt proud of the fine appearance" of the regiment, and his journal noted: "General Gibbon attended our dress parade to-day and the regiment was in 'fine feather.'"[18] It may have been a bit fancy for farmer and pinery boys, but the volunteers were pleased with their tall hats and blue uniforms. "We have a full blue suit, a fine black hat nicely trimmed with bugle and plate and ostrich feathers," one Westerner wrote, "and you can only distinguish our boys from the regulars, by their [our] good looks."

Gibbon became proud of his brigade and the men became proud of him. "It was Gibbon who did much to teach us how to be soldiers," one Badger said. "Until we learned to know him, which we did not till he led in battle, we seemed very far apart." Another admired the general's coolness when Confederate cavalry charged a picket post. "The Gen'l," he said, "who wore the garb of a common soldier, arose, lighted his pipe, drew his revolver and stood by the side of a tree and said 'd—n 'em, let 'em come, I am ready for the first six of the pups.'"[19]

In the final assessment, it was Gibbon who provided the know-how to get the volunteers ready for battle. If they were already singled out in an army of Easterners ("the one distinctively Western brigade in the Eastern army," one said),[20] the units were among the best-drilled, a fact recognized by the Wisconsin and Indiana boys. The fine military appearance also impressed the dignitaries and brightly arrayed belles who came from Washington to see and admire them. It was Gibbon (with Haskell and others) who gave the regiments discipline and professional training and prescribed a uniform that set the soldiers apart. If given a chance, the men of Gibbon's "Black Hat Brigade" believed, good results would ultimately follow.

Gibbon explained that "mere efficiency in drill was not by any means the most important point gained. The habit of obedience and subjection to the will of another, so difficult to instill into the minds of free and independent men became marked characteristics of the command. A great deal of the prejudice against me as a regular officer was removed when the men came to compare their own soldierly appearance and way of doing duty with other commands, and although there were still malcontents, who chafed under the restraints of a wholesome discipline and would have chafed under any, these were gradually reduced in number and influence."[21]

That was why a soldier such as "Tough One" John Cook accepted Gibbon as "boss soldier" and why, finally, the men came to call Gibbon "Johnny, the War Horse." One Wisconsin officer explained: "The men who carried the knapsacks never failed to place an officer just where he belonged, as to his intelligence and bravery. Even if they said nothing, yet their instinctive and unconscious action in battle, placed upon the officers the unavoidable brand of approval or disapproval. For no regiment acted well its part under fire and great danger, without the officers had the confidence of the rank and file."[22]

One officer who won respect was Rufus Dawes, and he left an assessment of Gibbon. The general, he said, "soon manifested superior qualities as a brigade commander. Thoroughly educated in the military profession, he had also high personal qualifications to exercise command. He was anxious that his brigade should excel in every way, and while he was an exacting disciplinarian he had the good sense to recognize merit where it existed. His administration of the command left a lasting impression for good upon the character and military tone of the brigade, and his splendid personal bravery upon the field of battle was an inspiration."[23]

10.

Hindquarters in the Saddle

For a time that May of 1862 near Fredericksburg, Virginia, it seemed Gibbon's Brigade might get into the war. "The men received the announcement that they would probably be needed for a fight with a tremendous shout," said Rufus Dawes. "They said 'a year's fight was bottled up in them and it was spoiling to come out.' It transpired, however, that there were not enough rebels in the vicinity to accommodate our men with the desired fight. A strong feeling possessed us that we were to be a mere side show while others performed the real acts of war." Another Badger grumbled in a letter home: "I hope we will give hail Columbia and then the thing will be played out. As it is it is on its last legs and I wish I could get a chance to hit them one blow."[1]

To his father Edwin Brown of the Sixth Wisconsin wrote in frustration of the Western brigade being held at Fredericksburg, and he mistakenly blamed the corps commander, General McDowell, and not Washington. The "whole secret of it is the *imbecility* or *disloyalty* of McDowell at the doors of the War Department," he wrote. "But by preventing any men of whatever grade from visiting Washington on any pretence and by his continued presence there, he bids fair to thwart the wishes of *his entire command*. Thus the Country if they do not suffer from his treachery or the betrayal of that command to the enemy, will at least have to pay the expenses of 30 or 50,000 troops in the field who will not be permitted to strike one blow at treason or rebellion. . . . If McDowell had given McClellan his *hearty cooperation* Richmond would be ours today. As it is if McClellan should be defeated in the approaching great battle which will doubtless determine the fate of the Southern Confederacy, the loyal American people have no one to *blame*, no one to *curse* but McDowell and the *Blindness* of the War Department."

The division commander, Rufus King, said Brown, "is a sluggard, a man of no force of character, or he would not be here with his division. . . . But King will play up the 'gentleman General' have luxurious headquarters, dispense hospitality to *notable individuals* get up parades shows for their edification, have fine bands playing evenings around 'these Head Quarters' pass the wine cup around to his satellites and friends, ride splendid horses when he goes out to see be seen attended by his parasites *and staff*. Ah! It is a great thing for men Bankrupt *politically & financially* to hold high place in the Army . . . without rendering it any aid in its death struggle with rebellion. Too many men who are entirely satisfied with the *place they hold* have been appointed as Generals. Why? When the war is ended they will go back to the *obscurity from which they came.*"[2]

The news from Richmond went from bad to worse, and by early July it was clear to everyone that George McClellan's advance—started in such bright hope—was a failure and that the grand offensive was in disarray. McClellan had brilliantly moved his large army by water and then by land to the very gates of Richmond, but there he was stopped in a series of sharp battles which became known as the Seven Days. The very magnitude and savagery of the fighting had left McClellan shaken. Finally he withdrew his brigades to a base of supplies at Harrison's Landing, where he endlessly complained he had been defeated by the failure of Washington to provide him with the reinforcements requested.

One of those uncommitted reserves was McDowell's Corps, held back at Fredericksburg to protect Washington, and the news of the reverse was greeted with dismay and alarm in the Western regiments. "There has been terrible slaughter, but we are well satisfied that Mc-Clellan is safe," the Sixth Wisconsin's Julius Murray wrote home. "We did not have half force enough. When we get there we will make them skedaddle, where ever we meet them we drive them back, but it must be admitted they fight like devils."[3]

Much of the rebel success at Richmond was later credited to the bold maneuvering of Robert Lee of Virginia, who assumed command of the secessionist forces upon the wounding of Joseph Johnston. McClellan, protesting he was overwhelmed by superior forces (in fact, he outnumbered the Confederates), bitterly blamed a list of real and suspected enemies for plotting against the success of his army. In reality, the Federal defeat was not due to clever scheming but McClellan's own puzzling inability to seize a single initiative when facing the unexpected. It was the men of the Army of the Potomac, by courage and stubborn fighting, who kept defeat from turning into disaster. They were no longer fresh volunteers—a conclusion presented by a Wisconsin officer even as McClellan moved on Richmond. "I believe the boys are as patriotic now as then, only an inexperienced person might not think so, if he should happen along about the time something goes wrong, and hear them cursing the war, and the generals, and the country, and sometimes even the cause that brought them here," he wrote. "They are not so ardent and fiery, experience has tamed them. They are cooler, and I believe fight better and endure more. . . . The mass of the army is true and tried."[4]

In August, worried about Washington, the War Department ordered McClellan to move portions of the Army of the Potomac from Harrison's Landing to a Union position along the Rappahannock River. It was a decision based on the mistaken assumption the Confederate army was of such numbers that it could protect Richmond while mounting an extensive offensive. With McClellan under a cloud, the new Federal hero was John Pope, who had been brought from the West with much fanfare to lead a new "Army of Virginia" created by combining forces in Washington and northern Virginia. One of the units shifted to Pope's new army was McDowell's Corps with a brigade of Western soldiers.

Pope, a native of Kentucky, graduated from the U.S. Military Academy in 1842 and served in the Mexican War. He was a captain in the regular army at the start of the sectional crisis in 1860 and, upon Lincoln's election, tried to use his connections (his father was a judge of influence in Illinois) to advance his career. He even made it a point to travel with Lincoln on part of the journey to Washington before the inauguration but was rebuffed in his attempt to be named the president's military secretary. A Washington post unavailable, Pope accepted a commission as brigadier general of volunteers and was selected to command the Army of the Mississippi. He soon won newspaper attention (most of it through his own self-promotion) for capture of New Madrid and Island 10 on the Mississippi River. The successes caught Lincoln's eye and Pope was brought East, where he was directed to protect Washington, threaten Confederate rail lines in central Virginia, and develop a second front against Richmond.

Pope immediately got off on the wrong foot. His successes on the Mississippi River made him more boastful than usual, and he took a clumsy swipe at McClellan. "I come to you out of the West, where we have always seen the backs of our enemies," the general proclaimed to his new Army of Virginia. "I am sorry to find so much in vogue amongst you . . . certain phrases [such as] 'lines of retreat,' and 'bases of supplies.' . . . Let us study the probable lines of retreat of our opponents and leave our own to take care of themselves. Let us look before us and not behind. Success and glory are in the advance, disaster and shame lurk in the rear."[5]

Pope's words were ill-received. "General Pope's bombastic proclamation has not tended to increase confidence, indeed the effect is exactly the contrary," Rufus Dawes wrote home,[6] while Pvt. James Sullivan said: "General Pope who had captured the rebels that the gunboats had dislodged from Island No. 10 and New Madrid, and in consequence fancied himself the greatest general of the age, took command of all the troops in the vicinity of Washington not belonging to McClellan's army proper. He issued his first order dated 'Headquarters in the saddle,' and the soldiers, with their usual aptitude to ridicule all attempts at self-glorification on the part of generals, said that he must have his brains where most persons have their hindquarters, and immediately dubbed him 'Hindquarters in the saddle Pope,' and after events fully justified their judgement. After a series of the most silly and bombastic orders . . . in so far as one countermanded, modified or explained the preceding one, his literary display was finally interrupted by 'Stonewall' Jackson, who having performed his part in turning the flank of McClellan's army on the Peninsula, turned his attention to the direction of the Shenandoah Valley, where the rich harvest was ripe and awaiting shipment to Richmond."[7]

With Pope moving to threaten rail junctions northwest of Richmond, Lee dispatched Jackson and his soldiers to Gordonsville and began shifting his brigades by rail to Jackson's columns moving against two Union divisions posted at Cedar Mountain. On August 9, Federal forces, expecting reinforcement, attacked Jackson's army only to be soundly beaten by superior numbers. With the success, Lee boldly shifted additional forces to Jackson, hoping to strike a blow before Pope could be reinforced.

At the same time, Pope was consolidating his army, and among the soldiers ordered to Cedar Mountain were the "Black Hats" of Gibbon's Brigade. The Wisconsin and Indiana men, in service more than a year and drilled so long in the Washington camps only to be left behind when "Little Mac" went to Richmond, were finally headed to a battlefield. Except for some hard marching and skirmishing while on a raid or two, only the Second Wisconsin had seen real fighting.[8]

The march of Gibbon's Brigade of King's Division from Fredericksburg northwest to the battleground at Cedar Mountain began in haste and excitement. Orders "to strike tents and fall in" were received the afternoon of August 8, 1862, and "in twenty minutes" the column of some 1,900 officers and men, tightly closed by fours, was on the road. It all was done with quick, professional efficiency. The Western men were no longer the awkward volunteers who tramped away from Wisconsin and Indiana in 1861. Just weeks before, in writing a friend, a Wisconsin officer reported the "cowards have been sifted by the thousands out of the ranks, and the huge talking men, the braggarts and boasters have gone home. The men who are left are real warriors, and not the holiday party that you saw us when we went away." A Second Wisconsin man said his regiment was considerably reduced, but "I think what there are left of us are made of the 'real ould stuff.' I don't think it would be safe for any disease as the cholera, smallpox, or typhoid fever to attack us single-handed. Perhaps take the three combined they might make us *sick*— nothing more; for nothing short of a Minie [bullet] can kill us, or we should have been dead ere this." Another Badger wrote: "It is said that we have some hard boys. I will admit that; but when they get where there is any secesh they are not afraid."[9]

The thick, twisting column was moving quickly. One of the soldiers remembered the August sun as "scorching" and the heat "like a great hot sponge, which sucked the moisture out of every pore of the soldier's body." The water in the canteens was soon gone. "When a streamlet or spring was reached," he said, "it was lined with eager soldiers scraping the muddy bottom with cups in order to provide for their exhausted canteens."

The dusty hours passed slowly and the road seemingly had no end. When it rained, the roads "were soon over shoe top deep with soft mud," said Pvt. Chester Wyman of the Sixth Wisconsin. During the night, there was a brief halt during a rainstorm. "I looked for a place to sleep and as it was dark and still raining, I felt around and found a rise of ground that I thought would keep the water from running under me," Wyman said. "Laid down and slept the sleep of the innocent. In the morning as soon as it was light I looked around and found I was in a graveyard and I had been sleeping on a grave."

The column crossed the Rappahannock River at Kelly's Ford about 9 o'clock in the morning, said John Johnson of Stevens Point, then a sergeant in the Sixth Wisconsin. "At daybreak we made coffee at Stevensburg; we then resumed our march through Culpeper to Cedar Mountain, in a field to the right of the mountain, which showed unmistakably that a battle had been fought, bodies of men and horses laying around."

The column pushed on, finally halting as word passed along the ranks that Jackson and his brigades had withdrawn. The general feeling of the officers and men, said Johnson, was resignation. "So he has slipped away again. About all we had done so far was chasing Gen. Jackson, and we were anxious to come up to him and try conclusions. This was the general desire expressed."

Lt. Col. Edward Bragg of the Sixth Wisconsin never forgot the sight of his soldiers wading waist deep through the Rappahannock River: "In the bright moonlight, the men, trousers off and shirts tucked up, baggage and ammunition on the shoulder, stepping from stone to stone, in one of those beautiful moonlight nights for which Virginia is celebrated; and how, now and then, when a poor devil slipped from the stone and went, *ca-souse*, into the water, a great cry went up." To his father, Capt. Edwin Brown reported that "Pope was so badly scared that on the night we arrived he caused all the stores everything belonging to the army to be shipped on the R.R. He expected to be attacked as Jackson was largely reinforced." John Gibbon's quick look at the battlefield "disclosed evidence of a severe struggle, but from what I could learn it was not a very decisive one." Sauk County men said the brigade never had a harder march: "Weather muggy, hot, no rest except to make coffee, wading streams, marching in mud very little rations (hardtack tasted good those days)."[10]

The tired Wisconsin and Indiana men, who had covered 45 miles, went into bivouac near the battlefield. Other brigades in King's Division were much thinned by soldiers who could not keep up. "Straggling became almost a mania, some regiments not being able to account for half their men," one soldier said. "It was here Gibbon's brigade showed its wonderful discipline and high morale. Our regiments had comparatively no stragglers, not through the immediate influence of the officers alone, but a feeling of personal responsibility, each man for the man whose elbow he touched in ranks, and the responsive thought, 'I must not fail myself in the duty I demand of my comrade.'" There was bad news as well—the Third Wisconsin, with friends and relatives from home, had been in the battle,[11] and Brown wrote bitterly: "The Regt. [Third] suffered greatly in the fight but no mention is made of it. N.Y. & Penn Reporters monopolize all the glory for their own State troops, altho they never do as well as the new England &Western troops—The marches made by our Regt. were *the longest & most severe made this century*. We cut off Jackson's Communication with Richmond & then marched here to help whip him, and the Sixth Wis. never even got a Newspaper puff for it. Two New York Regts. who acted as our support *30 miles in our rear* got all the Newspaper Credit for what we did."[12]

Finally the Sixth Wisconsin and the other regiments established picket lines and set up camps. That night, John Johnson, in making the rounds, came upon a badly shaken Dennis Kelly of Fountain City. "Sergeant, I have seen ghosts or spirits," said the young soldier. Johnson wrote later: "I knew the man to be truthful, and told him to be still and I would examine the cause, being afraid that some of the men would raise a false alarm. I started in the direction of the field, and marched directly to the nearest point. There I found a dead body, interred very shallow, and a phosphorescent light oscillating from the head to the foot of the corpse. And so it proved in every instance. It being a very warm, sultry night and dark, must have been the reason of it, or some gas from the decaying bodies. Some of the corpses were covered so slightly, that the head and feet protruded from under the sod."[13]

The fallen soldiers, said Sauk County men, "had been buried so shallow in the trenches that the tops of the trenches were moving like gentle waves with living corruption. This is the only place we could distinguish between the scent of dead animals and human beings in the state of decomposition. The human is very much more offensive than the animal, but it did not affect our appetites, it was here not a question of what you should eat, but what you could get."[14]

"This was our first contact with one of the real horrors of war," said Rufus Dawes. Hugh Perkins of the Seventh Wisconsin wrote home: "Oh Herbert, I have been all over the battlefield, and it looks hard to see men buried like a lot of hogs, 12 to 15 together. But I suppose they feel as well as though they ever so nice a grave and coffin. We had nothing to brag of in this fight."[15] Another soldier observed: "Along our march we saw many graves and dead horses on both sides of the road. Trees a foot thick had been shot down. Our shells had reached the peaks of Cedar Mountains. There is a terrible stench from the dead horses. Many dead soldiers had not been buried by the rebels. Others had only a thin layer of dirt thrown over them." He added, "Our boys stole a lot of poultry and fruit. The officers, though against this, acted as if they didn't see anything. Only when it got too bad they raised hell with the soldiers."[16]

The brigade spent the week camped at Cedar Mountain and James Sullivan of the Sixth Wisconsin left a statement: "As reconnaissance developed the fact that 'Stonewall' had fallen back behind the . . . [river] and Pope immediately reported him in full retreat towards Richmond, completely demoralized, and, after compelling his army to remain encamped more than a week during the hottest part of the year, on the battle field, subject to the overpowering stench of decaying horses and half buried bodies, when fifteen minutes march would have placed them in an adjoining grove of timber where they would have shelter from the sun and have plenty of good water, and be removed from the filth and unwholesomeness of a battle field. . . ."[17]

To the soldiers it was apparent something was seriously amiss. Jackson's men were marching and the generals seemed unsure where. Other Confederate brigades were leaving Richmond, apparently en route to join Jackson, but McClellan's divisions were slow moving to the assistance of Pope's Army of Virginia, and later there were angry words, some claiming McClellan wanted Pope to be a failure.

By August 19 Pope decided "the movements of Lee were too rapid and those of McClellan too slow to make it possible, with the small force I had, to hold that line, or keep open communication with Fredericksburg without being turned on my right flank by Lee's whole army and cut off altogether from Washington." Pope's orders went out to his divisions to pull back, and in Gibbon's Brigade that was the beginning of what the soldiers called the "Haymarket March." Said John Cook: "It was not 'all quiet on the Potomac.' It may be quiet now, but it was the damnedest lively Potomac that I ever saw."[18]

On August 20 the brigade crossed the Rappahannock near the Orange and Alexandria Railroad, camping a mile from the bridge. The soldiers were puzzled and one wrote home, "We had been hunting the rebels, and now we were trying to keep them away from us." Gibbon "found everything on the other side in the utmost confusion. Wagon-trains, Divisions, Brigades, and Regiments were all mixed up, apparently in the most inextricable confusion, nobody seeming to know where to go and where anyone else was, and there was such a total absence of all order and authority as to produce a most painful impression on the mind."[19] Slowly the officers began to restore order, and there was excitement when rebel cavalrymen appeared across the river, but no serious shooting developed. Dawes recognized an ominous sight: "By the clouds of dust rising on all the roads [opposite the river], we could trace the advance of the rebel army."

The next day the enemy fired across the river ("The first artillery we had ever heard in actual battle," said Dawes) and a Federal battery came on the gallop, wheeled into position, and returned fire, "cheered by the excited shouts of our men." In his journal, William Riley of the Sixth Wisconsin wrote: "Our battery got the better of them in a few shots, showing a better practice, and more accurate shooting. Our shells burst close to their guns, while the enemy fired wide of their mark." Sullivan remembered "our fellows, who had never heard a rebel cannon before, but had been kept well posted about the 'black flags' and 'railroad' iron of the rebels by the warlike editors at home, and thinking that nothing else could make such unearthly screams, they said the 'greybacks were slinging railroad iron.'"[20]

More alarming was the order for Gibbon's Brigade to move to the right of King's Division. To do so the regiments would pass under the rebel guns. "We marched," Dawes said, "along in the rear of the batteries, now all placed in order of battle to fire upon the enemy. As we came into range of the enemy's battery, they turned their fire full upon the sixth Wisconsin. This was our initiation. The shells whizzed and burst over us and around us. The men marched steadily, keeping their places, and holding their heads high. They soon learned that a discreet and respectful obeisance to a cannon ball is no indication of cowardice."[21]

When the brigade reached the correct position, the Sixth was ordered to advance skirmishers to the river. It was the most perilous duty—the men in a thin line, each soldier separated from another by several yards, all thrown well forward of the main forces. Bragg was to lead the six selected companies with Dawes second in command. As the two placed their line, they could see Federal skirmishers moving out from Patrick's Third Brigade on the left.[22] The orders were for Patrick's men to take direction from the Sixth, but the New Yorkers pushed ahead without stopping. Bragg, trying to maintain the line, ordered his men to "a thick woods" before his deployment could be completed. On the left was Company E, and the Appleton and Fond du Lac men were "switched off and lost and no connection was made with General Patrick's skirmishers." The advancing soldiers, Dawes said, "swung away from the proper front, and in place of advancing toward the river, we gradually changed to moving up parallel with the river, opening at every step, the gap between us and General Patrick's skirmishers."

With Company E and part of B missing, the Sixth line came out of the woods a jumble to encounter a body of cavalrymen in blue coats. Dawes, all excitement, galloped forward to ask if they had seen any rebels. "Yes, Sir, plenty of them,—just in that point of woods, not five minutes ago," an officer responded. The Wisconsin men pushed on pell mell across an open field toward "that point of woods" only to be brought up short "by sharp musketry skirmishing" behind them. "It was," Dawes said, "Captain Brown with our lost company 'E,' and Lieutenant Charles P. Hyatt, with a platoon of company 'B,' gallantly driving this rebel cavalry, for such it was, across the river.... [W]e had been sent on a fool's errand by a rebel company, who were dressed in Union blue overcoats. Brown's and Hyatt's men killed and wounded several of the enemy, and captured a Lieutenant and two private soldiers. These officers and their men won the first glory for the sixth Wisconsin on the field of actual battle."

Finally, with the line halted, Brown and Hyatt's men came up amid welcoming shouts. Brown wrote to his wife: "Co 'E' *drew the first blood* [of the regiment]. . . . We came suddenly on a squadron of Reb. Cavalry and gave them a volley. They skeddadled in grand style. No other Co. did any damage."[23]

After a time, the skirmish line was withdrawn, and toward evening the regiment was again ordered to a point near the river. A rebel battery saw the movement and opened fire. Stern old Lysander Cutler halted and, all according to regulations, carefully established guides and aligned forward into the position before he would allow his soldiers to lie down. "You must get used to it," he told the men. Sullivan left a different memory: "Their battery finally got the range of our regiment, which was drawn up in double column by division, and a shot ricochetted through the regiment, doing no damage, however, except destroying Colonel Cutler's mess chest, and the old greybeard, who had been an indifferent spectator hitherto, ordered the regiment to 'fall in' and he marched it about a length to one side, out of the line of fire."[24] Of the matter, Dawes wrote, "Fortunately, the rebels were poor artillerists and did not hit us, so nobody was hurt. We learned to 'lie down' in battle later in our experience, without waiting to establish guides. Our experience the first day under fire, as we lost no men, was really valuable in showing the men, that artillery fire was not so dangerous as they had anticipated."[25]

Gibbon's Brigade remained under the rebel guns two days, and Dawes wrote in his journal that the Sixth Wisconsin was subjected to "several good shellings." On August 23 King's Division was marched to Warrenton, then to Sulphur Springs, where there was more artillery fire. "We had constant artillery practice with the enemy, and some encounters with skirmishers," Frank Haskell wrote home, "but we lost but few men, and a good school for us all, to become accustomed to the enemy's shells, and the aspects of battle."[26] Finally, August 26, orders directed King's Division to "march with the utmost haste" northeast to Centreville. During this period, Dawes said, "judging from the clouds of dust which we could see beyond the river," the rebels were also moving, and somehow Jackson's brigades had gotten "between us and Washington."

Word also reached the marching soldiers that Pope's wagon park had been attacked four days earlier at Catlett's Station. The enemy cavalry burned supplies as well as captured prisoners, dispatches, and baggage, including one of Pope's uniforms. In the dark Gibbon's wagon guard, along with the sick and lame, sharply defended the 21 brigade wagons. The attack came about midnight during a thunderstorm, which slowed the 400 rebel horsemen, who had to "climb over" a railroad track. Well-directed volleys by the 60 guards turned back four attempts to rush the wagons, although one horseman with a saber got close enough to slash the hand of one Badger as he scurried under a wagon.[27] "Our boys felt pretty good over saving our brigade train, *the only one saved,* from injury or destruction in the entire army train," said a Sauk County man.[28]

One rebel, Fitzhugh Lee, the nephew of Robert E. Lee, had a close call. In the darkness and confusion, he had ridden up and shouted, "Don't shoot boys, these horsemen are our men." But Pvt. Herman Kellner of the Sixth Wisconsin was not fooled. Almost helpless and having discharged his rifle-musket, Kellner, ramming another cartridge, cried out: "Shoot the son of a rooster (or 'words to that effect')— he's a damned rebel." In any case, the cavalryman left "as fast as a scared horse could carry him," the teller of the story said, adding: "The man on the white horse proved to be General, then Colonel Fitzhugh Lee. The general since the war has spoken of his Catlett's Station experience as being one of his closest calls to cross the dark river. If Kellner had a charge in his gun the moment he discovered that the man on the white steed was a rebel, he would have brought down big game, sure."[29]

Rufus Dawes said it "was a very gallant deed, and of especial value to us as all of our papers and much property were with the wagons."[30]

Private Sullivan in the Sixth Wisconsin said Pope "was startled by the news that instead of being in a demoralized retreat towards Richmond, 'Stonewall' was crossing the Rappahannock on his right flank and rear. Our whole force immediately started in pursuit and all the talk was (which we understood originated at headquarters) 'that Stonewall Jackson had got into a bag and General Pope was going to tie the string and keep him there.' But the next news was that 'Stonewall' had taken the army train and Pope's headquarters train at Catlett Station and the next news was that 'Stonewall' had captured . . . [Manassas Junction] and had telegraphed to Washington for and received, supplies and an entire new outfit for his army. Our men had lost all confidence in Pope's abilities and it was openly remarked in the ranks that McDowell was a traitor."[31]

During those hours, Gibbon had a disturbing conversation with two army friends, John Reynolds and George Meade, just up from the Army of the Potomac outside Richmond. Meade said he had asked Pope, "What are you doing out here? This is no place for this army. It should fall back so as to meet the rest of the Army of the Potomac coming up and by superior forces overwhelm Lee." Pope replied that he had "orders from Washington" to hold the Rappahannock line for 48 hours and by that time McClellan's men would be on hand to assist him. Pope "querulously added," said Meade, that the 48 hours had passed and the "reinforcements had not arrived."

It was hot and dusty, and the Wisconsin and Indiana soldiers marched thirsty "on the shortest possible allowance of rations." Gibbon, on nearing Warrenton August 27, sent officers ahead to have provisions placed along the sidewalks "so the men could pick them up and supply themselves as we marched through the town." Reaching the intersection, Gibbon found "the streets packed with troops, and trains slowly making their way forward, but everything else seemed to be hurried and confused." Irvin McDowell was on a nearby porch, and seeing Gibbon's soldiers halted, he sent orders "to push forward at once." Gibbon went to the general and "explained to him in person that my men were much in want of the provisions and it would take but a few minutes to make the issue, but he reiterated his orders to push forward the march and much to our regret, we were obliged to turn our backs on and abandon the much-needed food. This was all the more to be regretted since scarcely had we cleared the town than the road was found so blocked up in front that our progress was very slow and after marching till long after dark we bivouacked for the night only five miles beyond Warrenton."[32]

At Warrenton, Dawes saw "wagon-loads of hard tack and pork" being destroyed, but "the emergency seemed to be considered so great that the troops were not allowed to halt and fill their nearly empty haversacks, and some of our men were marching hungry." Sullivan recalled how "Gibbon made room on the caissons and limbers" of his old command, Battery B, "for the hard tack boxes and bacon we 'gobbled.'" A bitter Wisconsin soldier wrote in his diary that night: "The officers know how to take care of themselves. Nobody worries about us. They care very little."[33]

The weary soldiers trudged through New Baltimore and pulled up near Buckland's Mills. They were dirty, tired, footsore and hungry. The past weeks, they had been marched here and there, seemingly for little purpose (the weary soldiers making sour remarks about King's "Pendulum Division"). They had withstood artillery, skirmished against rebel cavalry, and tramped long miles over dusty roads with flat haversacks and empty canteens. "It was now march and skirmish with an occasional bivouac, frequently interrupted by the 'zip' of the bullet or the crash of the bursting shell," said one soldier. "The booming of cannon became a familiar sound." Edwin Brown of the Sixth Wisconsin wrote home: "This Country is all woods & hills & they lay in ambush for us everywhere. I am afraid Pope is not equal to the task before him."

As the men of Gibbon's "Black Hat" Brigade slept the night of August 27, Pope was issuing orders. Jackson and his brigades were behind Pope's army, but some of the McClellan reinforcements were reaching Washington and there seemed an opportunity to trap Jackson isolated from Lee's Army. Pope's gallopers went to his divisions, ordering them to Gainesville and Haymarket, not far from the Bull Run battlefield of a year before and near the farm of John Brawner. The next day was a Thursday—August 28, 1862—and, said James Sullivan, it would prove a date long remembered "in many a Wisconsin and Indiana home."[34]

11.
Come On, God Damn You!

While the men of Gibbon's Brigade slept alongside the Warrenton Pike, Jackson's brigades were marching, and it had not gone as smoothly as it would seem in the light of later developments. After the capture of the Federal supply depot at Manassas Junction, the hungry rebels gobbled everything in sight and burned what they could not carry off. Jackson then made the bold decision to await the arrival of the rest of the Confederate army. To do that he needed a strong defensive position and the place he selected was a low ridge north of the Warrenton Turnpike and west of the old Bull Run battlefield of the previous year. Jackson's reticence about disclosing his plans, even to his commanders, caused a muddle, however, and by daylight, August 28, only one Confederate division was on the ridge; the second was off near Centreville and the third at Blackburn's Ford. But by noon, Jackson's divisions were posted along the ridge and he was thinking of ways to prevent John Pope from concentrating at Centreville.[1]

For John Gibbon's soldiers the march started at 4 A.M., and it became immediately apparent another long day was ahead. Hatch's Brigade of King's Division was the first to move, followed by Gibbon's regiments and Battery B of the Fourth U.S. Artillery. Behind them were King's two other brigades and their artillery. Rufus King was ill from an epileptic seizure (in ranks, it was whispered that he was drunk) and routine decisions for the march fell to Gen. John Hatch, the senior brigadier. The thick column moved only a half mile before it came up behind stopped wagons. It went that way most of the morning—march and halt, march and halt, the men frustrated in the heat and dust. Gibbon's soldiers passed through Gainesville ("a cluster of two or three houses where the Manassas Gap railroad crosses the turnpike"), finally reaching a lane branching to the right. "Taking this we marched a mile or two farther and then halted," said Gibbon. "Orders were given for us to form a line of battle and then countermanded. We remained halted in this position for many hours, and everybody was busy speculating as to what was going on and what was to be done." The men stacked arms and boiled coffee. There had been artillery fire up the road near the old Bull Run battlefield, but the soldiers paid little heed.

There was some excitement when "quite a large body of rebel prisoners" (the Confederates had not been able to keep up with Jackson's fast-moving regiments) was herded past the halted Federal column. The rebels were dirty, used up, and threadbare, much stripped down for hard marching. One straggler looked over the Wisconsin men with professional interest, taking in the heavy wool coats, black hats, and profusion of belts and accouterments. "You uns is pack mules, we uns is race horses," he pronounced in a satisfied voice, as if everything was explained. "All old Jackson gave us, was a musket, a hundred rounds and a gum blanket, and he 'druv us so like hell,' that I could not stand it on parched corn." Maj. Rufus Dawes of the Sixth Wisconsin said his men began the campaign "absurdly over burdened," so the strong men often carried two knapsacks to help the "little fellows" along. "With us," he admitted, "ponderosity was a military science."[2]

During the halt Gibbon rode ahead and found Gen. Irvin McDowell and several officers on a hill using field glasses to look over the country to the north and east. "In that direction heavy clouds of dust could be seen rising above the tree tops indicating the movement of columns of troops." Nothing developed, and Gibbon returned to his halted soldiers. No orders were forthcoming, and, after a time, regimental officers requested permission to kill and cook cattle herded along with the column. "I could obtain no definite information in regard to our probable stay," he said, "and after hesitating sometime I gave orders to have the beef killed and cooked. This was done and the beef was eaten before any orders came."[3]

About 4 P.M., an orderly rode up with directions to march back to the Warrenton Turnpike and proceed east toward Centreville. The word from McDowell, the galloper said, was that Jackson was at Centreville and King's Division should "move rapidly" along the pike and "be in position to bag him in the morning." The tired soldiers, "who had lived on corn for several days, roasted and raw," said Lt. Col. Edward Bragg of the Sixth Wisconsin, "sprang to guns" and marched back up the lane. At the junction, they found McDowell and King looking ahead with their field glasses. The column was stopped a few minutes, then moved east on the pike. Hatch's Brigade was in the lead with skirmishers well forward, moving on each side of the road. One of Hatch's regiments was the Fourteenth Brooklyn, a famous New York State militia outfit still outfitted in bright red trousers. The thin line of New Yorkers could be seen moving over the fields near a house, barn, orchard, and woods north of the turnpike—the farm of John Brawner. The turnpike generally followed the crest of a low rise that ran parallel to another wooded ridge several hundred yards to the north. The distant ridge, the Sauk County boys observed, was "not quite so high as the Baraboo bluffs" back home.[4] Dawes watched "the line of their red legs on the green slope . . . but they discovered no enemy." The Sixth Wisconsin was in the lead, followed by the Second and Seventh Wisconsin and the Nineteenth Indiana. The guns of Battery B brought up the rear.

As with all Gibbon's marches the half-mile column was well-closed, the soldiers distinctive in their tall hats and frock coats, rifle-muskets carried "at will." In the distance was the dull thump of artillery, but the brigade, said one in ranks, moved along "the turnpike on that quiet summer evening as unsuspectingly as if changing camp." Gibbon recalled that "the sun was shining, the birds were singing." A Sixth Wisconsin private said there was "no thought of battle," and a third Badger called the march "leisurely," with the soldiers "chatting, joking and laughing in the usual manner." East of the farmhouse the turnpike passed through a "clump of trees" ("an ugly piece of woods," one officer said) where the road had been excavated leaving a three-foot embankment. Coming out of the woods at the top of the ridge, the soldiers "could look ahead for some distance over the flat country, partly fields and part woods." Dusk was approaching.

Gibbon was riding alongside the Sixth Wisconsin. "On emerging into the open ground beyond, I could see no troops, Hatch's Brigade having disappeared behind another piece of woods in our front." He rode to "a gentle rise on the north of the pike" where he paused to look around; behind him the leading companies of the Sixth Wisconsin were just clearing the woods, the low sun on their backs. "I happened to be riding a little ahead, and looking off on the left, about a mile distant, I saw some horses coming out of the woods. I looked closely, and one thing struck me as peculiar—there were a good many light colored horses. . . . The next thing I noticed was the size of the horses and I knew guns were coming 'into battery.' I turned around and said to a staff officer, 'Ride back and bring up Battery B on a gallop.' I had hardly got the words out of my mouth when I saw the guns go into position, and bang! bang! came the shells shrieking and bursting over our heads."[5]

The rebel battery, said Gibbon, was "within a short distance of the very place where only a little while before Hatch's Brigade had been in position." The movement was also seen by the marching soldiers. Pvt. Albert Young of the Sixth Wisconsin thought the horses were pulling "army wagons" and wondered what they were doing in the woods. One Sauk County boy turned to Pvt. Gus Klein of Sauk and said, "That don't look like any of our batteries." Klein shook his head and said something he would regret, "See here! We have been in the service over a year and except a few skirmishes, we have never been in a fight. I tell you, this damned war will be over and we will never get into a battle!" At that instant there was a puff of smoke on the ridge and a hissing shell whizzed over the marching soldiers. "We never saw so polite a bow made by a regiment as we made, men and officers, as it passed over," one Badger said. The shell exploded with a crash in the woods south of the turnpike. Never, said Gibbon, was a command "more surprised" than his brigade. "It is not necessary to tell the outside world how awfully scared we were. I know it, for there was no worse scared man in that brigade than I was."[6] Dawes agreed. "Surprise is no sufficient word for our astonishment," he said, recalling that "six cannon shots fired in rapid succession."

For an instant the Wisconsin men stood ready to bolt, then Col. Lysander Cutler's voice—heard on so many drill fields—came firm and steady: "Battalion, halt! Front! Load at will! Load!" The men "fairly jumped in their eagerness, and the iron ramrods were jingling, when— 'Bang! Bang!' went the rebel cannon again," said Dawes. The shells again missed the column, "but a poor horse was knocked over against the turnpike fence," just missing two officers of the Second Wisconsin. "Lie down!" Cutler ordered, and the soldiers, fumbling with cartridges and ramrods, scrambled to take cover behind "a little bank along the roadside." There, one Badger said, "We all dropped in place and the shells came thick and fast and we hugged the ground."[7]

From the rear the six guns ("Gibbon's own old pets") came up at a gallop amid swirling dirt, clunking wheels and excited shouts. The battery was handled with the smooth efficiency of the regulars and as it passed around the right of the Sixth Wisconsin a squad ran forward to kick apart the wood fence alongside the turnpike (one of the men jumping to the task, said Loyd Harris, was Matt Bernard, the former slave bound for freedom) and the straining horses pulled through the gap, wheeling the heavy guns into position on the knoll where Gibbon was waiting. Gibbon made a motion with his hand and pointed to the spot he had selected, calling, "Into battery, here!" Within minutes the six cannon opened fire, all terrible noise and smoke, the blasts flattening the grass in front of the muzzles. Gibbon and his aide, Frank Haskell, moved into the woods and rode ahead to watch the Confederate fire. Gibbon said later he was convinced it was only horse artillery. Farther left, more rebel guns opened, firing on the two brigades at the rear of King's Division. Gibbon saw that the accurate shooting by Battery B was knocking down the fire of the first rebel battery, and—thinking he might be able to capture the guns—he sent Haskell to bring up the Second Wisconsin. "I don't suppose that more than half a minute had elapsed before I got impatient (I some times do) and rode back to meet the regiment coming through the wood."[8]

Back on the turnpike it was all confusion, with the Wisconsin and Indiana men down in the road. The smoothbores of Battery B were firing with "loud cracks" in a swirl of smoke, rebel shells shrieking overhead and exploding around them. Up the roadway could be heard the thumping of more artillery, directed at Hatch's Brigade, a mile ahead. Behind Gibbon's men other Confederate guns were firing on the Federal column spread for more than a mile back along the Warrenton Turnpike. One Seventh Wisconsin man watched in wide-eyed astonishment as Lt. Frank Haskell jumped "his horse over the fence and rode up toward the battery to reconnoiter the enemy's position, and then turned and walked his horse back as calmly as though there was not a rebel within a thousand miles." Minutes passed; then, to their left, the men of the Sixth Wisconsin saw the companies of the Second Wisconsin come to their feet. "What luck!" a Sauk County boy grumbled. "There is the Second in again before us." The Second Wisconsin dressed the line, officers and file-closers in their places, then moved by the left flank into the woods. The boys of the Sixth raised a "lusty cheer" as the column disappeared. The men of the "Ragged Ass Second," who had been bloodied at Bull Run and bragged so long about it, were unknowingly marching into the waiting guns of half the Confederate army and were about to pay a terrible price for their boasting. John Pope's soldiers had found Jackson and his brigades.[9]

From the turnpike, the men of the Sixth Wisconsin could not see the advance but heard an "awful crash of musketry," said Dawes, "and we knew there was serious work ahead." Gibbon met the officers of the Second Wisconsin in the woods and told them it was a Confederate cavalry battery ahead and "if we can get you up quietly we can capture the guns." North of the small woods, "the regiment was formed into line and silently moved up the gentle slope in front," Gibbon said. "As soon as it reached the brow of the hill, a few shots were fired, a line of skirmishers was quickly thrown forward, the enemy's skirmishers were

*A Second Wisconsin man
with Austrian musket: Pvt.
Ernst Schuchart. Courtesy
of Tim and Mary
Spellman. Used
by permission.*

driven in, and the regiment advanced to the plateau beyond. As the picket firing opened, the guns which up to this time had continued to fire, became silent and the Second Wisconsin had not advanced much farther before a very heavy musketry fire was opened upon it."[10]

The fighting erupted with startling suddenness. The Second Wisconsin was marching in line of battle by the left oblique near the Brawner farm buildings when hit on the flank by musketry from a nearby farm and orchard. One Badger skirmisher saw to his immediate front a thick Confederate force marching "three lines deep." Then, said Gibbon, "the worst infantry fire begun I ever heard. I was more afraid than ever, and afraid that the regiment was scared, but it was not."[11] The Confederate fire "was terrific," said Thomas Allen of the Second Wisconsin, "bullets came thicker than rain and it seemed as if our whole regiment must soon be annihilated." To a soldier in Hatch's Brigade a mile ahead, the musketry made a sound "like that of hailstones upon an empty barn."[12]

The colonel of the Second Wisconsin was Edgar O'Connor of Beloit, a West Pointer selected to command the unit in the reorganization of the regiment after Bull Run.[13] Back in Wisconsin the dark-haired, stocky O'Connor was under a cloud for his statement to a local newspaper that the Union volunteers might need more training before being ready for a battlefield. In some Republican newspapers that gave rise to questions about O'Connor's loyalty, given his West Point training and friendships with Southern officers. To add to his difficulties he had a lingering bronchial illness and had to give commands in a whisper to an aide, who repeated them.[14]

In any case, O'Connor, who had fewer than 450 men in his line, had something to prove, and he halted the Second Wisconsin and held it steady under the fire. It was one of those moments that the soldiers of both sides always remembered—the small Wisconsin regiment alone in the open field, seemingly doomed as a thick Confederate line swept toward it. But "to the amaze of the Confederate leaders . . . ," one Badger said, "the Black Hats knelt in their tracks as though bidding them to come on. . . ." The Second Wisconsin men "bethought themselves of all they had told the Sixth and Seventh of what it meant to stand fire, and if fifty brigades, instead of five, had burst upon them, there were men in those stubborn ranks that would never have yielded an inch." In line the boys held "their pieces with a tighter grasp and expressing their impatience with low mutterings in such honest, if not classic phrases, as 'Come on, God damn you.'"[15]

Finally, satisfied with the range, the rebels almost upon him, O'Connor gave the order to fire and his regiment exploded with smoke and noise. As soon as the Second Wisconsin had started forward, Gibbon had sent for the Nineteenth Indiana to come in on the left and the Seventh Wisconsin on the right. Soon the three regiments were involved. The Confederate fire expanded left and right, the volume increasing, and Gibbon sent gallopers to the two brigades behind him on the turnpike asking for help.

The general also hurried up his own Sixth Wisconsin.[16]

12.
I Would Not Like to Hear It Again

The aide carrying the order to the Sixth Wisconsin was James Wood of the Second Wisconsin, and he came up on the gallop. "Colonel, with the compliments of Gen. Gibbon," he called to Lysander Cutler, "you will form your regiment by battalion front, advance and join on the right of the Seventh, and engage the enemy." Worried about his friends and comrades in his regiment, Wood blurted, "Colonel, for God's sake, go over and help the Second. They are being cut to pieces." Cutler was a New Englander, steady and reliable, and he was sitting on the rail fence by the roadside watching the developing fight with his field glasses. "Yes," he said, "the woods are full of 'em, get ready boys, for the fun is coming."

The old colonel ordered the regiment to "Fall in!" and said, "We can not let our comrades be slaughtered in that manner." The Badgers, down close to the rails along the north side of the road, were quickly up, pulled down the fence, and moved into the field. As the men dressed their lines, three soldiers ran up with their rifle-muskets and belts in hand—Pvts. Harry Dunn of Menekaunee, John Burus of Oakfield, and William Campbell of Mauston. Footsore and broken down by hard marching, the three had been in the ambulances but ran to join their companies at the first fire.

The Sixth Wisconsin advanced "in line of battle with full regimental front and step, and 'guide left,' as regular as if on parade," and Rufus Dawes recalled marching to his first battle "with something of the feeling that one would hurry to save a friend from peril." His horse "partook of the fierce excitement, and ran up the bank and leaped a fence like a squirrel." Ahead he could see the men of the Second Wisconsin: "They were under the concentrated fire of at least six times their own number of the enemy. Our regiment, five hundred and four men in

*Lysander Cutler. Courtesy
of the Milwaukee County
Historical Society. Used
by permission.*

ranks, pushed forward rapidly in perfect line of battle, field officers and
Adjutant E. P. Brooks mounted and in their places and colors advanced
and flying in the breeze. Colonel Cutler was on a large dark bay, well
known to all the men as 'Old Prince.' Colonel [Edward] Bragg rode a
pure white horse, of high mettle, which was skittish and unmanageable.
My own sturdy mare was always steady under fire."[1] Dawes said he
"never felt before in my life that feeling of intense horror that came over
me when on mounting that bank I saw the Second gallantly struggling
and staggering under the fire of not less than six regiments of the
enemy." To his right, Bragg, unable to control his horse, dismounted
and went forward on foot.[2]

As the Sixth Wisconsin climbed out of the road, Pvt. Albert Young of
Fond du Lac looked ahead to "a meadow sloping down in front of us for
some distance," then rising to a wooded ridge. "Slightly to the left of our
immediate front, and extending a long distance to the left from this

ridge came a line of fire—it was then early dusk—and much nearer to us and the road," he said, "but still on our left was another similar line of fire. We did not need to be informed that these lines of flame were reb and Union lines of infantry, and that the fight was an exceedingly hot one. As soon as our line was formed we were ordered forward. We knew we were in for it."[3]

In the Sixth Wisconsin line was Pvt. James Sullivan. "It was about 80 rods across the field to a strip of woods, and when about half way across I looked back and saw our colonel, Cutler, sitting on his big horse as straight as a rod," he said. "We had never been engaged at close quarters before, and the experience was new to all of us. I don't know how the others felt, but I am free to confess that I felt a queer choking sensation about the throat, but someone in the rear rank awkwardly stepped on my heel and I instantly forgot all about the choking feeling and turned to him angrily to demand if there was not room for him to march without skinning my heel; and we were jawing and fussing until the colonel shouted halt, and there, about six or eight rods in front of us was a heavy column, marching by the flank, which I supposed was part of our division and had no idea they were rebels. . . . The colonel gave the command: 'Sixth regiment, Ready! Aim—Aim Low, Fire!' and our regiment delivered one of the volleys by regiment for which it was noted." He never forgot the moment: "Every gun cracked at once, and the line in front, which had faced us at the command 'ready' melted away, and instead of the heavy line of battle that was there before our volley, they presented the appearance of a skirmish line that had rallied by fours, there being only groups left, here and there, but another line moved up and took their place, and we stood there, firing at each other, at short range, until our men fired away twenty rounds of cartridges and the rebs fell back and another line took their place, and we engaged them."[4]

The Sixth Wisconsin, said Dawes, "advanced without firing a shot," making a slow half wheel in line of battle "as accurately as if on the drill grounds." The Sauk County boys heard "a rip-rip, but did not fully realize the situation until the boys began to fall." The regiment was well to the right. "Through the battle smoke into which we were advancing," said Dawes, "I could see a blood red sun, sinking behind the hills. I can not account for our immunity from the fire of the enemy while on this advance." At a "short range," Cutler ordered the regiment to halt and fire. "The seventh Wisconsin now came forward and passed into the ranks of the second Wisconsin. Our united fire did great execution. It seemed to throw the rebels into complete confusion, and they fell back in the woods behind them. We now gave a loud and jubilant cheer throughout the whole line of our brigade. Our regiment was on low ground which, in the gathering darkness, gave us great advantage over the enemy, as they overshot our line. The other three regiments of the brigade were on higher ground than the enemy. There was space enough vacant between our regiment and the others for a thousand men."[5]

Private Young said it was "a difficult matter" to describe his emotions and "possibly impossible to describe any of them accurately. I had a good many and they were varied." The first thought, he said, "was that the prospects for getting killed were growing bright, and the question I first put to myself was, 'Are you a coward?' to this I without an instant's hesitation answered, 'Yes.' Should I run? I must have been very pale. It seemed as if my blood had stopped circulating. Waves of intense heat flashed in quick succession through my entire being. I trembled so I could with difficulty keep from dropping my musket, but I hung on to it because I realized I should soon have need of it if I were not knocked out very early by a rebel bullet." But Young kept moving. "My legs quaked so they would scarcely support my weight, slight though it was. Should I run? Although I could hardly move one foot before the other toward the enemy, I felt that were I to head the other way I could beat the record. My mouth had in an instant, as it seemed, become dry and parched. I was suffering a terrible thirst. With trembling fingers I managed to get my canteen to my lips and took a long draught. It did not quench the thirst by which I was consumed. Again the question presented itself to me, 'Shall I run?' I answered it in the negative, because I was too much of a coward to run. I was too cowardly to endure being called a coward by my comrades if I survived." In the dusk light he could see "a black mass was moving out from the timber in front, directly towards us. I will not be certain, but I shall always think my hair began rising at this time. At least something lifted my hat from my head, and I had to grab quickly for it or I should have lost it. But I caught it and pulled it down tight so it would not be liable to come off again. Just at this instant, our colonel's voice was heard giving the commands. There was not the suspicion of a tremor in his voice, while I could not, I felt sure, utter an audible sound."[6]

John Johnson said his Sixth Wisconsin was "in the middle of an open field, the confederates behind a fence, on the edge of the field in the timber." He stood and fired the ammunition he carried "and I do not know how many rounds I received from the killed and wounded in rear of our lines." Ahead in "an opening in the timber," the rebels "placed some artillery on rising ground, but they never fired a shot. We killed the cannoneers, as fast as they came up to load. On the right of our line there was a thicket of timber brush, which, we could see the enemy file into at a run to rake us in flank. Command, fire right oblique, Sixth Wisconsin, and I did not see one man go back out of that copse of woods. . . . They tried again and again to form, brought reinforcements time after time, and each time 'steady, boys,' would run along the line, and before they came to the fence they were a disordered mass, and our swift and sure fire kept them so during the fight. The rattle of our musketry sounded all along the line, like a piece of canvass tearing in a storm."[7]

The crashing first volley of the Sixth Wisconsin—fired at a point-blank range of 50 yards—brought a cheer from the embattled three other regiments that was answered by a "Whoop, Whoop, Whoop" yell from the rebels, a sound once heard and never forgotten. "There is nothing like it this side of the infernal region and the peculiar corkscrew sensation that it sends down your backbone under these circumstances can never be told," a Wisconsin man said. "You have to feel it, and if you say you did not feel it and heard the yell you have *never* been there." The men of the Sixth stood and fired, Cutler mounted and just behind the two flags in the center of the regiment. On the left Dawes watched the fighting: "It was quite dark when the enemy's yelling columns again came forward, and they came with a rush. Our men on the left loaded and fired with the energy of madmen, and the sixth worked with an equal desperation. This stopped the rush of the enemy, and they halted and fired upon us their deadly musketry. During a few awful moments, I could see by the lurid light of the power flashes, the whole of both lines. . . . It was evident that we were being overpowered [on the left] and that our men were giving ground. The two crowds, they could hardly be called lines, were within, it seemed to me, fifty yards of each other, and they were pouring musketry into each other as rapidly as men could load and shoot."

Pvt. Chester Wyman of the Sixth Wisconsin said his company fired at the flash of the enemy muskets "as fast as we could load and fire. I did not know what second I might get hit but I would give them the best I had in me as long as I could." The man next to him was knocked out of line, "apparently dead," then Wyman himself was hit in the right thigh. He tried a step, but his leg gave way and he fell heavily. Around him the firing again flared up.[8]

On the other end of the Sixth Wisconsin line was Capt. John Marsh of Irish Company D: "The sun was sinking behind the horizon when from my position near the right I saw a confederate officer to the left form his command as for a final effort to break our line. They were on rising ground, every man standing, boldly out from a sky radiant with the golden state of a summer sunset. Recklessly placing himself in front of the line, he gave the command to charge. Down they came at double quick over that green slope, their gallant leader waving them on. Men drop from the ranks by scores, but the column sweeps bravely forward until half their number lie bleeding on the ground. The living hesitate and the bold leader rides fiercely along the line to urge them on, but the leaden hail is too potent, and they fall back, but with the steady pace of veterans."

But it was not over: "Twice more they charge down that bloody slope only to be repulsed with fearful slaughter. Strange to say neither rider nor horse that led this gallant charge had fallen, when darkness shut off my view, and only the flashing guns marked the contending lines of friend and foe. A bursting shell in the darkness nearly blinds me and I feel that I am wounded near the knee, but I can walk and don't mind it. Every man in my company seems a hero, and, when a corporal, whom I had disliked, quietly says, during the hottest of the battle: 'Captain, my gun's so foul I can't get the cartridge down, can you find me another?' I felt like embracing him. He was soon supplied, for we had a surplus of guns just then, many a brave fellow having turned his in for the final settlement."[9]

All of Gibbon's regiments were engaged, the fighting furious in the gathering darkness. It was "a roaring hell of fire," said one Badger. "Retiring never an inch, with no confusion, now standing up, now flat upon the earth, now swaying backwards or forwards to get advantage of ground, the devoted 1800 blazed with fire. Line after line of the rebels confronted them and was swept away, or broke in confusion. Fresh regiments would again appear . . . and with a cheer would rush for a charge upon the 'Black Hats,' but their rebel cheer was drowned in one three times louder by the Badger boys, and their lines met the fate of its predecessors. No battle was ever so fierce before,—no men ever did better than did the men of Gibbon's Brigade."[10] At one point, said Dawes, the rebels "rallied and in a line lapping ours both ways there burst from that dark wood volley after volley by battalion that roared and crashed in a manner not surpassed in any action I have seen." The men "loaded and fired with the energy of madmen, and a recklessness of death truly wonderful, but human nature could not long stand such a terribly wasting fire. It literally mowed out great gaps in the line, but the isolated squads would rally together and rush up right into the face of Death."

The Second and Seventh Wisconsin were pressed together in the center, the Nineteenth Indiana to their left and the Sixth Wisconsin well to the right, leaving a gap. The Seventh had come up on the right of the Second. In the smoke, Lt. Col. Lucius Fairchild of the Second Wisconsin, sleeves rolled up and sword in hand, came over on the run. "For God's sake colonel, deliver your fire up to the left. We are all cut to pieces, and the enemy are advancing on us." William Robinson of the Seventh Wisconsin looked over the situation. The colonel was a stiff-mouthed Vermonter, who had served in the Mexican War before going off to the gold fields of California. "Battalion! Change front forward on tenth company!" Robinson ordered. "By company, left wheel—March! Forward—March!" "Company after company came into the new alignment along the foot of that slope, and poured in their fire, our right striking right into the enemy's lines along the edge of the woods, and they broke and fell back," said a Seventh Wisconsin man, adding, "who does not remember the cheer we gave?"

On the left the men of Indiana's Nineteenth "suffered terribly," one said; the "lines of battle were close enough to do effective work." At one point two companies were ordered to rush a rebel battery, only to have the Confederates surge toward the gap in the Indiana line. "The regiment great felt the loss of those two companies, and swung back a little," one soldier said. Gibbon came up on foot to help reform the line. The general left his "sorrel horse" tied to a peach tree and the animal broke loose and ran away, leaving the general on foot and "in a dangerous and exposed position."[11]

Gibbon, who would see much fighting during the coming months, said later "the most terrific musketry fire I have ever listened to rolled along those two lines of battle. It was a regular stand up fight during which neither side yielded a foot. My command exhibited in the highest degree the effects of discipline and drill, officers and men standing up to their work like old soldiers."[12] One soldier said it was "one of the most stubborn, tenacious infantry fights . . . that history has any record of," while a Seventh Wisconsin man called it "a stand-up-and-shoot fight in line of battle" and Capt. Edwin Brown of the Sixth Wisconsin described it as a "baptism of blood & carnage." Edward Bragg said it was a fight at "close range, from late in the afternoon until after dark, with old Battery B ringing its case shot and canister up and down the line, and the roar of musketry filling the air, deadening the cries and groans of the wounded as they fell and passed away." In ranks, Pvt. Richard Warham of DeSoto was shot through the arm. He tried to load his rifle-musket but could not, "then busied himself giving the remaining cartridges of his box to the comrades." Dawes watched a mounted Confederate officer ride within 20 paces of his line. "He was, of course, killed."[13]

The two lines were so close together, said Sauk County men, "that by the flash of the muskets we could see the enemy distinctly, as they could see us. We did not remember to have heard another order than the first given, except an occasional one from the officers, 'Give them hell! boys, give them hell!' For after the first volley we fired as fast as we could load." One of the Crawford County men, George Fairfield, said Battery B "was throwing shell over our heads which made it seem as if the heaven was a furnace." One of the Juneau County boys in the Sixth Wisconsin, John St. Claire of Summit, said he "shot 45 times at the Devils" and a member of his company recalled: "Many of our men fired forty rounds of ammunition without stirring out of their tracks. Our brigade could not advance and the rebels could not drive us one foot, and it was a straight stand up and take it between the two rebel divisions, and our brigade, in which the advantage of numbers, more than three to one, was on the side of Jackson and also that he had the cover of the timber while our men were in the open field."

The Western cheers "were promptly answered by the rebel yell," said a Seventh Wisconsin man. "They rallied, brought up reinforcements, and charged on our lines;—and didn't they make it hot for us? Bullets from front, at right flank,—the air full of them, whistling by our ears,—scratching our clothes,—burning our faces,—bullets seemingly everywhere. The sixth came in on our right,—the nineteenth Indiana on the left of the second; and as battery B got into position on a little hill to our rear, firing over our heads, gave them canister, and the charge was repulsed. Twice more they brought up more men and charged down upon us. Line behind line they came, their flags flying, and we plainly heard the voice of their commander, 'Forward! Guide, center!' On they grandly came; and as they got near enough, and we poured in our fire, through the dim and smokey light, we saw their ranks swept down grow thinner and beautifully less until the last man of them seemed to drop into the ground. And yet, again they came; and again their dim ranks outlined against the sky above the hill went out into nothingness."[14]

In the quickening darkness, both lines alight with the musket fire, the gap between the Sixth Wisconsin and the rest of the brigade was clearly visible. From the turnpike two regiments from Doubleday's Brigade double-quicked into the fight and Rufus Dawes always remembered how the Fifty-sixth Pennsylvania and Seventy-sixth New York came

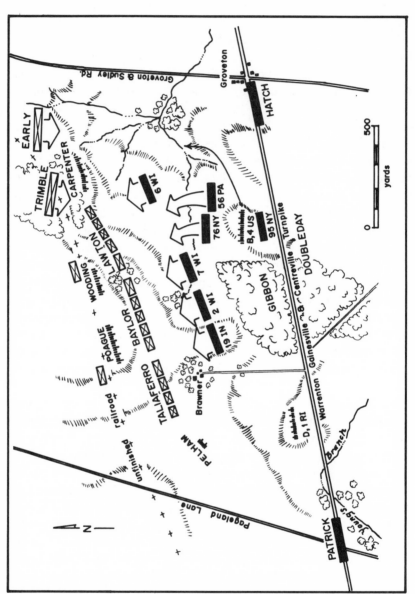

Battle map of the Iron Brigade at Brawner's farm. Drawn by John Heiser.
Used by permission.

into the gap and fired a crashing volley. "Hurrah! They have come at the very nick of time," he wrote a quarter century later, still feeling the excitement of the moment. The Confederates made three attacks against the Seventy-sixth New York—"the only genuine attempts at bayonet charges I have seen in this war."

Dawes rode to Cutler. "Our men are giving ground on the left, Major?" the colonel questioned. No sooner had Dawes replied, "Yes, Sir," when he "heard that tchug so ominous in battle." Cutler "gave a convulsive start, and clapped his hand on his leg," but "not a muscle of the old man's face quivered as he quietly asked, 'Where is Col. Bragg? I am shot.'" At the same instant, the colonel's horse, "Old Prince," was hit, but "he carried his master safely from the field." Dawes went to find Edward Bragg. To the left there was distant cheering and the two officers concluded that the Federal line "was again standing firmly." Said Dawes: "General Doubleday's two regiments by their opportune arrival and gallant work, aided much in turning the battle in our favor." Bragg was "always eager to push forward in a fight" and the lieutenant colonel advanced the Sixth Wisconsin several rods. "Soon the enemy came on again just as before, and our men on the left could be seen on the hill in the infernal light of the powder flashes, struggling as furiously as ever."

Dawes "could distinctly see Lieut. Colonel Fairchild, of the second Wisconsin and Lieut. Colonel Hamilton of the seventh Wisconsin, and other officers whom I recognized, working among and cheering up their men. Men who had been shot were streaming back from along the whole line. Our regiment was suffering more severely than it had been; but, favored by the low ground, we kept up a steady, rapid, and well aimed fire. As I galloped backward and forward along the line, my horse encountered ditches. Excited by the firing, cheering, and whizzing of the rebel shells, she would squat and jump a long distance in crossing them. How long our men withstood this last attack, I cannot estimate, but, in the history of war, it is doubtful whether there was ever more stubborn courage than was displayed by the second and seventh Wisconsin and nineteenth Indiana regiments on this field of battle." The only reason he wrote less of the Nineteenth, he said, was "because I could not see them so distinctly. Our line on the left gradually fell back. It did not break but slowly gave ground, firing as savagely as ever. The rebels did not advance. Colonel Bragg directed our regiment to move by a backward step, keeping up our fire and keeping on a line with our brigade. But one of the companies of the right wing ('C') became broken by the men marching backward into a ditch. Colonel Bragg halted the regiment to enable them to reform their line, and upon this ground we stood until the enemy ceased firing."

With the darkness, the soldiers on both sides unable to see, the fighting sputtered to a halt. The first battle of Gibbon's Western brigade, started in the thunder of artillery on a quiet August late afternoon and marked by the crashing of massed musketry, was ended. It was 9 P.M. The infantry fighting had lasted less than 90 minutes. Dawes found he "alone of all field officers in the battle remained mounted and unhurt."

Across the dismal field, said Albert Young, could be heard "the groans of the wounded, their cries for help and calls for water. It was more difficult to endure than going into the battle." George Fairfield said the calls "were the most pitiful sounds I ever heard." From the copse of trees in front of the regiment, said John Johnson, came "such lamentations . . . as 'O, God,' 'O mother, mother,' that would make the stoutest heart quail and shudder, even if they were enemies to our country. I would not like to hear it again."[15]

13.
Devil Take the Hindmost

Their first battle had not been like anything they had expected—no glory, no brave posturing, no panorama of marching soldiers, just a frantic scramble to load and shoot, load and shoot, again and again at the flashes of fire from the enemy; all noise and confusion. The line was a surging crowd; muskets fouled, hard to load, and hot to the touch. And it ended as quickly as it began, with the Sixth Wisconsin men clutching muskets and facing an enemy they could no longer see as officers pulled shaken soldiers to fill gaps and gathered details to assist the wounded. "Now was the hardest part of the battle," said one Badger, "to learn who of our friends were killed or wounded." Rufus Dawes recalled that the night was "very dark" and the men—officer and private alike—were surprised to discover the shooting was over. "Our one night's experience at Gainesville had eradicated our yearning for a fight. In our future history we will always be found ready but never again anxious."

In the darkness, "after an interval of quiet," Lt. Col. Edward Bragg called for "three cheers." The loud and defiant "Hurrahs!" echoed into the blackness, but "no response of any kind was given by the enemy."[1] Satisfied the fighting was over and his line secure, Gen. John Gibbon rode to the Warrenton Turnpike. He was convinced his brigade had been left unsupported and was, he admitted later, in "a very bad temper" when he came upon Rufus King and his staff sitting in a fence corner alongside the turnpike. Two other brigade commanders—John Hatch and Abner Doubleday—were also there. Hot words were exchanged, but Gibbon backed off after learning that Doubleday had sent the Seventy-sixth New York and Fifty-sixth Pennsylvania into the fight and that Hatch turned back but arrived too late.

A short time later the commander of the rear brigade, Marsena

Patrick, rode up and the five generals discussed the next move.[2] His orders, King said, were to march to Centreville. "From whom were those orders received," someone asked. "From General McDowell," said King. "Where was General McDowell?" another asked. No one knew. One thing was certain—Jackson's whole force might be in the woods just a few hundred yards away. "I was the junior general officer present," Gibbon recalled, "but none of the other officers expressed any opinion except General King and he seemed disposed to attempt to obey the orders he had received to march to Centreville. I strongly opposed this because I did not think it practicable to do it in the darkness, and as a better plan, proposed we should take the road to Manassas Junction with the hope that we might meet troops coming from there to support us. Still no one else expressing any opinion, either for or against the proposition, I took a piece of paper and by the light of a candle wrote what I proposed and showed it to the other generals, finally handing it to General King. They all agreed that it was the best thing to do under the circumstances and General King, after adding something in his own handwriting, signed it as a despatch to General McDowell." The action decided on, the officers returned to their commands to make ready for the march to Manassas Junction.[3]

The soldiers never forgot the calls of the wounded, the damp night air thick and greasy with the smoke of the fighting. Chester Wyman of Hillsboro, wounded in the right leg, was helped back to the woods and placed with the other wounded; it would be 10 days before he was finally taken to a hospital. In the Sauk County Riflemen, several were wounded, but none killed. William Clay of Delton had his arm just about shot off. Peter Stackhouse of Westfield was hit in the thigh. John Starks of Excelsior Township was wounded above the knee and Philip Hoefer of Freedom in the neck. Phil Nippert of Freedom was shot through the legs. Bill Lively of Ironton had a nasty leg wound. William Kline of Sauk was limping because of a rebel buckshot, but his brother, Augustus, was unhurt. Jim Whitty of Winfield was nicked by a bullet— the first of his four battle wounds. But Sauk County had stood up to rebel bullets, and one soldier wrote, "The boys all did well."

Across the fields could be seen flickering torches and lanterns as soldiers from both sides searched for fallen friends and messmates. "We found all our dead and wounded along a line, a rod or two in width," a Wisconsin man said. "It was then very dark and once we got outside of our line and ran into the enemy's pickets, who fired on us but missed." Lt. Col. Lucius Fairchild formed the survivors of the Second Wisconsin on the roadway and was shaken to find so few. "Where is the regiment—have they scattered?" he asked. Out of the darkness, someone replied, "Colonel, this is all that is left of the Second, the rest lay on the field." With tears, Fairchild said, "Thank God, they are worthy of their name." Bragg sent Dawes to determine the location of the other regiments, and the young Ohioan had a near escape: "I came suddenly in the darkness upon a marching column. Fortunately, I kept still and soon discovered myself to be on the side of a rebel regiment. I rode quietly along for a short distance with them and turned off into the darkness unheeded." Dawes finally found Gibbon, and the order he received was for the Sixth Wisconsin to remain in position. Dawes could hear the enemy "caring for their wounded and burying their dead. We could hear their conversations, but ordered our picket line not to fire or in any way to disclose our proximity." Some lost Confederates came out of the darkness into the Wisconsin line, where they were disarmed. They were Jackson's men of Ewell's Division, they said,[4] and the Johnnies asked with friendly curiosity about the soldiers in the "big hats" they had been fighting. Told they were Wisconsin and Indiana men, one Confederate private nodded and said that one of his officers had remarked, "It was no use to fight them damn fools; they did not know enough to know when they were whipped." Edwin Brown reported proudly in a letter to his wife that an Eighteenth Georgia soldier said it was the first time his brigade "ever turned their backs to the foe." The rebel had then asked "if we were *not western troops, saying they knew we were not Yankees.*"[5] Toward midnight, the Sixth Wisconsin moved back a short distance to the edge of the timber, where the weary soldiers bivouacked for an hour or two.

"While here," said Capt. John Marsh, "the Seventy-sixth New York, marching by the flank, usual route step, passed in front. The colonel was near the center of his regiment and opposite me when he gave the command: 'Seventy-sixth New York, halt.' The head of the column, however, kept on and the rear closing up. 'Seventy-sixth New York, won't you halt?' shouted the colonel, but it didn't, and the colonel pleaded: 'Seventy-sixth New York, you have behaved so well tonight, won't you halt?' But on they went with steady tread. . . ."[6]

It was the kind of thing to stampede a regiment, especially one staggered and battered in its first fight, but the Wisconsin men, drilled so hard the past year at Madison and outside Washington, stood steady in the darkness. It was about a half hour after midnight. "We marched back through the wounds to the turnpike," Dawes said. "Painful to relate, to this woods many of our wounded had gone when shot in the battle. They were now scattered about under its dark shadows, suffering and groaning and some were dying. In the pitchy darkness we stumbled upon them. This was the battle for which we had so long been yearning. On the turnpike we found hasty preparations for retreat and at about one o'clock a.m. we silently filed away into the darkness, muffling the rattling tin cups, and turning our course toward Manassas Junction." Edwin Brown later wrote his father: "We were obliged to leave our dead unburied, and those of our wounded that we were unable to move to the tender mercies of the Rebels. Doctors & nurses were left to wait on them. Lieut. [Jerome B.] Johnson was left with many others. I regretted it much but could not help myself."[7]

Near the turnpike the Badgers came upon two of the regiment's ambulances. The one horse rig driven by Thompson Jones of Sauk County was in a tangle in the ditch.[8] But the soldiers crowded around, "picked the whole outfit up and turned it around and he started for the top of the hill in view of us." While this was going on, George Harp of Baraboo, driving the four-horse ambulance, got his lead horses in the gully "and how he got them out, we never knew, but he was on hand to draw off our wounded, just as he always was in a fight. No better soldier than Harp ever served his country." Ludolph Longhenry of the Seventh Wisconsin was "among the last" to leave the battleground. "I was all alone. The Seventh Regiment had marched ahead. As I was leaving I came across one of our wounded . . . shot through the lungs. I gave him the last drink of water from my Canteen. But I could do no more." Longhenry pushed after his regiment. "Just before sunrise I left the dangerous rebel area. Every now and then a sharp-pointed bullet whizzed past me."[9]

Brigade Adjutant Frank Haskell said men and officers were somber as the column left behind the wounded; transporting as "many as the ambulances would hold we silently took up the line of march for Manassas Junction." Pvt. James Sullivan of the Sixth Wisconsin said the men were "bleeding, angry, hungry, tired, sleepy, foot-sore and cut to pieces." The march from the bloody fields on Brawner's farm was the hardest of the war. Drained of all energy by the hot emotions and numbing fear, the bone-weary young men were just able to put one foot ahead of the other. The column moved with little talking over the scuffling feet, the dull clink of accouterments, and the creak of the wagons and ambulances. "I never saw men more in need of sleep," said one soldier. "We would halt for a few minutes and half would go to sleep, each man sitting or laying down upon the spot where he halted."[10] Now and then the quiet night was broken by a soft sigh or the jarring cry of a wounded man. But to be left behind was more feared than enduring the weariness or the agony; so they walked through a seemingly endless night.

The soldiers had been up since before sunrise of the previous day, had marched a score or more hot, dusty, and thirsty miles, then had been thrown into what many regarded as their severest battle of the war. Capt. John Marsh was just about played out. When the division about 1 o'clock in the morning resumed its march toward Manassas, he said, "I found my wounded knee too painful to walk, but Maj. Dawes . . . kindly dismounted and helped me on his horse, saving me a journey to Richmond as a prisoner of war."[11] Dawes himself recalled: "As major I rode at the rear of our regiment. Presently there sifted out from the marching column numbers of wounded men, who had been struggling to keep with their comrades and to avoid falling into the hands of the enemy. I saw Captain John F. Marsh, who had been shot in the knee, drop to the rear, and dismounting from my horse, I lifted him to the saddle, marching through on foot myself. My steady old mare did the service of a good Samaritan. Each stirrup strap and even her tail were an aid to help along the weak and weary. The cry at such times is for water, water. There was none left in the canteens. But we deemed ourselves very fortunate."[12]

The next few hours were very hard. "I would travel a few rods, then finding myself going to sleep as I walked, my gun dropping out of my hand," said one Badger. "I would start up with a sudden jerk, and then for a short distance, with supreme effort, would march along, trying to keep awake. Many times since then have I been tired, footsore and weary, but I cannot recall one instance where the feeling of fatigue was so great as one this night's march from Gainesville. When we halted at Manassas Junction in the morning, I dropped down in my tracks and was immediately lost in slumber, from which I did not awake, until the sun was several hours high, and shining in my face."[13]

John Gibbon called it a "sad, tedious march" and "contrary to expectations we met nobody on the road and reached the vicinity of the [Manassas] Junction just as day was breaking. Here a halt was made, our poor, tired men lying down alongside the road for a much-needed rest, whilst steps were at once taken to supply them with food and ammunition. . . . The Junction was a scene of desolation and ruin, long trains of cars which had been filled with supplies for our army, were now a smoldering mass of ashes, the rebel troops, first supplying themselves, having set the balance on fire two nights before."[14]

With dawn came a sober realization. "I hardly knew our brigade," said Private Sullivan of the Sixth Wisconsin. "It was so reduced in size and the men looked so dirty and powder-stained that I could scarcely tell my own tentmates, and it seemed as if their dispositions changed with their appearance. The intensest feelings of anger were manifested against the commander [Rufus King] who allowed one brigade alone and unaided to fight the best divisions in the rebel army. The remainder of the division had the excuse that they had no orders, and did not know that we were so hard pressed, but we thought they were pleased to see 'them Western galoots' get fits.[15] Our men halted and made coffee, and 'Little Johnny Gibbon' won the affect of the brigade for all time by his manly sympathy for his men. It may seem strange that our brigade was allowed to be cut to pieces without getting help, but that seemed to be the way with Pope's army, 'Every one for himself and the devil take the hindmost.'"[16]

Frank Haskell said "none of us could look upon our thinned ranks, so full the night before, now so shattered, without tears. And the faces of these brave boys, as the morning sun disclosed them, no pen can describe. The men were cheerful, quiet and orderly. The dust and blackness of battle were upon their clothes, and in their hair, and on their skin, but you saw none of these,—you saw only their eyes, and the shadows of the 'light of battle,' and the furrows plowed upon cheeks that were smooth a day before, and now not half filled up. I could not look upon them without tears, and could have hugged the necks of them all."[17]

Company commanders surveyed their organizations, and regimental officers made their reports. When the general determined the "frightful loss," one soldier said, "Gibbon dropped his head and wept most bitterly. His sorrow was as sincere as that of the father who had been bereft of his children." Even four weeks later, "whenever the losses were referred to, his eyes would fill with tears and he would ask that the subject be dropped." It was recalled that the fighting removed all dislike for "the strict disciplinarian, and how great became the admiration and love for him, only those who have witnessed similar changes can appreciate."[18]

In the Sixth Wisconsin, eight were killed, 61 wounded, and three missing; Col. Lysander Cutler was among the wounded. The losses in the other three regiments were worse. The Seventh Wisconsin lost 164 of 580; the Nineteenth Indiana, 210 of 423; the Second Wisconsin, 276 of 430. Initial reports showed that 725—more than one-third of the brigade—were casualties. Eight of the brigade's 12 field officers were wounded, with Edgar O'Connor of the Second Wisconsin killed; he had been "shot four times," Dawes wrote in his journal. Col. Solomon Meredith of the Nineteenth Indiana was hurt when his horse, "Old Roan," was shot in the neck and fell on the colonel's leg, the saddle saving him from serious injury. All three field officers of the Seventh Wisconsin were wounded; Col. William Robinson was carried bleeding from the field. Lt. Col. Charles Hamilton was shot through the thighs but maintained his seat in the saddle as his boots filled with blood. Maj. George Bill suffered a slight head wound. In the Second Wisconsin, Maj. Thomas Allen was shot in the neck and left arm but did not leave the field. "Our Col. fought bravely until killed and the Lt. Col. [Fairchild] was under the hottest fire but escaped unhurt," Allen wrote home. With no field officers available in the Seventh, Gibbon consolidated the Second and Seventh Wisconsin under Fairchild, the senior field officer on his feet.[19]

That King's Division marched away from Jackson's front to Manassas Junction the night of August 28 was later called a tragic error by John Pope.[20] Pope's Army of Virginia was scattered. One division had been ordered to the Thoroughfare Gap to contest the arrival of the rest of the Confederate army, but the Federal commander retired on approach of the columns of Confederate Gen. James Longstreet. Hearing King was taking his division to Manassas Junction, another Union general, James Ricketts, took his soldiers and marched to Bristoe. Pope insisted later that it was the worst move King or Ricketts could have made—if they had maintained their positions, the two might have kept Longstreet's soldiers from reaching Jackson. Upon hearing King's engagement August 28, Pope became convinced that Jackson was in full retreat to Thoroughfare Gap in the Bull Run mountains and Union forces could be hurled at the rebels while King and Ricketts blocked their retreat. Actually the situation was much different. Jackson was not retreating—he was digging in along his strong defensive position. His lines of communication to Longstreet were open, and the head of Longstreet's column was already through the gap and bivouacked within supporting distance. Not expecting Longstreet before Saturday night, or even Sunday, Pope issued orders for an attack on Jackson. Even as his gallopers went to the divisions, Federal skirmishers were already exchanging fire with Jackson's men along the turnpike east of Groveton. Other Union forces joined in, and soon an engagement was in progress.

In their camp along the railroad at Manassas Junction the morning of August 29, the Wisconsin and Indiana men cooked the fresh beef ration and boiled coffee. In Company K of the Sixth Wisconsin, Tommy Flynn, who hailed from Knightstown, Indiana, went over to the Nineteenth to see how his friends fared. He brought back pork and sugar, and the Juneau County boys "dined in high pomp as the result of his efforts." The brigade's ammunition wagons also came up and the Wisconsin men each drew 60 rounds. About midmorning they began to hear the "heavy sound of cannon and an occasional ripple of musketry," seemingly very near the place where they had fought the previous night.

Rufus Dawes, sleeping alongside the roadway, awoke to the "heavy tramp of hurrying feet" and found a thick blue column moving back along the very road the Sixth Wisconsin had covered the previous night. The soldiers were Fitz-John Porter's, just up from McClellan's Army of the Potomac (the tough veterans a "happy sight to see," said one Badger), and they were marching to the sound of the fighting. Porter's men had withstood the battles outside Richmond several weeks earlier, and they were fresh and in good spirits and filled with contempt for John Pope's soldiers, especially those dirty specimens in fancy plumed hats standing alongside the road to gawk and cheer. "We are going up to show you 'straw feet' how to fight," one infantryman called to the Wisconsin men. Soon a "running fire of disparagement" was being voiced by both sides. One of Porter's regiments was the Fifth New York, a colorful Zouave organization still outfitted in baggy red trousers, and as it passed a frustrated Badger went to the road with narrowed eyes to raise his fist. "Wait till you get where we have been," he yelled. "You'll get the slack taken out of your pantaloons and the swell out of your heads."[21]

After the regiments passed, Gibbon's Brigade and the rest of the division fell in behind Porter's men. They marched back along the very road traveled the night before, and the Westerners could hear fighting and see dust clouds stretching away toward the Thoroughfare Gap. In ranks that was regarded as Jackson on the run for safety. "The cannonading is getting stronger and closer," a Wisconsin soldier wrote in his diary. "It sounds like the continuous thunder of a storm: boom-boom-boom-boom. We now have hope seeing a quick ending of this unhappy war."[22]

At the junction of the Manassas-Gainesville and Manassas-Sudley roads, Porter's column continued toward Gainesville. He had been directed by Pope to attack Jackson's right—an order Porter never followed or was unable to follow—and the road took him into one of the bitter controversies of the war. At the junction, staff officers waved King's men up the Manassas-Sudley road. They soon reached the Warrenton turnpike, where the soldiers found Irvin McDowell on his horse. "We have been driving the enemy all day," the general called. "Give him a good poke boys. He is getting sick." McDowell was wearing what one Badger called "the oddest looking hat I ever saw"; it was believed in the ranks that McDowell wore the distinctive headgear "so the rebels could distinguish him, and not direct their fire in his direction." The division was finally halted and formed in two lines of battle, but Gibbon's regiments were detached and marched to the right, climbing the hill north of the Warrenton pike to support Federal artillery. In the Second Wisconsin, soldiers recognized the ground on which they had fought the first battle of Bull Run a year earlier. It was near sunset. To the left the fighting was dull and indistinct, but evidently severe. "Listening to this musketry, we deemed ourselves exceedingly fortunate to have escaped a fight," said Dawes. "A few artillery shots from the enemy whistled over us, but we soon fell into a profound and much needed slumber."[23]

A long time afterward, following an examination of the records, Dawes sat down to write a history of his regiment and in it was a bitter summary: "On the afternoon of this day, August 28th, 1862, was lost the only opportunity that occurred in that campaign to attack Jackson with superior forces while separated from Lee. The verdict of history is likely to be, that the opportunity was 'lost in the woods.' The best blood of Wisconsin and Indiana was poured out like water, and it was spilled for naught. Against a dark background of blunders, imbecilities, jealousies and disasters in the Pope campaign, stands in brief relief the gallant conduct of our heroic leader, John Gibbon. Whatever history may do for others, his fame is as safe as that of the faithful and gallant heroes of the brigade he commanded."[24]

But that realization was still ahead, and the Wisconsin and Indiana soldiers slept in line of battle wearing belts and accouterments, riflemuskets at hand. "We understood," said Private Sullivan of the Sixth, "that Lee had been beaten and tomorrow would finish the job, and that the much dreaded 'Stonewall' was bagged with his army, but the next day brought a very different story."[25]

14.
The Little Colonel

With Col. Lysander Cutler severely wounded, Edward Bragg took command, and it was an event that would prove far-reaching in the chronicles of the Sixth Wisconsin. The young soldiers were troubled by the loss of the fatherlike "old colonel" (a description used only out of Cutler's hearing), but the Badgers were not uncomfortable having the "little colonel" as the "boss soldier."

Edward Stuyvesant Bragg had been with them from the first. As a young man Bragg had moved from New York State to Fond du Lac, where he practiced law and began to make a name for himself. With Fort Sumter he was among those calling for maintaining the Union by arms, if needed, and to make his point he abandoned his law practice. "I am in favor of suppressing the rebellion," he told a war meeting at Fond du Lac. "I want these young men and my neighbors to enlist. I will set the example." Bragg then walked to the table and signed his name.

He immediately began raising a company from his hometown and nearby farms and villages. The new organization, he decided, would be "Bragg's Rifles," and that said something about the man. To his new comrades Bragg's restless energy created a good impression. "He takes on the duties of a soldier as naturally as a tree takes on the burden of her fruit," one soldier said. "He observes shrewdly, combines and infers rapidly, and intuitively separates important things from unimportant. He hates sham pretension and gives and demands perfectly straightforward and frank intercourse." Rufus Dawes wrote home that the 37-year-old lawyer-turned-soldier was "the brightest man in the regiment," and a Shawano County volunteer reported: "Capt. Bragg is a gentleman, every way qualified to command and he will do all that lies in his power for the comfort of his men."[1]

Bragg (who would use his soldier days as a springboard to a long

*Edward S. Bragg. Courtesy
of the State Historical
Society of Wisconsin.
[WHi (X3) 11286]*

political career) was one of those complex individuals produced in the
volunteer organizations during the Civil War—a mix of ambition and
patriotism, part politician, part soldier. He was a man of ability although sometimes petty. His letters to his wife were filled with bitter
complaints against the elderly Cutler (whom he felt blocked advancement) and many questions about what the people back home were
saying about him. One of his lieutenants noted that Bragg "seems to be
engaged in fishing for some higher place and not in promoting the
health or good feeling of the Company."[2]

But the boys in ranks came to admire Bragg and his "awful vocabu-
lary" while handling the regiment. "He is rather under medium height,
does not talk much, and when he does speak it is in a low tone," one
soldier said. "But . . . he was like fiend when fighting, raving and
storming at his men and urging them on to the more daredevil acts,
himself leading the way." Another described the captain as "small and
wiry; eyes and hair black as coal voice penetrating" and recalled how

Bragg once comforted a wounded soldier with a pat on the back, telling him, "You're all right, chicken."[3]

There were, of course, a score of Bragg stories and one of the best involved a Massachusetts clergyman down to see the Army of the Potomac. When the churchman came to the Sixth Wisconsin, he confided to the regimental chaplain that he was "much pleased with the general appearance of the men," finding them a "clean and orderly set, who drank and gambled much less than soldiers in other regiments." The reason, the clergyman said, "must be due to the example of your colonel. . . . They feel the force of his beautiful Christian spirit, and they are afraid of shocking him by the use of profane language." The churchman asked as to what "denomination is Colonel Bragg a member?" The honest chaplain ("recalling some of the highly picturesque expletives which the colonel was apt to use while in action and the sultry anathemas which the men of the Sixth directed at the enemy along with the bullets") coughed "violently to smother a laugh" and replied, "Well, really, Brother Clark, I don't know to what church Colonel Bragg belongs. I never asked him, and I have never heard him say anything that would give me a hint."[4]

From the first days of the regiment Bragg was a camp favorite. But that Saturday, August 30, 1862, on the field of Second Bull Run, his reputation was still to be established. He would first have to lead his volunteers through one of the darkest days for the Union arms.

The sun rose clear, and "all was as quiet as a Sabbath morning at home." In their bivouac the men of Gibbon's Brigade awoke to distant skirmish fire that sounded, one said, "like a dozen carpenters shingling a roof." From the hilltop they had a "fine view" of the Union army— "divisions, brigades and regiments"—arrayed before them, the dark columns moving in the distance toward various positions. Farther on, out of sight behind a woods, were the Confederate lines. But the minutes became hours and little developed. Some of the soldiers went back over the hill to start small fires. "We dared not to make coffee there as the smoke would show where the infantry was and the rebels would commence to shell us," one Badger said. The rumors, said Rufus Dawes of the Sixth Wisconsin, were very thick and "a question I heard seriously discussed" was whether Jackson would get away without being "bagged."

The morning wore on and John Gibbon rode off to find army headquarters. He came upon John Pope and several officers to the rear of his position but found no tents, guards, or flags, just a scattering of cracker boxes for seats. Pope was very animated, and to Gibbon he complained of "the inaction" of Fitz-John Porter. Porter had done nothing the previous day while the rest of the army was fighting, Pope said. "That is not the way for an officer to act, Gibbon." Gibbon was surprised at Pope's tone. "I knew Porter's reputation as a soldier well and felt confident that he was not a man to stand by and do nothing when he ought to fight," Gibbon recalled. "But I knew little or nothing of the military situation and said nothing."[5] It was late afternoon when Pope became convinced the enemy was retreating. The general could not have been more wrong and, to compound his mistake, he began issuing orders for a pursuit.[6]

King's Division, under command of John Hatch due to King's illness, was marched to the Warrenton Turnpike, then west a half mile before being formed north of the road. Gibbon's regiments were in two lines with another brigade in front of them, also in two lines. Ahead was the woods and beyond that, out of sight, a railroad embankment that would prove to be full of rebels. The Union line stepped off. As it reached the woods Gibbon ordered his regiments into a single line, the Sixth Wisconsin on the right. Ahead the advancing Federals disappeared into the foliage. The Sixth Wisconsin had gone about six rods when musketry erupted to the front. "We pushed on without delay or halt," Gibbon said. The "underbrush was thick and impassable for horses" and mounted officers had to go on foot. "It was with difficulty that any alignment could be preserved. Bullets came thick from the front and very soon shells were bursting among us, coming from the left." The line slowly worked through the underbrush, the regiments tangled as bullets and what the men called "scraps of railroad iron" tore through the tree limbs. "We pushed on," said Dawes, "advancing as the lines in front of us advanced and lying down on the ground when they stopped." Without warning the Federal line in front gave way in disorder. A New York regiment behind the Sixth Wisconsin also "took the contagion and ran away not having fired a gun."

Somewhere ahead, the rebels "raised a tremendous shout, and poured in a heavy fire of musketry. The sharp artillery fire of the enemy which enfiladed our line, added to the panic and confusion." In the noise and smoke Bragg came up, shouting left and right, "Sixth Wisconsin, kneel down! Captains, keep your men down! Let nobody tramp on them!" Gibbon was also there, a revolver in his hand. "Stop those stragglers!—Make them fall in!—Shoot them if they don't," he ordered. "Stop them or shoot them like dogs." Kneeling, with bayonets set, the Sixth Wisconsin received the swarm of fugitives, the line bucking and jerking as soldiers and officers clubbed, cuffed, and cursed the fleeing men in a frantic effort to halt them. Finally the wave of running soldiers passed, some halting, others never stopping in their panic to reach safety.

The woods and underbrush in front was suddenly empty of soldiers and the firing stopped. "We know well what that portended," Dawes said. "The rebels were advancing in pursuit." Gibbon ordered Bragg to throw forward a company as skirmishers and selected was the second platoon of Company K. "It was a fearful duty to go into the face of an advancing army," Dawes said, but the skirmish line, under the command of Capt. David Quaw, deployed and moved into the woods. They had not gone far when a flurry of bullets rattled through the trees. The first shots killed Levi Gardner of Fountain City "dead in his tracks" and upended Hoel Trumbull of Lemonweir.[7] "Trumbull had his rubber blanket folded up very narrow (about 3 or 4 inches wide) and it was around his waist under his waist belt," said a comrade. "He was running forward when a bullet hit him on the waist belt and rubber blanket and he turned the completest somersault I ever saw, and some of us laughed heartier at it than at the antics of a circus clown." Trumbull was on his feet as quickly as he was knocked down, gasping for air.

The thin line of skirmishers moved deeper into the woods, the Wisconsin boys snapping off shots as they dodged from tree to tree. A short distance ahead they came on Confederates and there was sharp firing. The Juneau County boys dug in, said Dawes, the "panic and retreat of our own troops and the exultant shouts of thousands of rebel soldiers did not daunt these men." Quaw called, "Tree!"—jumping behind a sapling, where he admitted "I must have shrunk to the dimensions of a wafer." The tree was jerked by a dozen bullets and Quaw recalled his skirmishers before the Confederates could get in another volley.[8] Pvt. James Sullivan, who had taken "shelter behind a small tree," did not get the order. "I began to peg away at the Rebs until I exhausted the 20 rounds that was in the top compartment of my cartridge box, and when I stopped to refill it I saw I was alone and I dug out of there in a hurry. The regiment had advanced further into the woods and moved to the left and I finally found them laying down and the Rebs were trying to shell them with shell and case shot, and the tree tops and limbs were falling in all directions. I was very angry at [John] Ticknor, thinking that he had carelessly left me there alone and not yet having arrived at the dignity of using . . . 'a good mouth filling oath,' but still clung to the 'cuss' words of my boyhood, I asked him with an indignant 'dog gone' why he had left me there to fight the whole rebel army alone. Lt. Colonel Bragg ordered me to lay down, and all the satisfaction I got from Ticknor was, 'Lay down, Mickey, you damfool, before you get killed,' and I lay down and transferred my cartridges to the upper part of my cartridge box."

Soon all Federal troops in the woods except for the Sixth Wisconsin had withdrawn. The regiment was under the fire of sharpshooters, said Dawes, with "quite a number of our men killed or wounded by them." But nothing transpired, one soldier grumbled, "till the state of affairs were reported to the General and orders received as to what should be done." Those long minutes in the smoke-shrouded woods were trying. "A bullet would strike a man who would writhe, groan and die or spring up, throw away his impediments, and start for the rear," said Dawes. "Our men peered through the leaves, shooting at the puffs of powder smoke from the muskets of the rebels. As I walked along the line, some men of company 'I' said: 'Major, don't go near that tree.' I was not aware what tree, but had wit enough to jump away. Spat, went a bullet against the tree, cutting a corner from my haversack. They had noticed that the tree had been several times struck by the bullets of a sharp shooter."[9]

One soldier ("hugging the earth to escape the thick-flying musket balls from in our front") was astonished to find Edward Bragg behind him. "Our colonel stood erect and motionless, alertly watching every development, ready for any emergency. And when the enemy brought artillery into position on our left and began throwing shells which came down the line and through the thick timber with a hair-raising clatter, he never moved nor even appeared conscious of the appalling danger."[10] It was that instant Bragg became—in heart as well as title—the "little colonel" of the Sixth Wisconsin.

Ahead of the Wisconsin men a wounded New York soldier begged for water. Unable to take the horrible cries any longer, Charles Lampe of Milwaukee ran forward with a canteen only to be shot dead. Henry Petit of Lynxville took a ball through the body and "crying loud enough to be heard a mile" fell into the arms of Sgt. August Miller. "What's the matter you great calf?" Miller asked roughly. "I'm killed! Oh my God! I'm killed!" "Well," said Miller, "what the hell is the use of making a fuss about it?" Petit was carried to the rear. He was out of the war and on his way home, where an unexpected legacy from Europe and an easier life awaited him. One of the New York soldiers collared by Gibbon no sooner dropped down among the Wisconsin men when he was shot and killed. A rebel sharpshooter also clipped the hat of Edwin Brown, the officer claiming later the Confederates were using "globe sighted target rifles."

Milwaukeean William Bickelhaupt, shot through the lungs, was lying nearby and Dawes could hear "the poor little boy, for such he was, in plaintive broken English telling his comrades what to write his 'Mutter.'" Half crazed with pain and fear, Bickelhaupt's mind wandered between the fighting and home. "Oh, I am dying," he cried. "I am killed. Tell my mother I was a good soldier." Then his body lurched and he shouted, "Give them hell! Give them hell!" before falling back, his bloody chest heaving. A few seconds and he began again: "Tell her that I did my duty in battle—Poke it at 'em, boys! Poke it at 'em!—Tell her that I . . ." Bickelhaupt lay wounded three days before being taken to a hospital, where he seemed to be recovering, then infection set in and he was dead within the month.[11]

John Gibbon told Bragg and Dawes that he had no orders to retreat and he should stay until he got them. Finally, convinced no staff officer could bring such an order, the general directed Bragg to form skirmishers to cover the retreat. The squads deployed and Bragg ordered the Sixth Wisconsin to face about. "But the moment we turned our backs we received a galling musketry fire and heard the exultant shouts of the enemy in our rear," one soldier said. "Our commanding officer and Adjutant Haskell saw that we would be destroyed in no time, if we did not face them. To do this was a difficult maneuver, under the circumstances, and I never saw it executed during the war but that once; but we accomplished it, and retreating backwards, towards our line, facing the confederates."[12]

There was no better soldier in the regiment than Pvt. Francis Deleglise of Appleton. "No one had a brighter, better kept uniform," said a comrade. "His rifle was as clean as a rifle could be made, his spare clothes and blankets were always folded just so, and he was sure to get everything in the way of rations that belonged to him and he knew just how to cook them." But Deleglise had one mannerism troubling in a soldier—lying down while shooting. (Two days previously at Brawner farm Edwin Brown had come upon the private flat on the ground, working his rifle-musket with cool deliberation. "Private Deleglise, why are you lying down?" the astonished officer asked. Deleglise looked back and replied, "Because I can get better aim, Captain." Brown had paused, nodded, and walked down the line.) In the woods at Second Bull Run, Deleglise was again "on the ground loading and firing" when the Sixth Wisconsin withdrew. "It had become necessary," said Jerome Watrous. "The enemy had gotten around on both flanks and still had a force in front. That was the force Frank was giving special attention and he didn't hear the orders to fall back. One of his comrades rushed back, caught hold of his coat and gave him a yank and told him to get back quick. . . . Without the least excitement, but with a little longer stride than usual, he went back to the command, about faced and resumed his deliberate firing."[13]

The Sixth Wisconsin moved out with "a slow backward step" and Gibbon soon discovered all Federal troops had withdrawn. Bragg again faced the regiment by the rear rank and took a steady double quick toward the Union lines. At the edge of the woods he ordered the color bearers forward to wave the flags to prevent Federals from firing on his line as it came out of the trees.[14] Then, said one soldier, "taking long, quick strides himself, his regiment imitated him." Another Badger said the Sixth Wisconsin "emerged from trouble" in "splendid order" and "great old cheers went up from the spectators." The command "moved as steadily as it had in battalion drill. . . . Going ten or fifteen rods in that manner the little colonel gave the commands, 'Halt!' 'About, face!' 'Shoulder arms!' 'Ready, aim, fire!' 'Recover arms!' 'About, face!' 'Forward, march!' and again they moved forward in quick time twenty or thirty rods more. There was another 'Halt!' another 'About, face!' another volley, another 'About, face!' and another march to the rear. That is the way that Western regiment fell back."[15]

It was a "full three quarters of a mile over the open fields to the place where our new lines were forming," said Dawes. The Sixth Wisconsin, "alone upon the plain, in full sight of both armies, marched this distance." At one point the line passed through a small orchard and the regiment's flag tangled in the branches and disappeared, causing disruption. Frank Haskell came up on his horse. He took it all in and that "prince of good soldiers"—as Sullivan called him—called out, "By heavens, these colors must never go down before the enemy." The flag was already up and Haskell, facing the regiment and marking time by pumping his sword up and down, called "Left, left, right, left" as he had done on the drill fields of the Washington camps and "the regiment straightened up and marched as well as it ever did on review." Rufus King reported that the Sixth Wisconsin, "the very last to retire, marched slowly and steadily to the rear, with column formed and colors flying, faced the front as they reached the main Federal line and saluted the approaching enemy with cheers and a rattling volley." King, said Dawes, was in error. "We should have killed our following skirmish line by such firing."[16]

Gibbon's Brigade was placed in support of Battery B on a rise commanding the Warrenton Turnpike. Some two dozen Federal guns were arrayed on the hill, the Sixth Wisconsin between two batteries, one facing west and the other south. It was late in the afternoon and the Wisconsin soldiers could see heavy columns of rebel infantry moving toward their left flank. To the front, several hundred yards ahead, a Confederate line advanced to the edge of the woods. "By raising on our hands and knees we could see the magnificent corps of Longstreet coming toward us in close column by division, the closest formation at that time of infantry," a Sauk County boy wrote. "Their artillery was opening a close and destructive fire on the guns in front of us," one of the Juneau County boys recalled, "and canister and case shot were flying all directions." A canister or grape shot Ed Symon's haversack as it lay on his thigh and "scattered his stock of hardtack and coffee in all directions, and he mourned more over the loss of his 'grub,' as he called it, than if it had been an arm."[17] A solid shot also careened through the six guns of Battery B cutting the tail of "old Tartar," the bay horse ridden by Lt. James Stewart. "The shot gave the horse a deep cut across the rump, the scar of which lasted his life-time," said Dawes. Never forgotten, said James Sullivan, was one rabbit ("so much scared by the tremendous noise") which took shelter under one soldier or "the man whose leg was shot off and was making such good time for the rear by the aid of his musket."[18]

Dawes left a description: "We could see regiment after regiment of the enemy moving in column by division, and forming into line of battle as they advanced upon our men. . . . Our batteries were all actively firing upon the advancing columns of the enemy. Their artillery was also in action. The solid shot and shell struck around us and whizzed over us. Occasionally a horse would be killed by them, and one man's head was carried away entirely. Such sights very severely test one's nerves. A solid shot will plow into the ground, spitefully scattering the dirt, and bound a hundred feet into the air, looking as it flies swiftly away like an Indian rubber playing ball."[19] John Johnson of the Sixth Wisconsin barely escaped one cannon ball. "The shot must have struck the ground in front of us, then I could see it as plain as if we were playing ball," he said. "The instinct of boyhood was predominant in me and my left hand stretched out to catch it. It just touched the top of my left shoulder."[20]

The scene below was ominous. The Federal lines were in the fields in front of the woods. "Regiments would sweep splendidly forward into the front line, fire a crashing volley into the woods and then work with great energy," an officer said. "But they quickly withered away until there would appear to be a mere company crowding around the colors. The open fields were covered with wounded and stragglers, going to the rear."

In the Sixth Wisconsin line, the soldiers turned to watch as a Massachusetts regiment supporting an Ohio battery on their left broke in panic, the fleeing soldiers taking "shelter in a ditch (that had been used as a rear [privy pit] by all hands while we had been on the field) much to our indignation and disgust." Pvt. Tom Flynn, watching in amazement, said to the men near him, "There is not divils enough in the confederacy to make me put my head in that ditch."

The battery was left without support and the commander ("a brave German officer") galloped to Bragg "crying worse than a whipped schoolboy." "Mine pattery vas gone, mine pattery vas gone," the officer said, "shouting and swinging his hands." Bragg, watching "in his usual cool, indifferent way, with one eye shut and the other not open," told the German, "We'll take care of your battery." The German rode away. Gibbon came up and sent an order to the artillery to hold fire. The German was soon back. "Got in Himmil! General, why you no say shoot, by my battery! By Jesus Christus, why you no say shoot?" Gibbon gave the officer a cold look. "Go to your battery, Captain, and obey orders when given," Gibbon said.[21]

Gibbon watched "masses of the enemy" approaching "a bald hill in front of the Henry House," both lines disappearing in smoke and the rips of musketry. At the same time, a Confederate line came out of the woods and advanced on the German battery. The Second and Seventh Wisconsin, consolidated under Lucius Fairchild, had been placed behind the brow of the ridge, one wing on each side of the German guns. The thick Confederate line advanced with deliberate step. "When we . . . found the Johnnies flanking us on both sides and saw those double-shot Napoleon guns, we knew there was to be music," one Badger said. Gibbon waited until his infantry could "see every detail of their outfit," then commanded, "Batteries, ready! Aim! Fire!"[22]

The hilltop exploded. The blasts "tore great bloody gaps in the Rebel lines and piled the dead and mangled in rows like hay raked in windrows in a hayfield," a Badger said. "It was an awful slaughter." The Confederates were "pretty close when the front line arose and fired, cutting them badly and turning them about after they fired one volley without much effect. . . . The bullets came over our heads like a shower of hailstone." As the artillery smoke drifted away, the Second and Seventh Wisconsin poured in a volley that halted the rebels "right there and the order to fix bayonets and charge caused them to conclude that they did not want that battery, and they scampered back for the woods as fast as they could go, under a withering fire of all the guns could bear on them." An Irish private, taken by the scene, called out, "Set them up on the tother alley, boys, they're all down on that!"

The remark brought laughter, and despite the perilous situation, the tension was somehow broken.

15.
The Army Ran Like Sheep

The laughter no sooner faded when it was apparent the Federal line was in danger. To the left, the Wisconsin men could see Union brigades being driven in confusion over the fields. It was the Confederate advance of Gen. James Longstreet and his veteran soldiers plunged forward in a sweeping attack that would destroy John Pope's Army of Virginia. "This outflanked our position," said Rufus Dawes, "and it was evident we must soon draw back our line."[1]

Out of the confusion behind John Gibbon's line an officer rode up, identifying himself as on the staff of Joseph Hooker. The order he carried was to retreat. "General Hooker was almost a stranger to me and belonged to a different corps," Gibbon said later. "I called the attention of the officer, bringing the order, to the importance of the position we held, especially in view of the fact that our troops appeared to have retaken possession of the hill near the Henry House and that if we fell back, the whole line would have to do so and requested him to so state to General Hooker." The officer soon returned and the order was the same—fall back as Pope had ordered "a general retreat." Hooker himself was seen riding among the batteries, ordering the guns and supporting infantry to retire. "Regiments moved steadily by the right of companies to the rear, the batteries moved also in retreat," said Dawes. The Sixth Wisconsin, marching in double columns, left the position at the double-quick, halting at one point to wheel into line and fire at Confederates threatening a battery. "A rebel line in our front rose up from the ground and advanced slowly after us. It was a strange sight, our blue line slowly retreating and the long gray line slowly and quietly following." When the Federals stopped, the rebels halted and lay down on the ground. Now and again the rebels would shout, "Get, you sons of bitches, get!" and, one Badger explained, "We got, not talking back," while a second added: "I am proud of our Brigade, but we ran. How I skedaddled with my short legs. . . . In fact, I wished I hadn't been born." There was no dishonor in this, he explained. "We stood when commanded to stand, and when ordered to go—we got!"[2]

In ranks the soldiers were troubled. "We understood when we were placed on that ridge that it was the key of the battlefield, and if keys of battlefields are of any use to win battles," said Pvt. James Sullivan, "I fail to see why we did not win, as I am very sure we held the key and were not driven an inch by the rebels, nor did our pieces have to 'limber to the rear' until we were finally marched off the field."[3] Gibbon led his brigade across a valley and up a hill, passing "a great pile of knapsacks and other equipment, lying in a piece of timber where they had been left when their owners had gone into action."[4] Before pulling out Gibbon saw Hooker watching the Confederate advance and he rode over to explain his hesitancy to retreat. "That is all right," Hooker said, adding "some complimentary remark" about the way the brigade had behaved which, said Gibbon, "at once excited my pride and attracted me to him."

On his way to catch his soldiers Gibbon found Irvin McDowell. As the two shook hands McDowell said with a smile that he had heard Gibbon had been killed. Gibbon assured him that was not the case and spoke with enthusiasm of his Wisconsin and Indiana soldiers, just then marching past. "If you have such troops as that," McDowell said, "you shall act as a rear guard and be the last, except myself, to pass Bull Run!" Gibbon was puzzled. "I must admit that up to this time I had not got it through my head, that there was such a thing as a *retreat* or that we were to be a rear guard."[5]

Gibbon's Brigade was placed on a ridge alongside the Warrenton Turnpike near the Robinson house. The six Napoleons of Battery B were unlimbered. "The sun was now just disappearing and the atmosphere so thick with smoke that the eye could not reach to any great distance," Gibbon said. "We could not see any of the enemy's movements but the sound of cannon was still heard both to our right and our left."[6]

Out of the darkness came a horseman riding in an erect fashion, an empty sleeve pinned to his tunic. It was Maj. Gen. Phil Kearny, who had lost the arm in the Mexican War. He was one of the most famous soldiers of the Army of the Potomac and he was furious.[7] "Whose command is this?" the general called. Gibbon identified himself and said he was the rear guard. "You must wait for my command, sir," Kearny replied. "Yes, I will wait for all our troops to pass to the rear," said Gibbon. "Where is your command, General?" "Off to the right, don't you hear my guns? You must wait for Reno, too," Kearny said, referring to Jesse Reno's division. Gibbon asked the location of Reno's position. "On the left—you hear his guns? He is keeping up the fight and I am doing all I can to help." Then Kearny fixed Gibbon with his eyes and blurted in a bitter tone: "I suppose you appreciate the condition of affairs here, sir?" When Gibbon did not reply, Kearny said again, "I suppose you appreciate the condition of affairs? It's another Bull Run!" "Oh! I hope not quite as bad as that, General." "Perhaps not," Kearny said. "Reno is keeping up the fight. He is not stampeded. I am not stampeded, you are not stampeded. That is about all, sir, my God that's about all!" With that, Kearny was again off in the darkness. Two days later he was shot dead at Chantilly. In one of his last letters, the general wrote, "The army ran like sheep, all but a General Reno and a General Gibbon."

As the darkness closed around the battle ground, the firing faded and stopped. It was 9 o'clock. In the valley below, Gibbon could hear rebel officers forming their lines. After a time, convinced the fighting was over, the general rode to the left, where he found a brigade of Reno's command and a battery. "The Brigade and Battery Commanders urged me to order them back, but I was adverse to doing this in the absence of their proper commanders." Finally Gibbon gave Reno's soldiers the order to retire, leading the column to the Warrenton Turnpike. Riding back to the front he was also told that Kearny's troops had gone to the rear. He was about to retire his own brigade when an officer rode up in the night and called out in a cheery voice, "What the devil are you ordering my troops off the field for Gibbon?" It was Jesse Reno. He listened to Gibbon's explanation, then said, "All right, all right. All my troops have gone back, and now you can leave as soon as you please."[8]

James Sullivan of the Sixth Wisconsin said it was midnight when the regiments—after building bright fires to confuse the enemy—"leisurely fell back all night, crossing Cub Run next morning, where we halted and formed lines across the road to stop the pursuing rebels, but they did not choose to attack. We continued our march to Centreville and Sumner's corps, which had come up to support Pope, came forward and relieved us and after marching, starving and fighting a week, without a night's rest, we lay down in the mud and rain and slept as only the tired soldier can when he has a chance."[9] Gibbon also began to realize the truth of Kearny's assertion. He found the Warrenton Turnpike "blocked up with a mingled mass of stragglers, wagons, artillery, ambulances, and wounded, some of whom were in hand litters as they had left the field." His column, still in formation, fell in behind "the moving mass" on the march to Centreville. The scene at Centreville "baffled description," said a Sauk County man, who saw officers of all grades, from all branches of service, milling around "looking for their commands and mobs of men looking for their organizations. Infantry, artillery, cavalry, ambulances, wagons and all the impediments used in an army all mixed up with dire confusion."[10] Jerome Watrous of the Sixth Wisconsin later measured the tangle of wagon trains, artillery, cavalry, and infantry against the Union retreat of First Bull Run. "But it was a different class of men," he said. "They had seen service; they had been in a number of hard battles; they had learned how to fight. It was not their fault that a great victory was not won at the second battle of Bull Run. They had lacked competent leadership. It was fortunate for that defeated army and Washington that Lee's army had been so severely punished that it did not follow up its advantage. At no time, in all of the four years of the war was Washington so disturbed or in such great danger. . . . The country was shocked and discouraged."[11]

The regiments bivouacked at Centreville. A picket line was deployed at the rear of the brigade, at the front, and on both sides. "Nobody knew when the next blow would come," said Edward Bragg of the Sixth Wisconsin. "Ignorance of the situation, and disorder and lack of discipline among the troops was the rule." Rufus Dawes was one of the officers placing the sentries. "Our men, after the privations, labor, and intense excitement of three successive days in battle, were unfitted for such duty," he said. "One man placed on a picket post in the woods, in the bewilderment of his senses, got himself faced toward our camp instead of toward the enemy." As a detail went to relieve him, the weary soldier mistook them for the enemy and fired. Killed by the lone shot was Rudolph Fine, one of the Hillsboro boys of Company I.[12] Gibbon wrote with bitterness, "Again had faulty strategy defeated us, and again the folly of attempting to command armies in the field from a distance had been demonstrated."[13]

The next day, September 1, 1862, the Western regiments—"in regular form with no demoralization"—led the retreating army the six miles toward Fairfax Court House. Two incidents were remembered. The hungry soldiers came upon a wagon train carrying fresh bread. "We had been tightening our belts for several days to help relieve the feeling of hunger," one Badger said. "As the wagons passed we got on each side and with our bayonets speared out the whole contents of the wagons. Real fresh bread don't go far with a half starved soldier." The second incident revealed Gibbon's dark side. One Badger recalled how the "exhausted, tired, footsore soldiers" were unable to keep up the pace, and Gibbon, mounted and accompanied by a one-horse spring wagon carrying his "bedding, provisions, canned fruit, etc.," ordered the drum corps to play the "Rogue's March" to shame the stragglers. The soldier added bitterly that it was "the only instance on record . . . outside of his own cruelty, barbarity and indecent humidity, where the outrage was imposed on volunteer soldiers unless sentenced by a court martial."

Late in the day there was more fighting, to the right, and Gibbon's regiments were formed in line of battle during a heavy storm; the noise of the distant artillery and musketry, intermingling with the roll of thunder, producing a startling effect. "The darkness incident to a sky overcast with heavy, rolling clouds, lighted up alternately by flashes of lightning and the flames of artillery, made a scene long to be remembered," said Dawes. The Warrenton Turnpike was a tangle of wagon trains. At one point there was a panic, with "wagons two or three abreast and the mules going at a full gallop, followed by a sudden crash and a jam, and wild cursing and shouting by the drivers."[14] The sound was the fighting at Chantilly as Union forces blocked an attempt by Jackson to get around the Federal right. Phil Kearny was killed.[15] The next day the marching brigade was passed by an ambulance carrying Kearny's body, which had been sent in from the enemy lines under a flag of truce.[16]

When the regiments finally approached Upton's Hill six miles from Washington, Bragg had his colorbearers wave the flags to prevent "being fired upon by the Union guns in the fort upon the height, so demoralized were they with the crushing defeat that the Union army had received." As the weary soldiers marched to their old camps a welcomed announcement came down the line—McClellan had been given command of the defense of the capital. The news was greeted with loud yells, and John Hatch, a McClellan partisan, swung his sword over his head and led the men in the cheers, which Dawes said were given with "an uproarious good will and repeated."[17] Jerome Watrous later explained the matter: "There was a loud call for a new leader to gather up the reins, reorganize the army and enter upon the next campaign. Where was the leader? There was no time to lose. McDowell had twice been defeated at Bull Run. He wouldn't do. Pope . . . had met disaster. He wouldn't do. President Lincoln did what he believed was the best thing to do. He named Gen. McClellan." Lt. Frank Haskell wrote home: "Poor, lying Pope was played out. The man alone who is fit for the place, McClellan, took the army." Bragg used harsher words: "Pope is a braggart & a villainous perverter of facts & McDowell too fussy & confused, to have any combinations successful." It was the McClellan news, said

Gibbon, that sent the "weary fagged men into camp, cheerful and happy to talk over their rough experience of the past three weeks and speculate to what was ahead."[18]

It was also at Upton Hill that the German commissary sergeant of an Ohio regiment "gave bacon, and hard-tack and coffee, without a requisition or a receipt, to keep the men alive during the night." The Western volunteers were defeated, disgusted, and dispirited but not despairing, and there was satisfaction they had performed with bravery. "Great as our loss has been it is better than defeat," one Badger said, "and everybody feels proud of belonging to 'Gibbon's Brigade,' commanded by John Gibbon, or 'Fighting John' as our boys call him." Haskell wrote his family he had been in the battles of the past three days, but "I have no touch of bullet, ball or shell upon me. I cannot give you particulars or write more, as the terrible weariness of a long fight is upon me."[19] Hugh Talty of Company K, Sixth Wisconsin, told the soldiers of his cook fire, "Arrah, if the big ginerals wus wurth a cint, we'd show thim rebels what dilgant hands we were at fightin." His nephew, "Mickey" Sullivan, agreed. "The feeling was universal that the miserable result of all our hard fighting was due to lack of skill in our commander and the meddling interference of the war department in keeping several different armies to protect Washington, neither of which was strong enough for any purpose but that of defeat. Pope, McDowell and several more of that ilk were relieved from command, and 'Fighting Joe' Hooker took command of our corps. Our brigade camped at Upton's Hill and once more received enough to eat."[20]

The news of McClellan's return made the soldiers "jubilant in consequence," but James Sullivan and tentmate Erastus Smith "had no inclination to throw up our hats for anybody unless he had done something to deserve it. We reserved our cheers for future use."[21] But there was, Sullivan said, a belief "the blunders of the past months would not be repeated, and we might at least expect good common sense at headquarters."[22] He gave this assessment: "I know that our part of the army had no idea that we were defeated, and I think, had he [Pope] been an energetic commander, with two fresh corps coming up to his support, and his centre and right wing intact, there was no occasion for Pope to retreat from Bull Run, leaving his dead and wounded uncared for; many of the latter of whom died for want of care before the ambulance corps and citizens of Washington went out and brought most of them in." Sullivan concluded: "During the sixty days that Pope was in command the army had one uninterrupted series of disasters, and although they fought well and lost heavily, there was no talent to direct the men.

Pope blames Fitz-John Porter,[23] but the enlisted men of the army thought that he should blame his own ignorance and self conceit, for, if he had handled his army half as well as Porter's men fought at Bull Run, the result would have been different. . . . [B]ut Pope, who had come there to show the 'Army of the Potomac' how to fight, had to have some excuse for his ignominious failure. I don't wish to be understood as being unfair and prejudiced against Pope any more than against any of the other military failures of the war; but when Pope took command he made such a braying of trumpets in his own praise as to render him particularly conspicuous."[24]

The assessment of Rufus Dawes was more measured. "General Pope made a grave blunder when he assigned the ingrained hero worship of General McClellan, which feeling can be little understood now, because conditions akin to those affected us have passed away. Such a feeling, as that for General McClellan, was never aroused for another leader in the war."

The return of George Brinton McClellan to partial command of the army was unavoidable. The Army of the Potomac, an organization created and inspired by "Little Mac," was, as one soldier put it, "smarting under criticism and its own frustration that it had disappointed its own hopes and those of the people." Richmond had not fallen two months earlier; John Pope was a failure at Bull Run; the Confederate army was again threatening Washington; and, as Dawes said, "there were those even in high position, who seemed to glory in the fact." Abraham Lincoln, against the advice of others and unsure of the loyalty of his army, pursued the only course left to him—McClellan was restored to the soldiers who loved him. The move cheered the officers and men, for the most part, and added a light step to the weary volunteers who had failed a second time on the fields around Manassas Junction. Common and severe throughout the army, said Dawes, was "animadversions against the President himself, for what was called 'interference' with the plans of his Generals."

Edwin Brown of the Sixth Wisconsin was just about played out. "What is reserved for us in the future I don't know," he wrote home. "We have been out generalled. Jackson, Lee & Longstreet are too much for 'the Pope' and McDowell, who have commanded the army since we left Culpepper. The troops have no confidence in either of them. They *curse* them continually as the *cause* of our disasters. When the army heard that McClellan was restored to his original command, 150,000 voices broke forth in a *multitude of grand old cheers*—The soldiers have faith in him whether politicians do or not—Gen. Pope is the greatest imposition that has been palmed off on a credulous army or people. McDowell even, *is a giant* in comparison to him." There was more: "Most of the New York & Penn. troops behaved badly, did not stand fire well, broke & run in confusion when the thing became hot. New England troops did well and so did Western. So far as I could judge, *this was universal*, yet those that make the best time get the most NewsPaper puffs. They buy correspondents to *fight their battles on paper*. I must say this the Rebels fight furiously desperately, madly, and *have great system in their madness*. We always have to fight them in strong positions generally in the woods, and their sharpshooters play the very devil with our officers and artillerists." Also of concern was Brown's own health. "As to myself," he wrote his father, "*I have seen enough of the horrors of war*, imagination cannot picture it, it is too horrible to write about. I am weary, worn out. I don't weigh over 115 pounds, and would like to seek repose with my family & friends. I have been on every march. In every place of danger, that my Co. & Regt. have. I have been broken so much of any rest, have had such hard fare that I am very weak, tired and thin. I tried to get leave of absence for one week to rest in Washington but was refused. What the end will be I can't tell. probably a fit of sickness." At the top of the letter Brown wrote a troubling sentence: "I don't know as I shall ever get a chance to come home—I think the south will maintain their independence."[25]

Privates, captains of infantry, even the president of the Republic, it seemed, were troubled and unsure, and outside Washington again stood a victorious rebel army. From Upton's Hill, Dawes wrote of the "terrible ordeal" of the past weeks. The regiment had been "in battle or skirmish almost every day from August 21st to 31st. Our brigade has lost eight hundred men; our regiment one hundred and twenty five. The country knows how nobly our men have borne themselves." There was one important sentence: "I have been at my post in every battle."[26]

16.
We Have Got a General Now

George McClellan worked in his usual efficient manner those first days of September to organize his army for a campaign he would fight with his usual caution. In the changes ordered, John Gibbon's four regiments became the Fourth Brigade, First Division of the First Army Corps, Army of the Potomac. The ill-fated and troubled Army of Virginia, fashioned by John Pope and whipped at Second Bull Run, passed from the army rolls forever. Gen. John Hatch was given command of the division, replacing Rufus King, who would leave the army for a diplomatic post. Irvin McDowell, with his strange battle hat, limited ability, and unfortunate luck, also left active service. The command of the First Corps was given to Joseph Hooker, a general of growing reputation. All of the developments were followed with interest in the Western regiments.

From Upton's Hill it was unsettling to the volunteers that by looking one direction they could see the flag on the United States Capitol in Washington and by turning to the other they could make out the red flags marking Lee's army. "You see we are back near our first starting point," a Wisconsin officer wrote home. "It is a sorrowful conclusion of a mismanaged campaign Pope has played out with the army." Peddlers again worked the camps, but the soldiers' pockets were empty. "Sutlers are asking outrageous prices," one reported. "Molasses 50 cents a bottle. . . . As a result the soldiers are obliged to steal."[1]

Long after the war Wisconsin veterans came to believe that the "disgraceful defeat" at Second Bull Run was caused by McClellan's desire to see Pope a failure. "The bulk of the Army of the Potomac under McClellan was within reach of that field and could have had a part in the battles of the three days," Jerome Watrous said. "It would be difficult to convince unprejudiced people who recall the condition of things during that frightful campaign of destruction, disorder and slaughter, that General Pope was not purposely left to fight the battle with his inferior force and suffer just such a defeat as came to him and his splendid army." To back his statement Watrous offered a story given him by a Fifth Wisconsin veteran. It involved another Fifth Wisconsin soldier, an orderly at McClellan's headquarters, and Watrous said it explained "why orders were not issued to hurry to the assistance of the Union army." The orderly was visiting his old company, just up from the Peninsula, during what would become the Second Bull Run campaign. "Boys," he told his comrades, "you will get orders to move tomorrow morning, early. You will prepare five day's rations. You will start for the battle, but you will not reach there." Why, what did he mean? he was asked. "I have heard talk at headquarters which would chill the blood," the orderly replied. "It is definitely settled that Pope must be defeated. A victory . . . would mean John Pope at the head of the United States Army; that would never do."

Watrous concluded: "An army corps and two or three divisions did move the next morning, but very slowly, and long before night went into camp, and started to the front the next day, our advance reaching Centreville and meeting Pope's army on the retreat to Washington. If the truth and all of the truth ever comes out pertaining to the second battles of Bull Run, every patriotic man and woman in the country will be shocked at the perfidy, the infamy, which prevented a great Union victory, instead of a disgraceful defeat, a rout."[2]

In the annals left by the "Calico Boys" of the Sixth Wisconsin, however, more important matters were talked of in the Upton's Hill camp at the time. The first involved Edward Bragg and the arrival of mail from home. In his packet were several letters urging him to stand as a "War Candidate" for Congress. The "Little Colonel's" reply did him honor: ". . . I shall not decline a nomination on the platform, the Government must be sustained, but my services can not be taken from the field. I command the regiment, and can not leave in times like these."

The second incident occurred in Washington. Col. Lysander Cutler, while recovering from his leg wound received at Brawner farm, bought a new uniform and went on canes to the office of Secretary of War Edwin M. Stanton to pay his respects. After some time in a waiting room, Cutler was finally admitted. As the old officer awkwardly approached on his canes, Stanton—always, it seemed, ill-tempered—looked up and took in the bright buttons and new coat. "What in hell and God damn nation are you doing in Washington?" he asked in his querulous voice. A man of steadier manners, Cutler halted a second, then replied, "If I had not been shot and a fool, I would never have come here. Good day, Mr. Secretary." The old colonel limped off without a backward glance, or at least that was the story repeated around the campfires.[3]

The final matter was closer to the soldiers' hearts. Rations were scarce, they recalled, and all they had upon reaching the Washington camps was fresh beef—so fresh, in fact, it was still on the hoof. The animals were killed at the rear of the companies and each man cut the piece he wanted or could get. Unfortunately, the soldiers could not cook the meat because of the lack of wood for fires. Accustomed to a full table back home, the Wisconsin men said it was two days before a regular issue of rations and even then, the hardtack and pork just would not do. Finally the Baraboo and Lake Delton and Excelsior Township boys, after consultation, went to Capt. David Noyes of Baraboo. A few months earlier, in a time of plenty, the company had sold extra rations and established a small fund for just such emergencies. It was agreed the captain would take some of the $300 he was holding, go to Washington, and buy food. The officer's return was greeted with a raucous hullaba-loo on the company street. Noyes was burdened with condensed milk, canned turkey, peas, beans, and other good things to eat. It was the first time many of the men had seen canned food (quickly discovering folding knives and bayonets useful in opening the containers), and the occasion was marked by the joyous statement of one soldier: "For two days, we did nothing but eat and sleep."[4]

But the rebel columns of Lee, Jackson, and Longstreet were again on the march, this time into Maryland, where various opportunities seemed available. Gen. McClellan faced serious obstacles as he began to respond. The command structure of the Union army was unsure and the men in ranks still shaken by the defeats of recent weeks. In a short time, by hard marching and fighting, Lee and his soldiers had all but lifted the siege at Richmond, had won victories at Cedar Mountain and Second Bull Run, and now threatened not only Washington but Maryland and Pennsylvania as well.

On September 5, 1862, orders went to the Confederate brigades, and the next day the columns pushed across the Potomac River south of Frederick, Maryland, a direct threat against Washington and Baltimore. Lee hoped his overworked quartermasters might find it easier to feed the always hungry Confederate soldiers in the fields of Maryland and Pennsylvania. A campaign there would also allow the farmers of Virginia to harvest their crops unmolested and, possibly, just possibly, a stunning victory might produce European recognition of the new Confederacy. But never was an army so unready for invasion as Lee's Confederate Army of Northern Virginia—ammunition stocks and supplies were nearly exhausted, the army's horses and mules were thin from lack of forage, the infantry was ill shod, and supply wagons were dilapidated. The morale of the Confederate soldiers, however, was first rate, and they moved along the Maryland roads with a certain dash and step always remembered by those who came out to watch them.

Lee's bold venture turned sour from the first. The expected flood of Maryland recruits for his army never became more than a trickle; the straggling of weak soldiers thinned the long columns, and the Confederates were unable to linger at Frederick because the area was soon stripped of forage and supplies. But with a Confederate army in range of Washington, no Federal soldiers could be dispatched to threaten Richmond.

For the Westerners, the Federal pursuit of Lee began at 10:30 P.M. on September 6 when marching orders reached Gibbon's Brigade. The column was quickly assembled in the darkness and hurriedly tramped to Washington. Then, in that puzzling way armies move, it was halted on the street in front of the Executive Mansion, where Pvt. John Johnson of Stevens Point curled up for a "good nap, on the pavement, up against the fence enclosing the grounds of the White House."[5] Sauk County men said the night was "terribly hot and sultry" and the lawn of the President's house was thickly strewn with played-out soldiers. In the dim lantern light, they could "see the tall form of the President ('Old Abe,' as we called him) in shirt sleeves, water pail and dipper in hand, stepping over and among the boys lying around all over the grounds, giving them water to drink."[6] The night passed quietly and with the dawn the order to "fall in" was given. It was first thought the regiments were en route to Georgetown, but they were marched north to Maryland. The next day, Sunday, September 7, the column pushed on, stopping briefly near Brightwood so the soldiers could boil coffee. "We have to carry our knap-sacks again. Corn, potatoes, apples . . . are being taken from the country-side because we had only crackers and coffee with us. We went into camp about eight miles north of Washington on the road to Frederick," a Wisconsin soldier wrote in his diary.[7]

The marching was at "a tremendous pace," one Badger said, with the weather "very warm, and the clouds of dust nearly suffocating." The marching soldiers pushed toward Rockville, Maryland, "with only the shortest possible halts and no stoppage for coffee." In his diary, a Wisconsin soldier tracked the progress of Gibbon's Brigade:

> September 8, Monday—All kinds of rumors are floating around but no one knows definitely where we are going.
> September 9, Tuesday—We resumed our march toward Frederick. Five crackers for rations. Now and then we see the Stars and stripes floating over farm houses. Some farms are abandoned. This is a great orchard country. In the forest can be found enormous sweet grapes in abundance. This is beautiful country, with great farms and beautiful girls.
> September 10, Wednesday—After an all day march northward, we camped about sundown near Slideltown.
> September 11, Thursday—We marched today to a small community called Lisbon.
> September 12, Friday—We marched today through Poplar Springs, Ridgeville, and toward Newmarket, where we bivouacked. Yesterday the rebels had abandoned Newmarket.[8]

On one brief halt, Capt. Edwin Brown of the Sixth Wisconsin wrote his wife the letter of a man obviously near the end of his rope: "I have just time to write you a line—nothing more. You are doubtless informed of the defeats of our Army *which explains our being here.* Three times has my life been in jeopardy, where danger was in *every inch of space.* You can say to your friends that your husband was no coward, where so many *showed 'the white feather.'*" There was more: "The troops had no confidence in Pope or McDowell, therefore many behaved badly. The only troops that really maintained for themselves a good name *every where* was Hooker's & Kearney's divisions and Gibbon's Brigade of King's Division. The Army is discouraged, having no great confidence in anyone. They have more confidence in McClellan than any one else. None too much in him however. Rebels are in force in Maryland, we are 'massing' to meet them."

Brown added a personal note: "I am weary & sick if the enemy was off from our soil I should go to Hospital. Honor requires that every one *who has any patriotism left* should meet the insolent foe. Should I live to see them driven out of this State & away from Washington, *I will have rest at some rate.* . . . Kiss the babies for their war worn father. Good Bye Wife, E. A. Brown."

It was his last letter home.[9]

On the night of September 13, the brigade near Frederick, John Gibbon rode ahead to the town to visit McClellan's headquarters. Seated in McClellan's tent, he was struck by the orderly conducting of affairs.

McClellan, expressing himself freely, at one point took a folded paper and, holding it up, said, "Here is a paper with which if I cannot whip 'Bobbie Lee,' I will be willing to go home." He would not show the officers the document, but folded it to the signature—"R. H. Chilton, Adjt. Gen."—Lee's chief of staff. McClellan told the officers the paper gave the movements of every division of the Confederate army. "Tomorrow," he said, "we will pitch into his center and if you people will only do two good, hard days' marching I will put Lee in a position he will find hard to get out of." Gibbon was taken by the confidence shown by his old West Point classmate and his own growing sense the army had "a General who knew his business and was bound to succeed." Made bold, Gibbon told McClellan, "Well, we will do the marching and I have a command that will do its part," and he added praise for his Western regiments and said the command was much reduced. Another regiment should be assigned his brigade, Gibbon said—a Western unit. The general listened with interest. "You shall have the first western regiment I get," he promised. Gibbon rode back to his brigade in "better spirits than I had been in for a month."[10]

That same night of September 13, Maj. Rufus Dawes wrote his mother a rather thoughtless letter for a young soldier to send home. "Our army is moving up again to the battle field. Probably before this reaches you the conflict will be over. If so, you will know that I was there. My health is good and I am ready to take my chances. Do not feel that our task is easy or sure of successful accomplishment. The battle will be desperate and bloody, and upon very equal terms."[11]

The document in McClellan's possession became the famous "Lost Order" of the Maryland campaign. It revealed to McClellan that Lee's army was widely separated. As at the beginning of the Manassas campaign, Lee had boldly divided his army, but a copy of the marching order was lost (an event never satisfactorily explained). It was found by a detail of Union soldiers and was quickly in McClellan's hand. He now not only knew the location of Lee's columns but had the opportunity to attack first one and then the other wing of the Confederate army, possibly destroying both. McClellan soon had his army in motion, but when Lee realized McClellan was deploying to attack him, he began concentrating his scattered forces. To delay McClellan until Jackson could capture the Federal garrison at Harper's Ferry, Lee dispatched a portion of his army to South Mountain, where the Union columns would have to pass to attack the Confederate army.

In Gibbon's Brigade, reveille came at 4 A.M., and the soldiers would remember the "fertile valley" and how the day came bright and warm—

"as beautiful a morning as one could wish to see," one soldier said[12]—and in the distance the soldiers could make out the spires of the town where church bells were ringing in what Rufus Dawes called a "rejoicing at the advent of the host of her deliverance, the Army of the Potomac." To the southwest was the dull mutter of cannon, later determined to be Jackson's attack on Harper's Ferry. Below Dawes was arrayed the army: "From right to left along the valley below us, stretched the swarming camps of the blue coats, and every soldier felt his courage rise at the sight. Through a wooded and uneven country, by different and devious routes, the columns of the grand army had marched forward. We had known something of their progress, but had not so felt their power as they did now when they were concentrating before us. The deep feeling of almost affectionate admiration among the soldiers for the commander of our army, General McClellan, was often thus expressed: 'We have got a General now, and we will show the country what we can do.'"

At 8 A.M. the brigade, the Sixth Wisconsin in the advance, marched through Frederick. "Our entry into the city was triumphal. The stars and stripes floated from every building and hung from every window," said Dawes. "The joyful people ran through the streets to greet and cheer the veterans of the Army of the Potomac. Little children stood at nearly every door, freely offering cool water, cakes, pies and dainties. The jibes and insults of the women of Virginia . . . had here a striking contrast in a generous and enthusiastic welcome by the ladies of Frederick City." One Badger reported the encouragement "received from that loyal city helped us all through the balance of the day."[13]

To Gibbon it seemed the whole of the citizenry turned out to welcome the soldiers. "When Gen. McClellan came through he was overwhelmed by the ladies, they kissed his clothes, threw their arms round his horse's neck and committed all sorts of extravagances," Gibbon wrote two days later. "Those who saw it say there never could have been such a scene witnessed in this country since Washington's time. . . . The people all come out to speak to us as we pass and show their delight at the idea of the rebels being driven out of the state. There is no question of the loyalty of this part of Maryland." It was during a halt in the streets that Gibbon told his soldiers that McClellan himself, just the night before, told him two days of hard marching would lead to the destruction of Lee's army. (Cheers.) Gibbon said he knew they "would march well and without straggling." (More cheers.) And, he said, he wanted them as well to hoot and jeer "every man they saw along the road straggling from his command." (Loud cheers.) In addition, Gibbon said, McClellan pledged the first Western regiment received by the army would be assigned to the brigade, adding, "I supposed he made the promise because he knew of no better place where a new regiment could learn to fight." Of course, that brought the loudest yells of all, and the march resumed "with everybody in high spirits."[14]

The bright moment was too quickly over. The dusty column pushed along the roadway over hills and through the beautiful valley. One soldier said the "bright guns glistening in the sun," the long trains of wagons, the generals "with their fine bodyguards," and the stars and stripes floating in the breeze made it one of the "grandest sights we have ever looked upon." Alongside the roadway were citizens on saddle horses, and the soldiers called to the riders "they would get to the rear mighty quick when the first gun was fired, which proved to be true in a few short hours."[15] Stragglers began to appear, and Gibbon moved forward a detail and the brigade drum corps. As the guards gathered in the footsore soldiers and pushed them along, the drum corps rattled "The Rogue's March" and the "stragglers were thus forced forward amidst the laughter and jeers of our men." One poor soldier was singled out. "Look at that fellow, hasn't he a regular hospital gait," a Badger said in a loud voice. "Wonder if he has been to the sick call, this morning," a comrade responded. Soon the stragglers began to disappear from the roadway. "What was of more importance to my command," Gibbon explained, "a strong spirit of opposition to straggling was created and it became an honorable ambition to remain in the ranks, instead of constantly inventing pretexts to fall out."[16]

One remembered encounter involved a camp favorite of the Sixth Wisconsin, Pvt. Bill Palmer, whose "great good nature and natural dry wit" eased many hard mile for the Sauk County boys. The company was at the rear of the column when McClellan and his staff passed with a great show of bright buttons, swords, and fancy horses. Stepping out of ranks waving a $5 banknote, Palmer confronted one elegant staff officer. "Here, old man take that," said Palmer. Confounded by the appearance of the soldier and looking him square in the face, the officer questioned, "My man, what do you mean?" "Nawe, you just take it," said Palmer, drawling it out "in his Yankee Vermont twang" so the boys could hear him. "When I left Wisconsin I said that the first galoot I met with a longer nose than mine had to have a fiver—so here 'tis." The staff officer waved him away, but Palmer persisted, and finally the officer pulled down in the saddle and spurred off without a backward look. Of course, from that moment on, Bill Palmer was known throughout the brigade as "Nosey" Palmer of the Sixth.[17]

At 11 A.M. the column reached the Catoctin Mountain, where fences and trees showed marks of a skirmish. From the summit the soldiers had a view of the Middletown valley. Beyond the valley, eight miles away, was the smoke of battle and the dull sound of firing on South Mountain. The column received a warm welcome at Middletown, the people excited by the artillery in the distance and "bloodstained soldiers" making their way back from the fighting. Rufus Dawes, hearing a colonel of an Ohio regiment had been wounded, made inquiry and found it was Lt. Col. Rutherford Hayes of the Twenty-third Ohio, a man to be heard from in the history of the nation.

The column pulled up some distance past Middletown and turned into a field, where the soldiers stacked arms back of a creek along the base of South Mountain. "Here we laid down alongside the turnpike, which crossed over the Mountain in front of us, and saw a systematic movement of the troops begin, which we could plainly see from our elevated position," said Pvt. John Johnson of the Sixth Wisconsin. "The army was disconnected. The right wing moved up the mountain about two miles from us on our right. The left wing started up about one and one-half to our left. We could follow the course of our troops as well as the Confederates, by the smoke of their musketry rising above the timber, and when they came out in the openings, they were in plain view. Both wings of our army were pressing the Confederates back towards the gap, where the turnpike crossed over the mountain, but when the line of troops had pressed them back to within one-half or three-quarters of a mile of the gap, the fighting was stubborn, and it seemed that both of the wings had all they could do to hold their ground. The Confederates held the pike, and about one half mile on either side all the way up the mountain. We felt very good, that we would have seen a splendid view of a battle, and enjoyed it out of harm's way, seeing where our boys would push them back, or when our shells would do some good execution in the rebel rank, until we grew quite hilarious, when the drum call to fall in was heard."

To the officers it was announced that Gen. Joseph Hooker, commanding the First Corps, wanted to carry the crest before dark. The regiments were marched one way, then on the National Road for half a mile before turning left into a field where lines were formed—the Seventh Wisconsin and Nineteenth Indiana in the first, the Second and Sixth Wisconsin in the second. On the right of the turnpike, the Sixth was placed 40 yards to the rear of the Seventh. In the ranks, Dawes said, were about 400 men. An Ohio battery was also in the field, firing shell toward South Mountain.[18] Ahead, the soldiers could see a valley, "beyond which by a steep and stony slope, rose the South Mountain range." To the right, "long lines and heavy columns of dark blue infantry could be seen pressing up the green slopes of the mountain, their bayonets flashing like silver in the rays of the setting sun, and their banners waving in beautiful relief against the background of green."[19]

In ranks, the Sauk County boys noticed George Miles of Reedsburg was solemn and quiet, and he was asked what was bothering him. "You fellows would be quiet too, if you knew you would be killed tonight," he replied. His friends tried to laugh him out of the dark mood, telling him they had been chasing rebels for a week and had seen none and there was about as much chance of a fight as of going home. Later in the afternoon, a Sauk County man who was troubled by Miles's premonition found an officer and asked that Miles be kept behind. As Miles "was as well liked by the Captain as he was by the rest of us, the Captain ordered him to go off on some detail." But Miles "was on to the situation" and refused. "I came here to do my duty and although I know I shall be killed I shall go in," he said.[20]

A short time later, the soldiers of Gibbon's Brigade saw that the Federal lines moving up the slope to the right were having "a hot time in dislodging the rebels from their strongly fortified position." Then an orderly galloped to Gibbon and "the boys commenced to brace up." The order soon came down the line. "Attention, Battalion!" "Load at will!" "Shoulder arms!" "Forward by file right, MARCH!"

Ahead up the National Road was Turner's Gap on South Mountain where, said Pvt. James Sullivan of the Sixth Wisconsin, Gibbon's "Black Hat" Brigade was destined "to become famous."[21]

17.
The Iron Brigade of the West

Turner's Gap at South Mountain was a good place to defend and hard to attack. Heavily wooded in places, the slopes were steep and rock-strewn, with the passage so narrow that determined men with artillery could withstand a much stronger force. The problem facing the Confederates was one of numbers—there were not enough of them to hold the gorge and approaches very long. To make the assault the Union brigades were deployed in a wide front astride the National Road. Once both flanks were engaged, Gibbon's Western Brigade, assisted by Battery B of the Fourth U.S. Artillery, was to attack the gap as a demonstration.[1]

In preparing his advance, John Gibbon placed the Nineteenth Indiana and Seventh Wisconsin, in line of battle, on either side of the turnpike with the right two-gun section of Battery B poised to move up the roadway in support. The Second Wisconsin was behind the Nineteenth left of the roadway and the Sixth Wisconsin behind the Seventh on the right, both support regiments in double columns. Each soldier carried 100 rounds of ammunition. "The turnpike is steep and winds up among the hills," said Frank Haskell, the brigade adjutant, in describing the advance. "The ground descends from both sides to the turnpike,—is wooded save for a belt from one hundred and fifty to three hundred yards wide upon each side, and is crossed here and there with strong stone fences and abounds in good natural covers for troops,—altogether an ugly looking place to attack, the enemy's center, and held by artillery and we knew not how much infantry."[2] Deployed as skirmishers were one company from the Second Wisconsin and two companies of the Sixth Wisconsin. The assault force was no sooner formed when a galloper brought word that Union troops on both flanks "were making headway" and that Gibbon should advance. The brigade stepped off with "a hearty cheer," and Gibbon recalled that the "occasion was one to exhibit admirably, the drill and efficiency acquired by the brigade. . . ." Ahead, the sun was sinking behind the mountain, casting long shadows over the stone walls, fields, woods, ravines, and farm buildings alongside the road.[3]

It was easy going at first, the lines moving with a steady step, the massed brigade passing through fields and orchards toward the "heavily forested mountain where the rebels were hiding." The regiments had just started up the grade, facing the late sun, when the first Confederate pickets were flushed and there was scattered shooting. The thin line of men astride the turnpike drove "slowly up the mountain, fighting for every inch of the ground." On the right, the skirmishers were from two companies of the Sixth Wisconsin—the "Prescott Guards" under Rollin Converse and the "Lemonweir Minute Men" under John Ticknor. "Nothing could be finer than the conduct of these two companies," Rufus Dawes said, "or more gallant than the bearing of their young leaders." For half a mile the skirmishers pushed on in a "deadly game of 'Bo-peep,' hiding behind logs, fences, rocks and bushes."

The command of the skirmish line fell to Capt. Wilson Colwell of the Second Wisconsin, and his order was "Forward!" It was recalled later how there was a certain reckless bravery in the young officer's manner. Just days before, Colwell had been passed over for promotion to another regiment because of a false allegation back home that he had not "behaved well" at First Bull Run. "Colwell was naturally very sensitive, and this affected him so much that he went into battle determined to die," said a friend. "He even stated that he had no desire to survive the fight, and . . . he boldly stood up, fighting with the bravery and desperation, which has characterized him in every battle." Colwell was soon shot and carried bloody to the rear; he was dead within the hour. Lucius Fairchild of the Second Wisconsin wrote in his official report: "His place cannot be filled."[4]

It was classic fighting between skirmishers—one line pressing forward, the other retreating. At one point, the Juneau County boys of the "Lemonweir Minute Men" came upon a "cultivated field with a heavy wood on the right" and their line "extended from the woods down to the road." The field was full of boulders, some quite large, but the advance was steady. "Part of the men would fire and then rush forward while the others covered them and fired at the rebels, and then the rear line would pass through to the front," said James Sullivan, who was with the advance. Here and there, behind a boulder, three or four men would gather and hold it until the enemy was driven out of range. "The utmost enthusiasm prevailed and our fellows were as cool and collected as if at target practice, and, in fact, on more than one occasion . . . one would ask the other to watch his shot and see where he hit."

Sullivan, who was suffering from the mumps and whose cheeks had "reached a respectable rotundity," was with his "comrades in battle"— George Chamberlain of Mauston, Ephriam Cornish of Lindina, and Franklin Wilcox of Lemonweir. Dusk was at hand, the light fading, and the four were behind a large boulder, two firing from each side with Sullivan and Chamberlain working together. The boyish Chamberlain had left a circus to enlist, and it was said by his friends that he joined the army seeking relief from a hard life.[5] Sullivan and Chamberlain were the "stray waifs" of Company K and had "to suffer for all the misdeeds or mistakes, no matter by whom committed." It was a common remark, Sullivan said, that if Dawes "would stub his toe he'd put Mickey and Chamberlain on Knapsack drill," and "consequently we were inseparable companions and fast friends."[6]

The Confederate batteries posted at the gap began firing, but the rebels had trouble getting the range, generally overshooting the advancing lines. Whenever the skirmishers were checked, the two guns of Battery B would "wheel into action and fire shell at the houses, barns or thickets, where the rebels found a cover." John Gibbon rode back and forth on the high ground where he could watch his line. His repeated order ("in a voice loud and clear as a bell and distinctly heard throughout the brigade," said one soldier) was "Forward! Forward!"[7] There was no pause. The line reached a fence and just ahead, said one soldier, was a "large pasture full of logs, stumps, big boulders . . . behind which the skirmishers are having a picnic with the 'Rebs' in front, trying to dislodge them from the position and to make them get for the woods." From the gorge Confederate artillery got in a lucky shot—the shell exploding in the Second Wisconsin, killing four men and injuring five others. But Battery B responded; the Confederate artillery fell silent, and Gibbon again urged his line up the slope with repeated shouts.[8]

It was now harder going with the bullets coming from everywhere as the blue line pushed up the hill, the water in the canteens almost gone and the climb seemingly endless. The four regiments were nearing Turner's Gap. At Brawner farm near Gainesville two weeks before, the brigade fought alone in the darkness; at Second Bull Run, the bravery of the regiments was overlooked in the dismal defeat; but on South Mountain, the embattled Wisconsin and Indiana soldiers were in clear view of a hill where Gen. George McClellan and officers had gathered.[9] "Little

Mac" was watching the fighting when Gen. Joseph Hooker came up for orders, and what happened next became tangled in myth, a story told and retold at the old soldier meetings until no one was sure of the truth of it.[10] In a conversation with a Wisconsin veteran three years after the war, McClellan recalled this exchange:

> McClellan: "What troops are those fighting on the Pike?"
> Hooker: "General Gibbon's Brigade of Western men."
> McClellan: "They must be made of iron."
> Hooker: "By the Eternal, they are iron! If you had seen them at Bull Run as I did, you would know them to be iron."
> McClellan: "Why, General Hooker, they fight equal to the best troops in the world."

Hooker (said Jerome Watrous of the Sixth Wisconsin) "fairly danced with delight as he saw those blue lines of Western boys steadily moving up the long, high mountain facing showers of lead and storms of iron" and was so elated he pounded off without his orders. After dark, when Hooker again reached headquarters, in the flush of victory he called out to McClellan, "Now, General, what do you think of the Iron Brigade."[11] A few days later, in writing of Gibbon's Brigade, a Cincinnati newspaper correspondent reported: "This brigade has done some of the hardest and best fighting in the service. It has been justly termed the Iron Brigade of the West." There were conflicting stories, said Watrous, but "this is the true story of the origin of the name."[12]

But that would all come later, and on the rocky slope of South Mountain the Wisconsin and Indiana soldiers climbed and stopped to shoot, then climbed again, higher and higher, the fighting heavier and the darkness deepening, and always Gibbon's shouts of "Forward! Forward!" At one point, the Nineteenth Indiana stalled in the Confederate fire from in and around a farmhouse and outbuildings. Col. Solomon Meredith called for Battery B, and the two guns came up to throw what Meredith called "several splendid shots . . . causing a general stampede." One of the gunners was John Cook of the Sixth Wisconsin, who had joined the battery just two days earlier. "I did not know a hand spike from a fifth wheel, but I was there just the same," he said, "and when they wanted ammunition, it all depended on me whether I had it or not. You see I was a sort of promiscuous supernumerary fellow. That is, I just as leave be in Milwaukee as at South Mountain. The boys voted me thanks and said it was the greatest maneuver of the campaign."[13]

The brigade was now several hundred yards from its starting point, steadily pushing into the gorge. The rebel position was "one of great advantage," one Badger said, "and it was only by stubborn fighting that they were driven back." Ahead was a stone fence and the Johnnies poured in a heavy fire that slowed the Nineteenth Indiana and Seventh Wisconsin. The Seventh rolled over the fence "pell-mell, yet in good order," one said, then scampered through an "old pasture" toward a woods, the Confederate skirmishers running for cover just ahead. The Sixth Wisconsin was close behind.[14] Slightly right of the advancing Wisconsin men was the skirmish line of the Sixth's Company K and James Sullivan: "[George] Chamberlain, who was brave as a lion, kept continually rushing forward leading the squad and of course we had to follow up and support him. It was now sundown and being in the shadow of the mountain, it was getting dark very fast, and our fellows pushed the rebel skirmishers up to their line of battle, and our squad took shelter behind a big boulder and two of us fired from each side of it. The Seventh which was the line of battle behind us, opened fire and the skirmishers who had gradually moved to the right towards the woods had uncovered their front and were fighting the rebel skirmishers at close quarters. . . ."[15]

The sharpest fire came from a stone wall running along a ravine left of the Seventh Wisconsin. Commander John Callis pushed the right of his regiment forward to face the wall, only to expose his line to rebels in the woods. The Confederates "with a yell accompanied with a withering volley" opened on the backs of the Wisconsin men, but "the regiment deliberately wheeled back into line being at least ten minutes under this heavy fire without returning a shot." On the plateau in front of the stone wall, bullets coming in from left and right, the rebels poured "a most terrific fire" into the Seventh Wisconsin, said a Sauk County man, so that "it seemed no one could survive." One Seventh Wisconsin man said the bullets "flew as thick as hail"; another called it "a terrible fire"; and later the soldiers would puzzle over the fact that the enemy's shooting caused many wounds but killed few men.

Callis ordered a change of front. "It is done with the rebels pouring their musketry into us at a good round pace," said a Seventh Wisconsin soldier. "We were soon back into line. 'About face!' and orders are given to 'fire and load and fire at will!' We commence to fire. By this time it was quite dark; the rebel line was at the edge of the woods behind a fence; and all we could see of the enemy was a streak of fire as their guns were discharged."[16]

On the skirmish line, James "Mickey" Sullivan of the Sixth Wisconsin found the air full of projectiles that splattered off the rocks and thunked around him. "When the crash came, either a bullet split in pieces against the stone or a fragment of the boulder hit me on the sore jaw," he said,

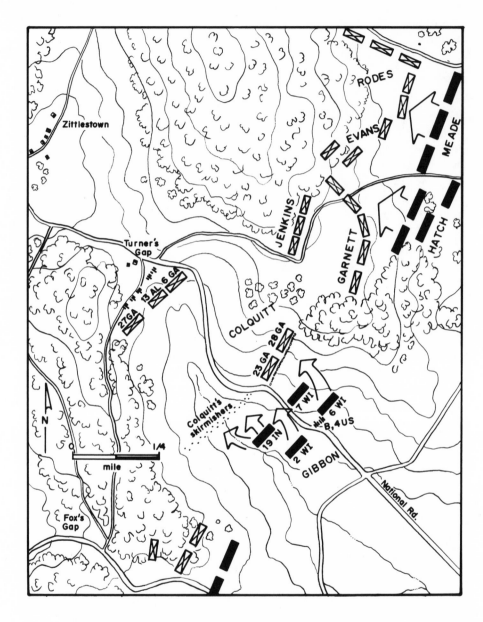

Battle map of the Iron Brigade at South Mountain. Drawn by John Heiser.
Used by permission.

"causing exquisite pain, and I was undetermined whether to run away or swear." Somewhere in the shadow of the rock, Eph Cornish cried, "Mickey, Chamberlain is killed and I'm wounded." There was another "crashing volley" and Sullivan felt "a stinging, burning sensation in my right foot followed by the most excruciating pain." He saw Frank Wilcox "topple over wounded." It was time to get out, the skirmish line having retired. Using his musket for a crutch, the wounded private hopped downhill "a good deal faster than I had come up." In the darkness the "sides of the mountain seemed in a blaze of flame," said Sullivan. "The lines of combatants did not appear more than three or four rods apart, but ours was steadily advancing. The pain in my foot and angry 'zip, zip whing' of the bullets prevented me from dwelling long on the sight, and I made the best of time down the turnpike which was lit up by the flashes of a couple of Battery B's guns, which were firing as guns never fired before. The two pieces made an almost continual roar and they were being pushed forward by hand at every discharge. The gap of the mountain seemed all aflame and the noise and uproar and cheers and yells were terrific."[17]

Behind Sullivan the Seventh Wisconsin stalled in front of the stone wall. "I remember firing my gun only a few times, and as I was loading up for another shot, something struck me in the right leg," said Zeb Russell of the Seventh. "I went down, of course. The first thought was 'the limb is shot off!' . . . I got back of the Company the best I could, perhaps a couple rods, more or less. . . . I got faint. Some one came along and I asked for a drink of water. He gave me a drink and asked where I was wounded. I said my leg was shot off. I felt down as far as I could reach, and found it was still there. About this time, another bullet came and hit me on the other foot. It lodged under the heel of my shoe; no harm done, but my heel was sore a great many days after, but I was thankful that I did not receive a bullet in some other tender spot, as they were coming thick and fast. . . ."[18]

In the noise and smoke, Hollon Richardson of the Seventh Wisconsin ran to the Sixth's Edward Bragg, waving his arm and shouting, "Come forward, sixth!" and Bragg displayed the coolness for which he would always be remembered. "Deploy column!" the lieutenant colonel ordered. "By the right and left flanks, double quick, march!" The regiment "responded to this impulsive force with instant action," said Dawes, and one man in his line recalled, "We came up on a run and just then the right wing of the Seventh Regiment were tumbling in every direction, from a withering, raking fire into their flank." The Sixth Wisconsin's left was now behind the Seventh, the right in an open field, and Bragg saw at once what needed to be done. "Boys, you must save the Seventh," he called, and, seeing Dawes, he shouted over the musketry, "Major! take command of the right wing and fire on the woods!" Dawes instantly ordered, "Attention, right wing, ready, right oblique, aim, fire, load at will, load!" The leveled rifle-muskets of the right wing crashed as one, the sound rolling over the hillside. The noise had hardly ceased to reverberate when Bragg called, "Have your men lie down on the ground, I am going over you." "Right wing, lie down! Look out, the left wing is going over you!" Dawes responded. Bragg took the left wing forward over the men of the right wing as they hugged the ground. The left wing volleyed into the woods, and the right advanced in the same manner over them and fired a third volley. The maneuver was repeated. "There were four volleys by wing given, at the word of command," said Dawes. One Badger called it the "nicest, quickest movement under fire that I saw during the war, and it must have been very destructive to the Johnnies. They received the volleys so rapidly that it could not have been otherwise, being in plain sight of them." Dawes concluded: "In a long experience in musketry fighting, this was the single instance I saw of other than a fire by file in battle. The characteristic of Colonel Bragg in battle was a remarkably quick conception and instant action...."[19] He always believed the crashing volleys by the Sixth Wisconsin "saved the fortune of the day." One captain of the Nineteenth Indiana, shot through the hips and rendered helpless, later told Dawes "that he 'cried like a child' when he heard those volleys so steady and fired at the word of command for, said he, 'I knew they (the rebels) couldn't stand that and I should not fall into their hands.' (Capt. Hart, Nineteenth Ind.)."[20]

The whole line was again shooting. "I had a plain view of them, when we first came up," said John Johnson of the Sixth Wisconsin. "There was a stone fence in front, 80 or 90 paces distant, and the Rebel line of Battle was in the rear of it.... After the third volley, we could see them no more for the bank of smoke laying in front of our line."[21] One soldier shot was George Fairfield. "The fire of infantry was incessant and forcible and the artillery roared to beat anything I had yet heard," he wrote in his diary. "It was while the battle was at its full strength and while the column was advancing I was wounded." Another soldier doing good work in the Sixth Wisconsin was Frank Deleglise. "If he had been going into a forest to chop trees he wouldn't have been any cooler about it than he was in that fight," said Jerome Watrous. "He loaded and fired with as much deliberation, taking special care to aim at an object, and that object was a man in uniform or a horse carrying an officer...." The soldiers, said John Johnson, "would kneel down and look under the smoke to see the flash of the Rebel muskets not to waste our ammunition. . . . There was sometime such rapid firing that our gun barrels became so hot that we could not hold them in our hands. I shifted my haversack on my left side and in firing would stick my hand inside of it to rest the musket and load the cartridges."[22]

From behind the stone wall came a shout. "Oh you damned black hats we gave you hell at Bull Run!" one rebel yelled, to which a Wisconsin man replied: "Never mind Johnny, it is no McDowell after you now." Dawes came upon one soldier "elbowing his way along, loading and firing," shouting at every shot, "Roll your tails, God damn you! Gibbon and McClellan are after you now!" After the Union line surged again only to be driven back by a flare of musketry, a Confederate called "Hurrah for Georgia!" which was answered by more Federal gunfire. Finally, after several long minutes, the rebel firing slackened, but the Confederates clung to the stone wall. The two lines were very close. The Federal canteens were empty, one Badger said, with "the mouth parched, the lips and tongue swollen and cracked caused by the powder taken into the mouth while biting off the end of the cartridges in loading." About that time, James Whitty of the Sixth Wisconsin was hit. He was on a rock firing away with the rest when a bullet tumbled him backwards. "For the love of God," Whitty cried in astonishment, "a 'Wild Irishman' is hit." He was carried out of the fighting. The Sauk County boys of Company A were going down at a fearful rate. Halfway up the mountain, George Miles of Reedsburg had been killed, fulfilling his own grim prediction. As he fell, his rear rank man heard him exclaim, "Tell my father I died doing my duty." John Weidman of Freedom and Jack Langhart of Prairie du Sac were also shot dead, and Richard Attridge of Prairie du Sac and George Rice of Baraboo were mortally wounded.[23]

Left of the roadway, it was the same. The Second Wisconsin pushed into the gap between the Nineteenth Indiana and the Seventh Wisconsin. The Indianans finally succeeded in flanking a stone fence and the Johnnies, caught in the front and right, began to retreat or surrender. The cry was again "Forward! Forward!" and the regiments scrambled up the hill toward the main Confederate line. On the right the advance again stalled under heavy enemy fire. "It was dark and our only aim was by the flashes of the enemy's guns," said Dawes. "Many of our men were falling, and we could not long endure it." Bragg took the left wing of the Sixth Wisconsin into a woods (the soldiers holding on to each other so as not to be lost in the blackness) and moved up the mountainside to where his soldiers could fire into the Confederate flank. He sent word back to Dawes to bring up the right wing, and the Badgers, stumbling in the brush and darkness, scrambled up "the stony side of the mountain" under fire, but "our gallant left wing fired hotly in return and the junction was completed." As the regiment moved into the woods, William Lawrence of DeSoto, who had been singled out for bravery at Second Bull Run, was shot. William Clawater of Bad Ax helped him to the cover of a tree and procured two blankets, one for the soldier's head, the other to cover him.[24]

The fighting again flared, but the cartridge boxes of the Sixth Wisconsin soldiers were empty, the rifle-muskets "dirty with bad powder" and so hot "it was not safe to load them."[25] The Badgers, one said later, had to wait until their rifle-muskets cooled and "we wish to remark that this is about as trying a place to be in as you could imagine with the enemy peppering you and you cannot shoot back." Most of the boxes were empty and the nearby dead and wounded stripped of cartridges. Of that bleak moment, Bragg said: "Ammunition commenced to give out, no man having left more than four rounds, and many without any. It was dark, and a desperate enemy in front." He told his men to cease firing and lay still. Soon the fighting stopped. In the quiet, a shaken Wisconsin soldier called out, "Captain, I am out of cartridges!" It was overheard by the rebels and there was another wave of firing, said Dawes, and "for a short time the contest was very sharp." But that too soon faded and the fighting finally ended.[26]

In the darkness, Edward Bragg could hear the enemy withdrawing. He waited for a time, then shouted, "Three cheers boys, the battle is won! Three cheers for the Badger state!" The defiant "Hurrahs!" echoed into the night. "The answer came from beyond the hill," said Dawes, "and we knew the victory was won." A few skirmishers crept forward, but pursuit was impossible. Bragg said his officers were unable to keep the soldiers awake and the men soon "fell fast asleep from exhaustion, without a cartridge in their boxes, and with their commanding officer and a captain as their pickets." John Johnson recalled that he was "so wet from perspiration that running my hand down my wool sleeve the water would run down in front of it."[27]

Finally Bragg directed Edward Brooks to carry a message back to John Gibbon. Lying nearby wounded was Joseph Marston of Appleton, and he heard Bragg say, "Adjutant, go and find General Gibbon. Tell him the Sixth Wisconsin is on the top of the mountain, that we are out of ammunition, but we will hold our position as long as we have an inch of iron left."[28] Brooks was soon back. It was impossible to furnish ammunition, the general had said, and he hoped the Sixth would soon be relieved—hold the position gained so long as there was "an inch of bayonets left." It was all very grim, said Dawes: "The night was chilly, and in the woods intensely dark. Our wounded were scattered over a great distance up and down the mountain, and were suffering untold agonies. Owing to the difficulties of the ground and the night, no stretcher bearers had come upon the field. Several dying men were pleading piteously for water, of which there was not a drop in the regiment, nor was there any liquor. Captain [John] Kellogg and I searched in vain for a swallow for one noble fellow [William Lawrence] who was dying in great agony from a wound in his bowels. He recognized us and appreciated our efforts, but was unable to speak. The dreaded reality of war was before us in this frightful death, upon the cold, hard stones. The mortal suffering, the fruitless struggle, to send a parting message to the far-off home, and the final release by death, all enacted in the darkness, were felt even more deeply than if the scene had been relived by the light of day."[29]

After a time stretcher bearers made the climb and began to carry off the wounded. A runner also reached Bragg with word the Sixth Wisconsin was soon to be relieved by fresh troops. "How glad we were to hear, they only can know who have experienced the feeling of prostration produced by such scenes and surroundings, after the excitement of a bloody battle," said Dawes. But the minutes passed and no soldiers arrived. The other regiments had long since marched back down the mountain. Brooks was sent again to find Gibbon. The general responded by saying the relief would certainly come. But the relief did not arrive. Brooks was again dispatched down the mountain to find Gen. Willis Gorman. He listened, but shook his head. "I can't send men into that woods to-night. All men are cowards in the dark," he told Brooks, who carried the message to the hill crest. Dawes wrote later that Gorman "forgot that the men who he condemned to shivering and misery for the rest of the night had fought and won a bloody battle in the dark. We were not relieved until eight o'clock in the morning of September 15th when the Second New York of Gorman's Brigade came up." In his journal, Dawes wrote with bitterness: "Some men may be cowards in the daytime."[30]

The Sauk County men of Company A said the ground was "so rough and rocky that more than one of the boys had to use his dead comrade for a pillow. It was fortunate that we were old enough in the service to sleep at any time." Remembering the long climb under fire and the savage exchange of volleys, one Badger said, "We who got through were happy."[31]

18.
Sharpsburg, Maryland

In the first light, the Confederates gone from Turner's Gap, Sixth Wisconsin men crept forward to examine the ground. "I regard this battle as one of the most complete victories of the war," Rufus Dawes wrote in his journal. "They had in the stone fence and rocks almost perfect 'cover' from our fire." The men found "many dead and wounded rebels" in front of their line. The injured Johnnies were from Colquitt's Brigade—the Sixth, Twenty-third, Twenty-seventh, and Twenty-eighth Georgia and the Thirteenth Alabama. Dawes and others came upon a Georgia soldier "wounded in the head, his face a gore of blood." The grisly aberration jumped up in fright and pain and tried to flee. "We could hardly persuade him that it was not our purpose to kill."[1]

At 8 A.M., soldiers of the Second New York ("who had been lying in the field . . . a safe distance in the rear, refreshing themselves with a good night's sleep, after a long and fatiguing march of some 10 miles," a bitter Lt. Col. Edward Bragg wrote in his report) came pulling up the slope. The Badgers were marched down the mountain, where they halted and began coffee fires. "We cleaned our muskets and ourselves, and we needed it," said Pvt. John Johnson. The men were black from the sooty musket smoke and "did not look anything like the trim Sixth Wisconsin soldiers, 'band box' and 'Calico Sixth' the rest of the boys used to call us."[2] Before the coffee was ready, however, the brigade was ordered to march back over South Mountain and that brought grumbling in ranks about certain officers needing to learn their business. "It was hard, but the men fell in promptly and marched along munching on dry hard tack. It was now 24 hours since they had had their coffee," said Dawes. Gibbon's Western Brigade was to lead the army's advance, the Sixth Wisconsin the forward regiment.

Informed the Confederates had left South Mountain, Gen. George

McClellan mistakenly assumed Lee was in headlong flight, and he sent a series of telegraphic messages to Washington announcing a great victory and claims that Maryland and Pennsylvania had been delivered from the hands of the rebels. It was not until late morning of the next day, September 15, that McClellan began a chase and, true to form, it was slow and methodical. By midday reports had reached headquarters that Lee's army had halted along Antietam Creek near the Maryland town of Sharpsburg.

East of South Mountain, Ludolph Longhenry of the Seventh Wisconsin was with the brigade ambulance train. Watching the army's movements, he made notes in his diary. "Two troops of rebel prisoners" marched through the Federal camps from South Mountain, then Federal brigades crowded the roadway; he counted "10 strong columns." There was also the distant sound of cannon to the west, and Longhenry marked the time—"10 a.m." More Confederate prisoners, many wounded, were herded to the rear. The day was very hot. The Union infantry was followed by long trains of artillery. For almost an hour Longhenry watched the procession of guns, and he was enough impressed by one battery of 20- and 30-pound rifles to record their passage. Finally, the road clear, the ambulances pulled onto the turnpike only to become entangled with baggage and supply wagons. It was a long time before the officers were able to unscramble the trains.[3]

In the tangle of columns following the Army of the Potomac was Pvt. George Fink of Milwaukee. Although newly recruited into the Sixth Wisconsin, Fink had previous service in the 90-day First Wisconsin Infantry and had been under fire early in the war. He was bringing from Washington 80 recruits, including himself. Fink had been handed a stack of descriptive lists and ordered to turn the new soldiers and their paperwork over to the commander of the Sixth Wisconsin. The small detail had marched all of September 15 before reaching South Mountain. "What we saw there was too terrible to tell," Fink said. "The dead, many of them had been left without burial. The bodies were decomposed. Dead horses, gun wheels, exploded shells and arms and accouterments were on every hand. The ruin and desolation made us read the meaning of war more plainly than we had ever had before." Hurrying on, by dusk the next day, Fink and his squad caught the army's wagons near Sharpsburg, where he found Otto Schorse of Milwaukee serving as brigade quartermaster. After a time, the wagons turned "into a secluded vale with the mountains rising on the east, north and south of us and a spur or steep hill on the west." The teamsters and recruits set up camp, said Fink, and "here we slept that night."[4]

His new regiment was not far away. The men of the Sixth Wisconsin—"footsore, sleepy, weary, battle-stained and hungry," one said—started the pursuit the previous day by being marched over Turner's Gap. As the column worked over the crest, it came upon Gen. Edwin Sumner's Second Corps. The tough old dragoon and Indian fighter (he was called "Bull" Sumner by his soldiers) had watched Gibbon's men fighting up the mountain and the general issued orders for his regiments to cheer the passing Wisconsin and Indiana men. Even Sumner and his staff came to the roadside to salute with swords and raised hats; the gray-haired general remaining uncovered until the head of the column passed.[5]

Coming up well behind his regiments, John Gibbon missed the display but stopped to speak with Sumner and his officers. Sumner's adjutant told Gibbon that the old general had ordered his corps to cheer the brigade "as a testimonial of the gallantry it had exhibited the night before in the fight which he had seen from the hill behind us." Gibbon was touched. "This action, on the part of Gen. Sumner," he wrote later, "was all the more gratifying from the fact that it was well known in the army that he was very much opposed to such demonstrations as not being proper for disciplined troops."[6]

Sixth Wisconsin men never forgot the salute. "It deeply impressed me at the time when I had but a scant idea of its meaning," said Loyd Harris, then a lieutenant in the Sixth Wisconsin. "But when later on, I came to realize its full meaning—that a distinguished corps commander could not pay a brigade a higher honor—I always felt like lifting my hat whenever General Sumner's name was mentioned." Jerome Watrous said it "was the only honor of the kind paid by the commander of a corps to a passing brigade during the war. The sixth led the march over the mountain, Lieutenant Colonel Bragg commanding, and was first to hear that memorable 'present arms!' first to see General Sumner and staff salute with swords; first to see the old general lift his hat to the officers and soldiers he had witnessed climb a high mountain in the face of a lead and iron storm. Forget such an event—such an honor? Not while memory remains unclouded." Lt. Col. Edward Bragg remembered it as "a very proud morning for me, although I had been on my feet nearly forty-eight hours without sleep."[7]

At Turner's Gap the men of the Sixth Wisconsin came to the stone fence of the heavy fighting the past night where dead Johnnies "were laying in squads alongside the road." The dead "lay pretty thick, all shot in the head, the balance of their bodies being protected behind the fence. There were no wounded, and it showed plainly that we had taken good aim in the dark, having nothing but the flashes of our muskets to guide us." Another soldier saw a field "strewn thickly with gray-backs. . . . Where our Brigade fought, over 300 of the thieves were keeled over, besides a great many wounded ones who had been carried off by their friends. Gen. Hooker, who commands this corps now compliments the Brigade by saying it is worth more than the other three Brigades in King's Division."[8]

The good shooting and hard fighting had also been noted by other organizations. Gibbon's regiments were getting a reputation, and it was not just because of their Western origins or distinctive hats. In the Washington camps, they had been King's "Wisconsin Brigade"[9] (a fact recalled with frustration by men of the Nineteenth Indiana) and then Gibbon's "Black Hat" Brigade. Now they were pointed out as stout fighters as well, and there was a story passed in ranks after South Mountain that made just that point. It involved a corporal of the brigade and the army's commanding general.

The soldier was with a detail taking back prisoners with orders to turn them in at headquarters. Finding the house to which he was directed, he entered and wandered the halls, looking for someone of authority. Coming upon a door ajar, the soldier opened it and found an officer writing at a desk. The officer turned, seemingly annoyed, and asked sharply, "What do you want?" The corporal was taken aback to discover he was face to face with George Brinton McClellan. "I have some prisoners, General, I am ordered to turn over to you." "Who are you and where do you come from?" The soldier's answer caught the general's interest. "Ah," he said, "you belong to Gibbon's Brigade. You had some heavy fighting up there tonight." "Yes Sir," said the corporal, "but I think we gave them as good as they did." "Indeed you did," said the general, "you made a splendid fight." It was enough to make a soldier awestruck, a corporal talking to the army commander, but the Westerner (a "youth of some considerable coolness," said Gibbon) added with a bright smile, "Well, General, that's the way we boys calculate to fight under a general like you." McClellan immediately stood, took the corporal's hand and said, "My man, if I can get that kind of feeling amongst the men of this army, I can whip Lee without any trouble at all." The corporal was soon telling his story, and the soldiers marveled over it—McClellan shaking the hand of an enlisted man and complimenting him on his brigade. "By such bearing as this," Gibbon wrote, "is the confidence of soldiers won."[10]

The whole matter, of course, was discussed in ranks as Gibbon's Brigade pressed forward pursuing the rebels. It was also remembered of those hard hours how the Newfoundland dog of Capt. Werner Von

Bachelle of the Sixth Wisconsin trotted with his master. The dog had come into the camps the past summer and been presented to the courtly Milwaukee immigrant. The captain had a fondness for animals and taught the dog "to perform military salutes, and other remarkable things." In camp, on the march, and in line of battle, the dog was the slight officer's "constant companion," and Dawes observed with truth that the pet was Von Bachelle's "most devoted friend on earth." With his European service, the German was widely admired; Dawes called him one of the "most highly qualified officers." But Von Bachelle, with his limited English and aloofness, had few friends, and his Old World training prevented casual associations with his countrymen in lower ranks. The quiet captain was also marked by a certain fatalism, and Edward Bragg often told the story of a conversation "under a holly bush" on South Mountain as the two "stood picket" for their sleeping soldiers. Von Bachelle, said Bragg, talked at length about his life before coming to America and his philosophy: "He fully believed he would not go [die] until his time came in regular order, and expressed as best he might that doctrine upon me."[11]

The marching column neared Boonsborough, west of South Mountain, where "old gray haired men, citizens of Maryland," gathered by the road to cheer the advancing soldiers. "They seemed almost frantic with joy," Rufus Dawes said. "They swung their hats and laughed and cried without regard for appearances." One old gentleman trotted alongside the mounted officer, telling him, "We have watched for you, Sir, and we have prayed for you and now thank God you have come." The old man jumped on a bank beside the road, shouting a welcome and thanking God at the same time, and when Dawes turned in his saddle for a final look, "the Nineteenth Indiana was responding with lusty cheers."[12]

The town seemed deserted; but as the first soldiers reached the streets, doors and windows flew open and the people thronged out to greet the Union army. "Flags that had been hidden in the darkest corner were now unfurled," Dawes said. The townsfolk had news as well— rebel infantry had passed through the town, moving in haste and some disorder, with officers carrying regimental banners; General Lee had been seen with the Confederate column. Word was also coming back that the Federal cavalry was gathering in hundreds of prisoners, stragglers and wounded left behind by the rebels. The Union columns turned left in the town, pushing on five or six miles over good roads and passing large farms before reaching Keedysville and the rear guard of Lee's forces. The Confederate lines were found spread west of town, several batteries at nearby Sharpsburg opening with case shot, the shells whizzing and bursting around the Federal columns but doing little damage. Gibbon's Brigade swung into a ravine for protection. No sooner had the soldiers halted when Union artillery came up on the gallop and wheeled into battery, opening fire with tremendous blasts. Unmindful of the guns, said Dawes, the men "rallied for the fences and building fires made their much needed coffee with little regard for the fragments of shell flying around."[13]

After a time, the major climbed the ridge overlooking the rolling countryside along Antietam Creek. The rebel line was clearly visible. First Corps Commander Joseph Hooker was there and he said to the officers around him that the enemy force was at least 40,000. McClellan and staff came up with a clatter and the general for a time studied the Confederate positions from the hill behind which the Wisconsin and Indiana soldiers rested.[14] At three o'clock, Gibbon's Brigade was ordered to move back out of the range of the rebel batteries; there it bivouacked. "Our greatly exhausted men were soon sound asleep," said Dawes.

The regiments lay still most of the next day, out of danger but close enough to get a good view of the artillery fire. The hours were spent by McClellan concentrating his army for a major push. He had 75,000 soldiers close at hand but was convinced (despite possession of the "Lost Order" showing Lee's army widely scattered) that the Confederates had 50,000 men on his front. In fact, there were only 15,000 rebels. By dusk McClellan was certain Lee's six divisions at Harper's Ferry had reached the field—bringing Lee's army to 100,000. In reality, the six divisions would reach Sharpsburg the next afternoon; even then, Lee would have fewer than 40,000 men.

At 4 P.M. September 16, 1862, the soldiers of the First Corps splashed across Antietam Creek below Keedysville, then on to the Hagerstown turnpike north of Sharpsburg. The Westerners had outmarched the supply wagons, and they filled pockets and haversacks with apples from nearby orchards, cutting down the branches to pick the fruit. While the movement was under way, Gibbon said, "McClellan made his appearance in the field and was received with great enthusiasm by the troops."

As light faded, there was artillery firing near Sharpsburg, but it sputtered away by 9 P.M., when Gibbon's soldiers finally reached the position assigned them on the extreme right. The men rested on the ground, formed in close column, muskets loaded and lines parallel to the Hagerstown turnpike. Gibbon recalled a certain uneasiness over the army's "very confused and huddled up condition, considering we were within range of the enemy's artillery." To add to the discomfort of officers and men, said Rufus Dawes, was drizzling rain "and with the certain prospect of deadly conflict on the morrow, the night was dismal. Nothing can be more solemn than a period of silent waiting for the summons to battle."[15] During the early evening there was nervous firing along the picket lines. Gibbon went to First Corps headquarters located in a barn near the turnpike where he found Hooker. While he was there, artillery erupted in the darkness and Hooker puzzled over it, telling Gibbon the enemy was firing into his own troops.[16]

Forward of headquarters, the Sixth Wisconsin men resting north of Sharpsburg were much changed from those marched from Madison a year earlier. The regiment arrived at Washington with 1,000 officers and men—now slightly more than 300 remained.[17] The winnowing had started even before the regiment's first battle as sickness, disability, promotions, desertions, transfers, and other circumstances cut the organization's number ready for duty. The Sixth had taken 500 into its first fight, suffering 17 killed, 91 wounded, and 11 missing at Brawner farm and over the next two days at Second Bull Run. Another 11 were killed, 79 wounded, and 2 missing at South Mountain. Some of the wounded and missing had returned, but the regiment was much thinned by hard service. Gone were some of the best. Old Lysander Cutler was in Washington recovering from his Gainesville wound. Farmer boy James "Mickey" Sullivan, shot in the foot, was on his way home; he would not return for six months. Reuben Huntley, one of the Yellow River boys, was dead on the skirmish line at South Mountain. "I never saw better work than old Huntley did," John Ticknor told his men with tears in his eyes.[18] So many faces were missing from the cook fires—William Clay of Delton, his arm about shot off at Gainesville; Patch Grove farmer Stephen Vesper, who wrote letters to his sister, dead at Brawner's farm; Milwaukeeans Charles Lampe and William Bickelhaupt, the first dead at Second Bull Run, the latter dying in a Washington hospital; Levi Gardner of Fountain City, dead at Second Bull Run; Rudy Fine of Hillsboro, shot dead by tragic accident in the retreat of Second Bull Run; circus boy George Chamberlain, dead at South Mountain; William Lawrence of DeSoto, dead at South Mountain.

But the "Calico boys" and the soldiers in the other regiments had proved something to themselves and the army in the weeks just concluded. At Brawner farm, for the most part alone and unsupported, they had stood up at point-blank ranges to the veterans of Jackson and fought them to a standstill. At Second Bull Run, the brigade was part of the rear guard of the defeated Army of Virginia. At South Mountain, the Westerners were singled out for bravery by Hooker, McClellan, and Sumner. In ranks of the Sixth Wisconsin, the soldiers approved of Edward Bragg and Rufus Dawes, who had fought the regiment with skill beyond their experience at South Mountain. Some company officers—Werner Von Bachelle of Milwaukee, John Ticknor and John Kellogg of Mauston, Edwin Brown of Fond du Lac, David Noyes of Baraboo, and Joseph Marston of Appleton—also proved worthy of confidence, but others were found wanting. "I call the Capt. a coward . . . ," Pvt. George Fairfield wrote home. "He will not run but he is so terrified that he can't give a command. At Bull Run . . . you would have thought he was trying to sneak up to a wild turkey. I did not see a single man in ranks but what stood right up like men. I was really ashamed of him."[19]

Also recognized was that the regular army discipline and endless drills enforced by John Gibbon and Frank Haskell had turned the regiments into an effective fighting force. "We will go in not eagerly, as ferocious stayers-at-home say, but willingly and to win . . . ," Dawes said. "A battle to veterans is an awful experience. There is not with our men the headlong recklessness of new men, who start it, acting as though they would rather be shot than not, and then lose their organization and scatter like sheep, but there is a conviction from much experience in fighting, that safety is best had by steadiness, persistence in firing, and most of all by holding together. So, with the inducement of pride, duty, patriotism and personal preservation, they will stand together until the last."[20]

The Army of the Potomac, organized by McClellan and pulled by political tides, was also changed. The "Boys of '61"—those patriotic volunteers who flocked to the Old Flag after Fort Sumter—now marched with a cooler passion. Betrayed by inept generals, ambitious officers, and influence peddlers who used the fortunes of the army for their own ends, the soldiers trusted George McClellan and worried among themselves that President Lincoln, by interference or delay, might frustrate the efforts of "Little Mac." There was also simmering anger for the stay-at-homes, the peace-at-any-price proponents, the bombastic newspapers editors, the war speculators, and the sutlers who preyed on the hapless soldier. Even the home folk did not seem to want to accept the reality—fathers, mothers, brothers and sisters, and friends not wanting to hear of the hardship of the soldier's life or of senseless killing, only of bright flags, heroics, and victory.

Those forces all pulled the men closer to the small circle of their campfires. They were keenly aware that the Army of the Potomac—despite the fighting, deaths, and hardship—had yet to prove itself to the country and that a showdown was near. In that unprecedented period when common soldiers could follow the war news in uncensored, partisan newspapers sold in their very camps, the men could see things were not going well—in fact, a pessimistic reader might find doom. In the West, despite a string of Federal victories, Confederate armies were again on the march; in the East, McClellan was a failure outside Richmond and Pope a failure in front of Washington. The war had also been brought to the homefront as lists of dead and wounded were posted and published. In faraway Wisconsin, some folks were making strident calls for peace, no matter the cost, and the Lincoln Administration faced seeming political disaster in the coming elections. In Europe, there were public claims that Northern armies would not be able to restore the peace and calls for recognition of the Confederacy. Lincoln himself seemed willing to turn the war to restore the Union into a war to end slavery.

But in ranks there was also a stiffening of resolve. "We have held our lives cheap and counted our blood of no value," Edward Kellogg of the Second Wisconsin wrote "in a weak and trembling hand" from the bed where he was dying of his festering Brawner farm wound. "We have dared and done all that the most exacting could require, but the stupidity of our leaders has squandered all this wealth of bravery and patriotism, and enthusiasm and energy, and has made all of no avail. We are not disheartened; we are willing to go on, even if it be in our own homes that we have to fall. We have been disgracefully beaten, but we are not conquered, and I humbly trust that neither Stonewall Jackson nor Robert E. Lee, nor things present, nor things to come, will be able to accomplish the feat. It seems to me that in spite of our undeniable reverses, the rebellion never before was in so fair a way to be speedily wiped out. I think the North may well feel jubilant at the prospect."[21]

One thing was certain—the pending battle might prove decisive, and the whole country was watching. The men and officers of Gibbon's Brigade would go into the fight, as Rufus Dawes of the Sixth Wisconsin said, "not eagerly . . . but willingly and to win." The next day was September 17, 1862, a Wednesday, and it would be the bloodiest day of the Civil War.

19.
The Cornfield

The shooting of pickets disturbed the long night, and morning came "misty and foggy" to the rolling countryside along Antietam Creek. In the gray light, Gen. Abner Doubleday, in command of the division because of the wounding of John Hatch at South Mountain, rode up asking for John Gibbon. "Move the troops out of there at once," Doubleday said. "You're in open range of rebel batteries." The drummers thumped the "long roll," but the men were in "heavy slumber" and it took "shaking and kicking and hurrying" to get them into formation. Off to the left flared the "sharp firing of pickets" and ahead was the thump of artillery. "Too much noise was probably made, which appears to have aroused the enemy," said Rufus Dawes. A rabbit, frightened by the clamor, came bounding along and sought a hiding place in Phil Plummer's coat, but "that poor, trembling thing" was left behind.[1]

Joseph Hooker, commanding the First Corps, arrived in a clatter of horses and staff officers as the ranks were formed. He was known throughout the army as "Fighting Joe" (a description he did not admire) and he was conspicuous with his "full regimentals of a Major General" and "large white horse." His blood was up and he called, "General Gibbon, get your brigade close column by divisions into line and follow me." Gibbon's Brigade stepped off. Behind the soldiers the six guns of Battery B of the Fourth U.S. Artillery opened with a crash, firing over the heads of the Badgers and Hoosiers. "We were hungry, ragged and dirty," a Wisconsin man said. "Before starting we pulled up our belts a notch or two. As we had very little to eat the day before and no breakfast at all, this was an easy thing to do."[2]

The thick formation had not moved 10 rods in the half-light before a Confederate battery opened fire. One shell whizzed overhead; a second passed harmlessly, then a case shot exploded with a lurid red flash and loud crack in the very center of the Sixth Wisconsin column. The blast sent bodies and equipment flying, ripping the arms off a Sauk County man and tearing Capt. David Noyes's right foot. Two men were killed outright and 11 injured. "This dreadful scene occurred within a few feet of where I was riding, and before my eyes," said Dawes. Pvt. Francis Deleglise of Appleton, ears ringing and half-blind, found himself the only soldier standing left of the gap, the explosion having swept away men on his right and behind him. His captain, Edwin Brown, was shaken but unhurt. Gibbon called it the "severest test of discipline" and worried the "shock would scatter the regiment like a flock of frightened sheep." But the voice of Lt. Col. Edward Bragg "rang out loud and clear, 'Steady, Sixth; Close up,'" and "stepping over the quivering bodies of dead and wounded comrades, the regiment moved to the front." Bragg said the "shock was momentary" and his "column wound out leaving the mangled bodies of their comrades on the ground." Moving without a halt the soldiers pressed forward until they came behind the shelter of a barn on the Joseph Poffenberger farm. Just ahead was a woodlot where the brigade halted to deploy, the Second and Sixth Wisconsin forming a line of battle followed by the Nineteenth Indiana and Seventh Wisconsin. "The artillery fire had now increased to the roar of a hundred cannon," said Dawes. "Solid shot and shell whistled through the trees above us, cutting off limbs which fell about us."[3]

The regiments were moving along a slight ridge marked by outcroppings of rock that carried the Hagerstown road south into Sharpsburg. Ahead a half mile, left of the road, was the farm of David Miller and beyond that his cornfield. South of the corn was a meadow and, farther on, a white church belonging to the German Baptist Brethren, a sect called "Dunkers" for their practice of baptism by total immersion. On each side of the road were stands of trees that would become known as the "West Woods" and the "East Woods."

From the Poffenberger farm Gibbon advanced his regiments, skirmishers forward. Rebel pickets around the Miller farm buildings with its garden and orchard opened "a vigorous fire," but the skirmishers "dashed across the field at a full run and the regimental line pushed on over the green open field, the air above our heads filled with the screaming missiles of the contending batteries." Lt. Frank Haskell came from Gibbon with orders "to advance as far as it was safe." Bragg gave Haskell a hard look and said, "Give General Gibbon my compliments, and tell him it has been damned unsafe here for the last thirty minutes." Then Bragg tugged down his hat and called, "Forward, Sixth Wisconsin!"

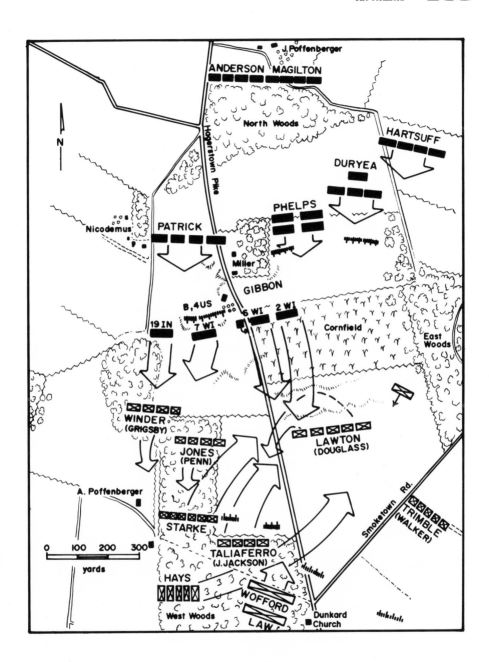

Battle map of the Iron Brigade at Antietam. Drawn by John Heiser.
Used by permission.

The regimental line reached the Miller farmyard. Cpl. Eugene Anderson of Mauston had just climbed over a fence and was standing sideways when hit. The ball struck him in the fleshy part of the leg below the right knee, glancing off the bone and lodging just under the skin. A surgeon would have to cut it out. He was left behind. The right wing of the regiment moved ahead, but the left was stopped by a fence around the family garden. Dawes called on the men to pull down the board paling, but despite frantic tugging and shoving by the soldiers, the fence held. He finally ordered the left wing to pass through a gate by the flank and "with utmost haste" reform in the garden. It was that instant Capt. Edwin Brown (that "good officer and genial gentlemen," Bragg called him) was killed. Brown, "almost worn out, and so lame that he could scarcely walk," was in a rush to clear the fence and lifted his sword and in a "loud, nervous voice" ordered "Company E, on the right by file into line!" when a projectile carried away part of his jaw, stilling forever the officer who so enjoyed the singing of the "hundred circling camps."[4] To the right, Sgt. Andrew Deacon of Fond du Lac heard the captain's "shriek" and saw Lute Murray of Shawano kneeling beside the officer. Deacon moved on, recalling later how Brown had said earlier that he would see the rebels out of Maryland, then apply for a furlough and if he could not get that, he would resign.[5] Brown went home to Fond du Lac to his wife and three children in a metallic casket, the lid soldered shut.[6]

The left wing scrambled over briars and flowerbeds in the Miller garden. Beyond the garden was a small orchard, and Dawes pushed to a rail fence skirting the front edge of the woodlot to catch the right wing. "Before us was a strip of open field, beyond which on the left-hand side of the turnpike, was rising ground covered by a large corn-field, the stalks standing thick and tall. The rebel skirmishers ran into the corn as we appeared at the fence. Owing to our headlong advance, we were far ahead of the general lines of battle." Bragg with "his usual battle ardor," ordered the regiment forward. "We climbed the fence, moved across the open space, and pushed on into the corn-field. The three right companies of the regiment were crowded into an open field on the right-hand side of the turnpike. Thus we pushed up the hill to the middle of the corn-field." Bragg said his soldiers had "a sniff of blood in their nostrils that morning, sweeping along like a storm cloud, over skirmishers and everything opposing." Behind the brigade, Gibbon brought Battery B to the Miller farm, where it "opened fire upon a foe, as yet, scarcely seen by the gunners." The advancing skirmish line in the field right of the corn was drifting away because the captain commanding, Bragg wrote with bitterness, "dodged behind a tree and grew there, letting his line go helter skelter without direction." Bragg called, "Move forward that line on the right!" But as his regiment pushed ahead his skirmishers hung back in the patchy morning mist. To the far left, musketry rattled as other Federal units advanced along the east edge of the cornfield, then, said Gibbon, a "terrific fire" flared "in the cornfield immediately to the left as well as in the woods to the right."[7]

The Sixth Wisconsin was astride the pike with German Company F in the pike and Companies G and K in the field. Farther west, the ground dropped away sharply. Seeing enemy artillery being pulled across the rise just ahead, Bragg told Capt. Werner Von Bachelle to take his company up the road to shoot the battery's horses.[8] The Germans quick-timed up the roadway only to be stopped by a blast of musketry from a heavy line of Confederate infantry that rose out of a clover field near the West Woods.[9] The volley knocked down men, splintered fences, and cut furrows on the pike. Von Bachelle, who was struck several times, fell on the roadway. Aware his wounds were fatal, he crossed his feet, drew down the visor of his cap, folded his arms, and died without a word. As the company fell back, the captain's dog, despite the urging of several privates, refused to leave his master's body and was left behind.[10]

Bragg quickly ordered the two right companies into the roadway, where the soldiers dropped down and poked the barrels of their rifle-muskets between the rails on the five-foot fence and opened fire. Dawes also halted his left wing and ordered the soldiers to lie down. "The bullets began to clip through the corn, and spin through the soft furrows—thick, almost as hail," he said. "Shells burst around us, the fragments tearing up the ground, and canister whistled through the corn above us." The destructive artillery fire (from "our own batteries," said Dawes) killed one Wisconsin officer and wounded another. "This has happened often in the war. The rebel artillery shot way over our heads." The dead officer was Lt. William Bode of Milwaukee, who was in the Hagerstown road, where his Germans were firing furiously when he was struck by a piece of case shot. In the field west of the road, Capt. John Ticknor of Company K received a painful but not serious wound from a shell fragment that knocked the breath out of him and left him spitting blood. He had previously been hit in the leg by a spent ball at Brawner's farm. His third wound would come July 1, 1863, near a railroad cut at Gettysburg, and it would kill him.[11]

In the smoke, falling stalks, and zip of bullets, Sgt. Maj. Howard Huntington of Baraboo came crashing through the corn, looking for Dawes. "Major," he yelled into Dawes's ear over the noise, "Colonel

Bragg wants to see you, quick, at the turnpike." Dawes found Bragg leaning on the fence, his face ashen. Bragg turned and said, "Major, I am shot," then the colonel's legs gave way and he fell heavily to the ground. "I saw a tear in the side of his overcoat which he had on," Dawes said. "I feared that he was shot through the body."

Bragg was hit just as the Second Wisconsin came up on the Sixth's left and the Confederates began to give way. "I thought my elbow fractured, as I had not then discovered the ball hole in the breast of my coat," Bragg said. "But the men discovered the hole in the side pocket, and saw the red lining & were sure I was shot through the body. To make sure I was not dead, I gave an order to withdraw the line on the right under cover of a fence, and there I must confess things began to look pretty dark. . . ."[12] Fearing Bragg was severely wounded, Dawes motioned to two soldiers to assist him. "Take a tent and carry him to the rear at once." The pair bundled the injured officer into a shelter half and carried him back through the corn out of danger. "Colonel Bragg was shot in the first fire from the woods and his nerve, in standing up under the shock until he had effected the maneuver so necessary for the safety of his men, was wonderful. I felt a great sense of responsibility, when thrown thus suddenly in command of the regiment in the face of a terrible battle," Dawes said.[13]

At the north end of the cornfield, Bragg found that only his left arm was numb and paralyzed and that he could walk. A few rods more and he came on John Gibbon, who asked, "Old man, are you hurt? You are very white." Bragg said he had been wounded and warned the general the enemy was "flanking the brigade." Gibbon dismounted and gave Bragg a pull from a flask (in a pious letter to his wife Bragg said the whiskey was "the first I have tasted since I have been in the service"). The spirits revived him and Bragg made his way to the rear.[14]

In the cornfield, the battle flaring up around him, Dawes stood at the fence alongside the Hagerstown road overlooking the companies in the turnpike while keeping an eye on the left wing amid the stalks. To slow the Confederate fire, Gibbon ordered the right two-gun section of Battery B forward to a position in front of two straw stacks southwest of the Miller buildings and deployed the Seventh Wisconsin and Nineteenth Indiana west of the road. Division commander Abner Doubleday, seeing the movement, ordered the New York brigade of Marsena Patrick to support the advance. In the corn, Dawes "noticed a group of rebel officers, whom I took to be a general and staff" near the West Woods. Getting rifle-muskets from the soldiers around him and taking rest on the turnpike fence, he fired six shots, reporting with satisfaction "they suddenly scattered." To the left, the thick, main Federal line came sweeping up through the corn and, at the order of Lt. Col. Thomas Allen of the Second Wisconsin, Dawes joined the general advance, calling, "Forward-guide left-march!" The soldiers of the Sixth Wisconsin were again up and pushing through the tall stalks. The movement divided his regiment, and Dawes, before running to catch his left, sent Huntington to Capt. John Kellogg with the order: "If it is practicable, move forward the right companies, aligning with the left wing." Huntington was soon back. Kellogg had said, "Please give Major Dawes my compliments, and say it is impracticable; the fire is murderous." As the left wing moved away, Dawes sent orders to Kellogg to get cover in the corn and to rejoin the regiment if possible. Huntington was struck by a bullet but carried the message to Kellogg, who ordered his men up only to have so many shot that he ordered them down again at once.[15]

With the brigade's wagons near the North Woods, Pvt. George Fink watched the fighting. "Shells were bursting in the air and falling like hail," he said. "The union line, which I afterwards discovered to be my own brigade was marching toward . . . the rebel line, and the men looked as if they were ten feet tall on account of the tall hats they wore, quite in contrast with the low, tight fitting caps of the volunteers and of the rebels. The rebels were in a cornfield and in the woods and at their rear about 250 feet was a fence. As the union men advanced up the slope, man after man would make a convulsive grab at some spot on his body, or perhaps merely drop his musket, then fall himself. It was a frightful thing to witness, for I was not near enough to tell whether or not those who fell were my best friends. Finally as the union men advanced, the rebels lay down and then a volley tore into the union men and was returned with more vehemence than that with which it was sent. The rebels jumped up and began running back. Some tried to get over the fence and could not and hung there until taken prisoners. The union men were firing at will and standing their ground."[16]

Except for the men in the turnpike, the Sixth Wisconsin was pushing through the corn on the right of a Federal line which was followed by a second. The men of the Second Wisconsin, to their left, had yet to receive or fire a shot. At the corn's edge was "a low Virginia rail fence" and a field running to the white church. "As we appeared at the edge of the corn, a long line of men in butternut and gray rose up from the ground," said Dawes. "Simultaneously, the hostile battle lines opened a tremendous fire upon each other. Men, I can not say fell; they were knocked out of the ranks by dozens. But we jumped over the fence, and pushed on, loading, firing, and shouting as we advanced. There was, on the part of the men, great hysterical excitement, eagerness to go forward, and a reckless disregard of life, of every thing but victory. Captain Kellogg brought his companies up abreast of us on the turnpike."[17]

The Fond du Lac and Outagamie County boys were falling at a frightful rate. As the line moved into the open field, Pvt. Nick Gaffney was shot and his tentmate, Francis Deleglise, stopped to help. Deleglise was still shaken by his own narrow escape from the shell which ripped his company and, convinced Gaffney was dying, drew a knapsack under his comrade's head before running ahead to find only four Company E men still in line under command of Cpl. George Eggleston. Deleglise bit the paper tail off a cartridge and was ramming the ball when the man next to him, while aiming, was shot in the head, splattering Deleglise with blood as the bullet passed into the soldier's left eye and out the right ear. Deleglise put down his own rifle-musket and pulled the soldier's knapsack under the blood-soaked head. Then, taking the loaded Springfield of the downed man, Deleglise fired the same instant a rebel bullet grazed his right cheek, breaking a tooth. Stunned and hurting, he turned back to the corn only to be hit in the left thigh, the bullet spinning him around and knocking him down.[18]

A Wisconsin officer called the slaughter "enormous." Pvt. Walker Barcus of Harmony was wounded and, finding he could not run, exclaimed, "Here is where you get your stiff legs!" Pvt. Reuben Sherman of Chippewa Falls shot at a rebel flag and saw it fall. He was boasting to men in the files around him that he had "fetched it" only to discover his own arm was paralyzed by a wound. Francis Deleglise hobbled back to the corn dragging his wounded leg, then dropped behind the fence to finish loading. He aimed at a color bearer in "a solid line of rebels 60 feet away," but a ball thumped off the upper right side of his forehead before he could pull the trigger. The thrice-wounded Deleglise ("not feeling equal, under the circumstances, to the emergency of a struggle with a solid line of advancing foes," he said later) dropped his musket, pulled off his cartridge box and belts, and limped back through the corn as best he could.[19]

The air was filled with a "hail-storm of bullets," said one Wisconsin officer. "Gainesville, Bull Run, South Mountain were good respectable battles, but in the intensity and energy of the fight and the roar of firearms, they were but skirmishes in comparison to this of Sharpsburg."[20] The Federal line was a surging crowd, the soldiers biting cartridges, ramming and firing over and over again. "Whoever stood in front of the corn field at Antietam needs no praise," Dawes would write 25 years later.

As the line pushed out of the corn, Rollin Converse of Prescott advanced his company. One of his privates was struck and called, "Captain, captain, I am killed! I am killed!" Converse told the man, "Go to the rear then." Converse had not moved a dozen more steps when he was shot through both thighs. Convulsively throwing his sword into the soft ground, he called to Charles Hyatt of Prescott, "Damn it, Hyatt, I'm hit. I can't run after them. Take command." Two privates of Company K, William Harrison of Lindina and Charles Abbot of Summit ("farmer boys of correct habits and upright characters and good education"), were shot and killed side by side. Pvt. David Cummings of Sparta went down, killed. Nearby were Franklin Gerlaugh and William Black. The Fredonia boys, both 19 and best friends, enlisted on the same day, shared a common birthday, and would be buried in the same grave. Gerlaugh was shot through the head, Black an instant later in the throat.[21]

The Johnnies slowly gave way under the heavy fire, but another thick line with red flags emerged from the West Woods. "Our whole line was driving slowly forward 20 yards in front of the corn" when the fresh Confederates pushed up, said Dawes. "Their volleys are murderous." In the swirls of smoke and the confusion, Thomas Allen of the Second Wisconsin ordered a change of front, wheeling his regiment right. He halted and ordered his men to pile fence rails for a barricade. The Sixth Wisconsin came in on his right and farther on other Federals extended the makeshift line. The supporting Union regiments had halted, but at the critical moment the second line advanced with a shout.[22] "The Fourteenth Brooklyn Regiment, red-legged Zouaves, came into our line, closing the awful gaps," said Dawes. "Now is the pinch. Men and officers of New York and Wisconsin are fused into a common mass, in the frantic struggle to shoot fast. Every body tears cartridge, loads, passes guns, or shoots. Men are falling in their places or running back into the corn. The soldier who is shooting is furious in his energy. The soldier who is shot looks around for help with an imploring agony of death on his face. After a few rods of advance, the line stopped and by common impulse, fell back to the edge of the corn and lay down on the ground behind the low rail fence."[23]

One of the last to leave the advance line was the Sixth Wisconsin's Bob Tomlinson. In his first days as a soldier, the young man from the Mississippi River country used to "swell and boast" about his prowess, but now he proved as good as he talked. "God, you ain't going back, are you?" Tomlinson asked, "disappointment in every feature," as an officer tugged at his sleeve. "Not yet," he said, "I have a few more cartridges left." Standing in the open field, Tomlinson deliberately fired his last rounds ("a target for hundreds to turn their guns on," one officer said) before he slowly walked back to the cornfield.[24]

Despite the shooting ("steady infantry work," one said) the yelling Confederates drove to the roadway fences to exchange point-blank shots with Wisconsin men crowded in the southwest corner of the cornfield. Thomas Allen of the Second Wisconsin was wounded, and one of his soldiers, Pvt. Horace Emerson of Portage, stared in horror as the man in front of him was struck in the face and the "blood and brains run out on my shoes." William Harries of La Crosse was shot in the left breast. He dropped his musket and started for the rear. Alexander Hill of Portage was struck by a bullet that drove into his groin a ring of keys carried in his pocket.[25]

In front of the Sixth Wisconsin along the Hagerstown road, here and there, Johnnies tried climbing the high fences and the fighting was "fast, furious and deadly." More New Yorkers from the supporting brigade of Walter Phelps, Jr., came into the Union line. The added musketry halted the rebels, but squads of Confederates clung grimly to the road and its fences. For 15 minutes the fighting raged, the two-gun right section of Battery B firing along the fence line and into the field west of the turnpike. Off to the right, out of sight, came "three cheers and a rattling fusillade" (the advancing Nineteenth Indiana and Seventh Wisconsin), and soon the whole Confederate line was running in disorder. "Bully! Bully!" a Badger soldier in the corn shouted. "Up and at them again. Our men are giving them hell on the flank." The musketry had been under way 30 minutes.[26]

The frantic attempt to capture the ground near the white church was not over. "Another line of our men came through the corn. We all join together, jumped over the fence, and again pushed out into the open field," said Dawes. "There is a rattling fusillade and loud cheers. 'Forward' is the word. The men are loading and firing with demonical fury and shouting and laughing hysterically and the whole field before us is covered with rebels fleeing for life, into the woods. Great numbers of them are shot while climbing over the high post and rail fences along the turnpike. We push on over the open fields half way to the little church. The powder is bad, and the guns have become very dirty. It takes hard pounding to get the bullets down, and our firing is becoming slow."[27]

But the Badgers and New Yorkers would not reach the small church. Pressed close to his soldiers, Dawes looked ahead and saw a "long and steady line of rebel gray" emerge from woods around the church. It was the division of John Hood and contained his famous Texas Brigade. The regiments had been called from their cook fires in a last-ditch attempt to stem the Federal advance and it was about 7 A.M. when Hood's 2,300 men crossed to the pasture south of the cornfield for a charge that would become fabled in the annals of the Army of Northern Virginia. The Confederates gave a loud yell and halted to allow the shattered first line to pass through, then fired a ripping volley. The bullets were "like a scythe running through our line," Dawes said. "The auspicious moment has passed. The great victory has passed away from our grasp. Five minutes sooner and our reinforcements would have broken the enemy into the ravine." The Wisconsin and New York soldiers now ran back into the corn. "The Sixth and its support were too weak in numbers to withstand this force," Bragg said, "and were pushed back, fighting as they went. It is not to be presumed they had a dress parade alignment after the blows they had given and received that morning, but every man of the Sixth acted as if *he thought he was the Sixth Wis., and had its honor in his keeping.*"[28]

It was "a race for life," said Dawes, and it was "now save, who can." The whole Federal line was in retreat—companies and regiments tangled and disorganized, cartridge boxes empty, and rifle-muskets fouled and hard to load. A bullet stung the calf of Dawes's leg but did not disable him. "Back to the corn, and back through the corn, the headlong flight continues," he said. The Johnnies, firing from the rear and fences along the turnpike, had the retreating Wisconsin and New York men in a vicious crossfire. Amid the swirls of smoke in the corn, the Wisconsin men fought singly and in twos and threes and in squads, making a stand here and there with a flurry of shooting, then retreating. Along the fences of the Hagerstown pike, the soldiers blazed at each other at murderous ranges of a few feet, bullets splintering rails and slapping through the stalks as Battery B's six Napoleons slammed heavy blasts of canister into the corn and at Confederates on the field between the woods and the pike.

When Dawes reached the slight decline north of the cornfield, he took the blue state flag of his Sixth Wisconsin and began to rally his broken regiment; several dozen men soon gathering around him. Every soldier able to hold a musket would be needed. The broken and disorganized regiments were coming out of the cornfield in groups of twos and threes. Just behind them, pursuing Confederates were surging forward with a yell toward Battery B and it appeared the six bronze Napoleons might be lost.[29]

20.
Give 'Em Hell!

The regulars and volunteers serving Battery B of the Fourth U.S. Artillery had been doing good work from first light. No sooner had the Second and Sixth Wisconsin reached the south edge of the cornfield than John Gibbon moved the guns ahead. The right two-gun section under Lt. James Stewart was the first to reach the advanced position west of the Hagerstown road in an open field forward of two stacks of straw. The two guns came up on the run, swinging around with much shouting and excitement, the wheels and horses throwing up clods of wet dirt. The artillerymen dropped the trails of the pieces with the practiced smoothness of regulars and prepared to open fire on "large bodies of the enemy, some 400 to 500 yards distant." From the rear came headquarters clerk Benjamin Meeds of the Sixth Wisconsin, who jumped in as a volunteer gunner. Along the fences of the turnpike and in the cornfield there was a terrible crashing of musketry. Ahead, groups of Confederates could be seen crossing the field toward the flank of the advancing Union infantry. The ground was undulating and Stewart called for spherical case shot with the fuses crimped to burst one and one-half seconds after leaving the muzzles. The two 12-pound smoothbores opened with loud cracks and within a minute the enemy give way in disorder.[1]

Ahead the infantry fighting was furious. Long rips of musketry were added to the booming of the cannon and the gunners began to hear the zip-zip of bullets. Accompanying Stewart was the battery's 15-year-old bugler, Johnny Cook of Cincinnati, Ohio. "No sooner had we unlimbered when a column of Confederate infantry, emerging from the so-called west woods, poured a volley into us, which brought fourteen or seventeen of my brave comrades to the ground," he said. "It was a sickening sight to see those poor, maimed, and crippled fellows crowding on top of one another [behind the straw stacks], while several stepping a few feet away, were hit again and killed." Stewart's horse was felled by bullets, spilling him to the ground. Unhurt, he ran to the limbers to gather a makeshift force of horseholders and drivers to take the places of downed gunners. At the same instant, the four Napoleons under Capt. Joseph Campbell rolled into position on his left. The six guns were soon in a line—three at the top of a gentle slope, two slightly advanced, the far left gun in the turnpike slightly behind the others. The ammunition limbers with horses and drivers were crowded into the narrow space bounded by the guns, the Hagerstown road fence on the left and the barnyard fence at the rear.[2]

Ahead in the drifts of smoke could be heard a "terrific fire," but Gibbon was unable to immediately determine the progress of his brigade. Wounded men were coming back out of the cornfield in twos and threes, and one of them was Lt. Col. Edward Bragg of the Sixth Wisconsin, who warned the brigade was flanked. The cornfield was now a hellish swirl of smoke and shouting soldiers, the air full of bullets and exploding shells.[3]

Thirty minutes into the advance Gibbon sensed the fighting was rolling back through the corn toward his bronze guns; gunners and horses were going down at an alarming rate and his brigade apparently was broken and in disorder. The rebels were pressing the retreating Federals from behind and with a murderous crossfire from the turnpike fences. Finally, out of the bloody shambles of the bullet-ripped field ("torn and broken and with thinned ranks," Gibbon said) came the survivors of the Sixth and Second Wisconsin and the New Yorkers of Phelp's Brigade.[4]

As the infantrymen fell back, the 12-pounder in the roadway blasted canister at Confederates working along the turnpike fences; the rebels were firing point-blank into the gun crews and horses. "It seems almost incredible that any man could have escaped in a battery working in an open field with veteran infantry under dense cover sharpshooting at it within 28 or 30 paces," one gunner said. The artillerymen switched to canister, then double canister. Capt. Joseph Campbell was shot. "He had just dismounted when he was hit twice, and his horse fell dead with several bullets in its body," said bugler John Cook. "I started with the captain to the rear and turned him over to one of the drivers. He ordered me to report to Lieutenant Stewart and tell him to take command of the battery." The steady firing of the six guns faltered and Gibbon feared his old battery might be lost.

Cook came upon a dead artilleryman who had been carrying ammunition. "I unstrapped the pouch, started for the battery, and worked as a cannoneer," said the young soldier. He would receive a Medal of Honor for his service of the next few minutes.[5] Nearby, Stewart frantically organized his crews to keep up the rate of fire. He came upon one infantry volunteer grimly jamming two complete canister charges in the gun he was serving. The lieutenant stepped in to show the man how to knock off the powder container of the second round against the hub of the wheel. The volunteer did as told but in the excitement mashed his finger under the heavy tin canister. After that, said Stewart, every second round went into the muzzle just as it came from the arsenal—powder and all.[6]

One of the gunners, Henry Klinefelter of Cottage Grove, a Seventh Wisconsin soldier serving as an artillery volunteer,[7] noticed the two right guns had stopped firing and looked over to discover that "all the men were shot down." Two or three of the injured artillerymen "crawled on their hands and knees several times from the limber to the pieces and loaded and fired those guns in that way until they had recoiled so far that they could not use them any more. Not until then were they entirely silenced." Another Seventh Wisconsin man transferred to the battery less than a week earlier was Horace Ripley of Bristol. Left with the limbers, Ripley helped a wounded sergeant to the rear and upon returning was given two horses to hold. One horse was soon hit in the flank and fell dying with Ripley trying to step free of the thrashing animal. "In a moment," he said, the other horse "had his bits completely shot out of his mouth, carrying away his whole under jaw." One of the regular artillerymen came out of the smoke up to the bloody animal, pulled a revolver, and "blew his brains out to put him out of his misery." The young Badger was brought forward to carry ammunition to one of the embattled Napoleons; enemy bullets soon left him and another man the only gunners serving the piece.[8]

It seemed the attack would carry all before it as the yelling Confederates drove forward into the blasts of double canister and musketry. In all of its service, from the Mexican War through Gainesville, Second Bull Run, and South Mountain, never had the six guns been under such attack. Pvt. John Johnson of Janesville, one of the Second Wisconsin men, was working a handspike with Sgt. Joseph Herzog to shift the gun to a new position when Herzog was shot through the lower bowels. Slumped against the trail of the piece in great agony, the tough regular pulled his belt revolver and shot himself through the right temple as Johnson watched in horror. Johnson said his gun fired 10 to 15 rounds of canister in what he said was "as fierce and murderous a combat as ever surged about a six-gun battery."

Back with the guns, men and horses were "falling thick and fast in the confined space," said Gibbon. Working the lone Napoleon on the turnpike, one of just four artillerymen still on their feet was Henry Klinefelter of the Seventh. The piece was on an incline and every time the gun fired, it rolled backwards. Gibbon was nearby. "In the hurry and excitement of the battle . . . the elevating screw was permitted to run down (as it will do in firing) until . . . the muzzle was sticking up in the air in such a way as to throw the projectiles entirely over the heads of the closely approaching enemy. . . . I called to the gunner to 'run up the elevating screw,' but in the turmoil he could not hear what I said."[9]

What happened next became "one of the cherished traditions of the battery." His artillerymen watching in astonishment, John Gibbon dismounted and shouldered Klinefelter and others aside. Straddling the trail of the gun, he ran up the elevating screw so the canister blast would glance off the ground into the Confederates. The general jumped away and nodded to pull the lanyard, saying, "Give them hell boys!" As the heavy gun bucked, he ducked under the smoke to see the discharge carry "away most of the fence in front of it." It produced "great destruction in the enemy's ranks as did the subsequent discharges, and at one of these, a sergeant of the battery (Mitchell) [Sgt. John Mitchell] was badly hurt by the gun running over him in its recoil. The enemy got so close to the battery in his desperate attempts to capture it, that the pieces were double-shotted with canister before which whole ranks went down, and after we got possession of the field, dead men were found piled on top of each other."[10]

How the rebels missed Gibbon was later a topic of campfire discussion. "His escape," one said, "was miraculous, as he wore the full uniform of a Brigadier-General, and the enemy was so close they could not help discerning his rank, unless the smoke obscured him." Bugler John Cook observed that Gibbon "was very conspicuous, and it is indeed surprising, that he came away alive."[11]

With the soldiers stumbling out of the smoke-shrouded cornfield was a Sixth Wisconsin man carrying his regiment's blue state flag and a rebel banner he found on the ground in the cornfield. Not sure what to do, he approached Gibbon, but the general (his hands full at the moment trying to save his guns) had no time for trophies. "Throw down the flag and take your place in ranks!" Gibbon said sharply. The young soldier, not one to disobey an order—especially from an excited of-

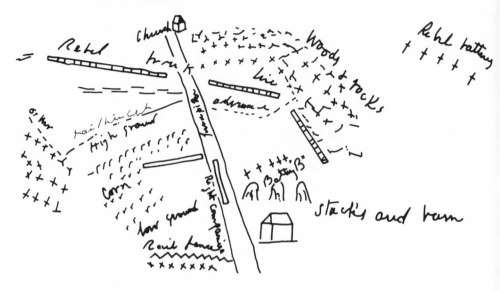

Sketch map of Antietam by Rufus Dawes from his Journal.

ficer—did as told. A few seconds later, Gibbon, "grimed and black with powder smoke in himself sighting these guns of his old battery," came upon Maj. Rufus Dawes at the edge of the cornfield rallying his broken regiment. "Hurrah for the Sixth! Three cheers men, for the Sixth!" Gibbon shouted. "Major, bring your men over and save that gun," he said pointing to the cannon on the roadway. Dawes had the state flag and, waving it over his head, ran to the artillery piece, calling, "Let every man from Wisconsin follow me!" (Later he wrote: "It did not seem possible then to carry that flag into the deadly storm and live.") But within seconds, "every 'black hat' within sight of the blue emblem of the Badger state gathered around it." Also coming up were men from the 20th New York State Militia—sent to support Battery B.

The Wisconsin survivors and some New Yorkers (Dawes said "about 200"; Gibbon recalled "a dozen or two men only") pushed forward and opened fire. The Wisconsin flag was planted near the lone gun in the pike and the soldiers rallied around it, frantically loading and shooting. It seemed everything was about to "go to pieces," said Gibbon, but "nothing could withstand the fire of those double-shotted Napoleons." Bugler Cook said the rebels "made three desperate attempts to capture us, the last time coming within ten or fifteen feet of our guns."

One Second Wisconsin man jumped in to assist the gunners. "Through that short and terrible ordeal, of less than ten minutes, in which Gibbon and those two guns literally filled the air with fence rails, haversacks, guns and limbs of rebel soldiers," the Badger volunteer "worked as if artillery was his forte." Nearby, Dawes was "fairly stunned" by "a report as of a thunderclap. The cannon was double charged with canister. The rails of the fence flew high into the air." At that instant, a line of blue infantry came sweeping from the right across the field in front of the battery, rolling the rebels into the cornfield.[12] It was the Nineteenth Indiana ("our gallant Nineteenth Indiana," Dawes said) and on its left was the Seventh Wisconsin, supported by three New York regiments. They came up with a steady step, fired into the flank of the Confederate attack and halted under a hot exchange of musketry with rebels in the roadway and in the corn. Then the Union regiments rolled forward with loud yells.

The Westerners had been halted in the West Woods when skirmishers of the Nineteenth Indiana saw Confederates closing in on Battery B. They sent word to Lt. Col. Alois Bachman, who was unable to see the rebels because his regiment was on low ground. Bachman took in the situation at once, called in his skirmishers and sent runners to the Seventh Wisconsin and the New York regiments that he was changing front for an attack. The Nineteenth Indiana—the Seventh Wisconsin on the left—moved to a rocky ledge and opened fire on the Confederates. Some Johnnies fled in disorder, but the others grimly stood ground. "Charge! Charge!" the Indianans began shouting. Bachman, the son of Swiss immigrants who had settled near Madison, Indiana, had been with them from the first. He pushed through his line and looked to right and left, then called out, "Boys, the command is no longer forward, but now it is follow me." Then, hat in hand and sword drawn, he led his yelling Hoosiers forward. The Seventh Wisconsin also cleared the ledge followed by the Twenty-first and Thirty-fourth New York supported by the Twenty-third New York. The cheering Federals sent rebels in the cornfield and along the turnpike running. One regiment—the Fourth Texas—in danger of being cut off, tried to move by the left flank, then halted and fired into the Seventh Wisconsin. The crash of musketry knocked back the Badgers and the Texans escaped.

To the right of the Wisconsin men, the Hoosiers drove forward alone, crossing the road into the cornfield, then wheeling right to follow fleeing Confederates to the brow of the ridge. There another line of infantry was waiting amid some abandoned artillery and it fired a murderous volley. One ball caught Bachman on his right elbow, turning him partially around, then a second shot went through his body, killing him instantly. The command fell to the youngest captain in the line—19-year-old William Dudley, who just months before had been quietly milling grain at Richmond, Indiana. It was a tough spot for any officer. As soon as Bachman's body could be carried to the rear, Dudley had the regiment fall back to the road, where it rallied. Three times the Nineteenth's flag fell and was lifted. On the left were Patrick's regiments and the Seventh Wisconsin, all the small Union organizations in disorder and rebels seemingly everywhere.

One Indiana soldier said later that it was "a gallant, but ill-advised charge," but the furious rush saved the six Napoleons. The quick and timely advance, said a Wisconsin officer, was made "regardless of consequences to themselves, but to protect Battery B, and save their Brigade brothers so hard pressed in the cornfield. It was bold, and was as bravely met, as the line of dead along that pike on that front testified more forcibly than word may do."[13]

No sooner had the Nineteenth and other regiments reformed alongside the turnpike when they were again fired on by Confederates pushing out of the West Woods. The Indianans gave way, but rallied, changed front, and again opened fire. The attack faded and Dudley withdrew his regiment to the rocky ledge, where it was joined by Patrick's New Yorkers and the Seventh Wisconsin. After a time, the cartridge boxes of the Nineteenth and Seventh empty, the two regiments fell back, leaving the New Yorkers. Patrick's men soon also withdrew to a meadow near the Miller barn to await ammunition and orders.[14]

No sooner had the Confederate assault been turned when Gibbon ordered his six guns to safety. The general never forgot those long minutes: "Double charges of canister belched forth in rapid succession from the mouths of the 12-pounders literally piled the dead on top of each other. The attack was beaten off, the bullets gradually ceased to come, and during the lull the battery was rapidly limbered to the rear and quickly withdrawn from its dangerous position, leaving the corner of the field thickly strewn with its dead men and horses, while the thinner ranks of the brigade followed after it."[15]

Also remembered of those hectic minutes were the actions of an unnamed Second Wisconsin private helping Battery B. "When the guns started to change position" the volunteer "hopped on a caisson with one of the regulars and had gone only a few rods when the thing turned over and came near breaking their necks. They got the thing righted and made another start when the caisson blew up; the full force of the charge went out of the end on which sat the regular, and blew him into shreds, while our man was only 'stood on his ear' in the apple tree tops (we had that morning cut off and piled in heaps,) from which he crawled, coolly remarking, 'For the first day in a battery I've been used rather rough.' He was a member of the battery about twenty minutes and was full convinced that 'that battery was inclined to take too many risks.'"[16]

It had been very close, Gibbon said later. "Had we succeeded even in getting the pieces out through the double gate-ways of the barn yard," he said, "there beyond was that long straight stretch of turnpike, perfectly under the command of the enemy the moment his riflemen reached the top of this little ridge up which the guns stood. A single horse killed or badly wounded in that narrow 'gorge,' and Battery B would be numbered among the trophies of Lee's Army." Edward Bragg said his Sixth Wisconsin men rallied to save the battery "as readily and cheerfully as for a companion in arms." The "guns had voices . . . and the voice of B had always been to them the forerunner of victory, and they loved the guns as if they were part of themselves." One gunner said it was the hardest service of the war. "The recruits of 1863, even with Gettysburg on their records, always took off their caps to the old Antietam boys whenever there was a campfire debate about prowess, and cordially yielded the palm to the Iron veterans who had braved the butchery of that fatal Cornfield on the Sharpsburg Pike."[17]

But all that was yet to be written as Dawes gathered his survivors on the turnpike. Gen. Abner Doubleday was nearby, and when the young major reported for orders he was told to remain in position. A few minutes later Gibbon came up and told Dawes to take his men back to the North Woods and await orders and ammunition. "Bullets, shot and shell, fired by the enemy in the corn-field, were still flying thickly around us, striking the trees in the woods and cutting off the limbs." He marched his regiment back into the trees and halted it in the best shelter he could find. There came the grim task of calling the roll and determining what he called the regiment's "dreadful losses." The Sixth had taken 315 officers and men into the battle and 152 had been killed or wounded. Two had been lost by Company C on skirmish duty on the right. Of the 280 men at the cornfield and turnpike, 150 were dead or down. Answering the roll in Company A were Lt. Howard Pruyn of Baraboo and Pvts. William Saare of Westfield, Gus Klein of Sauk, S. W. Keyes of West Point, and William Pearson and Lysander Vanleuven of Kingston. The Sauk County Riflemen had gone into the fight with 26 officers and men and now there was only "one stack of muskets left." It was like that through all the companies. "This was the most dreadful slaughter to which our regiment had been subjected during the war," Dawes said. As the Wisconsin men waited, they were joined by Capt. George Ely of Janesville, himself wounded, who brought 18 men of the Second Wisconsin and its colors. "They represented what remained for duty of that gallant regiment," said Dawes.

Within a few minutes, out of the battlefield came the powder-stained survivors of the Seventh Wisconsin and Nineteenth Indiana. They were also put into line. "The roar of musketry to the front was very heavy," said Dawes and, as he watched and waited, Braetan Morris of Cassville came up with the sword of a rebel officer he had captured. He gave it to Dawes as a trophy.[18]

The musketry marked a fresh Union assault into the cornfield. After a few minutes, into the woods where Gibbon's men waited came fleeing soldiers and wounded. "It soon became apparent from the tremendous number of stragglers and of missiles that crashed towards us," said Dawes, that the Federals were repulsed. Gibbon rode up. He had been to the front placing artillery when the assault collapsed before "a terrific fire of musketry . . . filling the whole open space between the East and the West woods with a disorganized mass of panic-stricken men." At the North Woods Gibbon found "a wild state of confusion and turmoil, many . . . men retreating from the firing coming out by their right flank up the Hagerstown pike and on both sides of it." But the survivors of his brigade, he found, were in a line. "You must hold this woods, men," the general called, and to impress the soldiers "with the importance of steadiness," Gibbon drew his sword ("a thing I never had done before in battle") to find the hilt guard damaged by a bullet. To the south, the "roar of musketry to the front about the corn-field and the Dunkard church had again become heavy."

Dawes had the brigade in a line—perhaps 500 soldiers in all—to drive back "at the point of the bayonet all men who were fit for duty at the front." It was Second Bull Run all over again. "Presently great regiments with boxes half full of cartridges came hurrying to the rear," said Dawes. With the retreating soldiers was Gen. Willis Gorman, the officer who had refused to relieve the Sixth Wisconsin at South Mountain because "all men are cowards in the dark." The officer was shaken by his turn in the cornfield and his appearance triggered some catcalls. "Make way," Gorman called to a Wisconsin man, "and let my regiment pass." But the private drew himself up and said, "I was put here, sir, to stop stragglers, and can't disobey orders." The red-faced general persisted, but the private refused to back down. "The regiment went around our line," Dawes said.

Ahead of the reserve position, Capt. John Kellogg rallied stragglers behind a stone wall near the Poffenberger house. Gen. Abner Double–day, puzzled by the line of men, came over, asking, "What regiment is this?" "A regiment of stragglers." "What regiment do you belong to?" "The Sixth Wisconsin, sir." "Are these Wisconsin men?" "No sir, Wisconsin men never run," Kellogg answered. Dawes called Kellogg's rally of stragglers "one of the most creditable affairs of the battle."

After a time the fighting faded and Federal troops came back through the woods and along the turnpike to a new line being put together behind the Black Hat Brigade. It was only "with great difficulty," said Gibbon, "a number of regiments were halted and re-formed." That accomplished, said Dawes, "Gen. Patrick moved us to the rear of a heavy line of batteries just where we slept the night before. Our active part in the battle was over."[19]

It was about noon when the Sixth reached the position, and the officers and men were "greatly astonished" to find Lt. Col. Edward Bragg with one arm looped up in a handkerchief sling. "Three hearty cheers were given with a will for we all had thought him killed," said Dawes. "He was severely wounded and unfit for duty, but he was there, and we had believed him to be dead." Bragg, of course, had a story to tell. He had made his way to a field hospital where he found the Sixth Wisconsin's surgeon, Dr. Oscar Bartlett. The two were good friends and given to bantering. "So you have come to see me," said Bartlett. "Have been expecting all the morning to be called to amputate your head. What is the matter, colonel?" "I don't know. If I did I wouldn't come here. I want to find out." "Where were you hit?" "In the arm. Can't you see?" "Is it broken?" "You are paid to tell me whether it is broken or not." The doctor ran his hands along the injured arm. "Bragg," he said finally, "if any other man in this army had been hit as you were he would have had a broken arm, but your arm isn't broken." "Thank you. Tie this handkerchief around my neck and hitch it to my hurt arm, doctor." "What are you going to do?" "I am going back to the regiment." "Better let me dress your wound first," the doctor said. "Never mind the wound; you can dress that to-morrow," said the little colonel, and then, after getting his arm hitched up, Bragg went to find his regiment.

Along the way he came upon a wounded soldier from his old company, Nick Gaffney, who had been shot in the cornfield advancing beside his tentmate, Frank Deleglise. "Hello Nick," said Bragg. "What's the matter?" "I am shot, colonel; I'm going to die." "No Gaffney, you are not going to die. Let me see your wound." The "pale, weak boy" pointed to a spot on his breast. "You're all right, chicken," said Bragg, putting his hand over the wound. "Take a long breath." It hurt Gaffney "like the cut of a knife" and the colonel's hand came away covered with blood. The shot had struck the soldier in the breast and gone clean through. Later, Bragg admitted that "I told the poor fellow he was all right, but I didn't believe it. I didn't see, then, how a fellow shot through the lung could survive." Gaffney went to a field hospital where a surgeon drew a silk handkerchief through his body. "It makes you shudder, doesn't it," said a comrade. "It made poor Nick Gaffney wince, but he uttered no sound." The wounded soldier recovered and was soon on his way home for good.[20]

Bragg never forgot the appearance of his broken regiment as it came up in the woods. "What grim-looking fellows they were which came back! Powder-stained, tired and hungry, but proud of what they had done, and ready to do it over again, so far as their numbers could permit." Out of the bloody cornfield, another Sixth man said, "came companies commanded by sergeants and with less than a dozen men of the hundred they had gone to war with."[21] The Wisconsin boys had been marching and fighting three days with empty haversacks; other regiments were in the same fix. "There were no rations left to supply the yearning, empty stomachs for food," Bragg said. He went back and found a sutler with two barrels of molasses cookies. The cookies were distributed and with "that they were content."

John "Tough One" Cook of Hartford, Washington County, got in the last word, not only for his Sixth Wisconsin but for all of Gibbon's Brigade concerning the events near Sharpsburg. He fought as a detached volunteer with Battery B, was wounded, and two decades later summed up September 17, 1862, with one brief sentence—"There was fun there."[22]

21.
Too Horrible to Behold

As the soldiers of Gibbon's Brigade waited in the North Woods, the fighting drifted to the south. It was in the early afternoon when a lone soldier came from the rear, asking after the colonel of the Sixth Wisconsin; George Fink had finally caught up to the regiment. Directed to Edward Bragg, Fink saluted and explained to the colonel that he had 80 descriptive lists to turn over with a squad of recruits. "He asked me if I couldn't wait until after the battle, as if he were to be killed the lists would do him no good," Fink said. "I explained I wanted to get into that battle as well as he did. . . . I do not like to tell just how profane the language used to me at the time, as I was used to it then." The boys gathered around the new arrival, firing questions about "families, friends and sweethearts back in Milwaukee." But orders passed along the line for the men to lie down. "The rebels were shelling us, but it did not last for a long time, and that was the last of the battle," said Fink.

Rufus Dawes said it was 4 P.M. (musketry "crashing" in the distance) when rebel batteries opened "a heavy fire of artillery" on the reserve position. "Our cannon, I believe about forty in number, replied with great vigor, and for half an hour a Titanic combat raged," Dawes said. "We lay as closely as possible to the ground." He and Capt. John Kellogg were sharing a ground cloth "when a large fragment of shell passed into the ground between us, cutting a great hole in the oil-cloth, and covering us with dirt. It was a mystery how this could be and neither of us be struck." In the ranks, a spent artillery shell, fuse sputtering, rolled up to Pvt. Tommy Moran of Milwaukee. The Irishman scooped up a handful of mud and slapped it on the fuse, calling out, "Boys, ten to one it don't burst." For a long second, the men stared in horror, then the shell lay inert and there was laughter.[1]

In the late afternoon the fighting finally ended except for some scattered shooting on the picket lines. Bragg always remembered his great frustration: "When night came, we had not much ground gained, as we had at ten o'clock when Hooker's Corps was relieved." It was generally supposed, said John Gibbon, "that the battle would recommence the next morning." But it did not, and both armies, spent and bleeding, held their positions. George McClellan, despite fresh soldiers on hand, mulled his next move and found danger; Robert Lee, always aggressive, could do nothing more because his small army was almost wrecked. After a time white flags appeared along the line and the day was spent gathering wounded and burying the dead under flags of truce. In his journal, one Badger noted the men were "tired and worn out and in need of rest and quiet."

The last of the fighting involved Ambrose Burnside's attack on the far right of the Confederate line, the final in a series of unsuccessful Federal assaults. Lee's army had been on the edge of disaster all day, but McClellan failed to press his advantage of numbers. At the critical moment, the "young Napoleon" held back, somehow convinced there were fresh Confederates in that clump of woods or behind that rise of ground ready to strike his army with an attack that could prove disastrous. Lee and his officers shuffled regiments from the left of their line to the center to contain the Union blows. Late in the day, the Confederate brigades marching hard from captured Harper's Ferry arrived in the last instant to save the rebel army. Even then, the day could have been won, but McClellan never recognized the opportunity.

His soldiers paid the price. The exact numbers may never be determined, but slightly less than 12,500 Union men were dead, wounded, or missing, compared with more than 10,000 Confederates; roughly one of every four Federals and one in three Confederates. The total was 22,700 (3,600 killed outright; more of the wounded to die in the days ahead) and September 17, 1862, came to be "the bloodiest single day of the Civil War." Of the 800 officers and men of Gibbon's Brigade, more than 340 were killed and wounded, about 42 percent. Of the four regiments, the Sixth Wisconsin suffered most, with 150 casualties of less than 300 taken into the fight. Next was the Second Wisconsin with 18 killed, 67 wounded, and 6 missing—a loss of 91 from 150. Battery B had gone to Antietam with 100 officers and men; 9 were killed and 31 wounded, and 26 horses killed and 7 wounded. Also wounded was Gen. Joseph Hooker, shot in the foot.[2]

The tough Wisconsin and Indiana men had seen Brawner's Farm, Second Bull Run and South Mountain, but nothing prepared them for the bloody fields of Antietam. "The piles of dead on the Sharpsburg and

Hagerstown Turnpike were frightful," Dawes recalled. "When we marched along the turnpike . . . the scene was indescribably horrible. Great numbers of dead, swollen and black under the hot sun, lay upon the field. My horse as I rode through the narrow lane made by piling the bodies along beside the turnpike fences, trembled in every limb with fright and was wet with perspiration. Friend and foe were indiscriminately mingled." One ghastly apparition left a lasting impression: "In front of the haystacks where Battery B, Fourth U.S. Artillery, had been planted was seen a horse, apparently in the act of rising from the ground. Its head was held proudly aloft, and its fore legs set firmly forward. Nothing could be more vigorous or life-like than the pose of this animal. But like all surrounding it on that horrid aceldama, the horse was dead."

The ground in places, said Gibbon, was "literally covered with dead bodies, they being especially numerous in the open field in front of Battery 'B' along the fence bordering the turnpike. In the cornfield, the bodies, in some cases, were piled on top of each other." It was there, he said, that "many a gallant Wisconsin man met his death. They were lying side by side with the dead grey coats and the peaceful cows which were caught there between the two fires and fell riddled with bullets." To Bragg the battlefield was "too terrible to behold without a shock. I never want to see another such. I counted eighty rebels in one row, along the fence in front of us lying so thick you could step from one to the other, and in others, they lay as in heaps, mowed down, and many of our brave boys with them. So it was everywhere." The rebels "fought like demons—but for once, they met their equals in pluck & muscle. They are the dirtyist, lousyist, filthiest, piratical looking cutthroats a white man ever saw. There are no redeeming characters that I have seen. Officers & men, one all alike—in filth & rags." One dead Confederate was the "major of the 1st Texas." The officer, Bragg said, with "fiery courage worthy of a State having an 'Alamo' for its nursery cradle, was killed in the lines of the Sixth Wis. He was wearing a lady's watch, presumably a talisman given him by a wife or fiance, which was sent to . . . headquarters to be returned to the donor."[3]

The grisly scenes left the men shaken. "I was detained to help bury the dead. It was an awful sight," a soldier wrote home. "Some were killed so instantly that they never changed their position. Some was sitting up in the very act of loading, with their cartridges in their mouth and gun still in their hands. The Rebs fight like mad men. They will not leave the field until they are badly whipped and sometimes they don't get a chance to leave them alive." Another Badger called it "gruesome" and wrote in his diary, "Dead men and horses lying in grotesque shapes along side each other. Now and then the rebel dead would be found lying in heaps or long wind-rows, but some would be seen scattered about our people." The men of his regiment, a third soldier wrote, were "much astonished at the number of rebels lying dead in a perfect line of battle, presenting a horrible appearance and stink from the effects of the sun, their blackened corpses lying in every imaginable shape." A Second Wisconsin soldier had trouble putting the scene into words. "I thought I had seen men piled up and cut up in all kinds of shapes but never anything in comparison to that field," he wrote home. To Julius Murray of the Sixth Wisconsin it was "a terrible battle" although he and his son, Lute, "come out safe and are both well." Murray served as an ambulance driver while his son fought in the cornfield. "Luty has been in every fight and has fought bravely, his pants were cut open on the knee and several parts of his clothes bear the marks of bullets," Murray wrote. "I am proud of him, but he shall not go into anther fight if I can prevent it, and I think I can when the whole company [E] has been cut down to 13. I think we have run our share of risks. . . . Several shells burst over my head, where the pieces went only God knows. At any rate, altho I could hear them whizzing, they did not hit me."[4]

In the letters, diaries, and journals was a disturbing refrain, an off-hand manner in dealing with death and suffering. "I have had a full realization of the horrors and excitement of the battle field, and you can hardly comprehend its horrors after the battle is over. It is cheering and fighting while it lasts and under the excitement you do not much mind the shells bursting over your heads, the solid balls tearing up the ground and cutting trees down around you, the incessant peal of musketry amidst the universal din," Murray wrote. "You become callous to those falling around you dead or wounded, in fact, we have all become callous, and the sights of dead piled up in every direction on which we would have looked with horror a few months ago, we carefully examine now to see which is friend or foe." Pvt. Hugh Perkins of the Seventh Wisconsin wrote, "I have seen some hard times and a good deal more than I expected to. My comrades and tentmates have fell on each side of me, and I am still alive and without a scratch. I have had the balls come so close that they made my face smart, but it didn't break the hide. It has got so that it does not excite me any more to be in action than to be in a corn field hoeing, or digging potatoes." Pvt. Horace Emerson of the Second Wisconsin reported that one man of his company "was hit five times and layed on the field 30 hours before he was taken off. He died. He said the men took his canteen and haversack telling him that he may as well die one way as another. He was mortally wounded being shot through the bowels which is sure death but slow."[5]

The burial details faced a grim task. George Fink went to the field, where he found Michael Basel, Leo Gotsch, Jacob Mueller, and John Schilcke of his Company F from Milwaukee. They had buried Capt. Werner Von Bachelle and were burying Lt. William Bode. The captain's body had been found on the turnpike. Von Bachelle was on his back, "his feet crossed and his arms folded, his cap drawn forward over his eyes, like a soldier taking his rest, his body riddled with bullets, his field glass across his shoulder shattered into innumerable pieces and his faithful dog . . . lying across his body dead." Edward Bragg counted a dozen wounds. "He was a soldier of fortune and died as he desired—a soldier in the front line of battle." The dead of the Sixth were buried under "a locust tree on the right of the pike and in the field proximating to the church, well up to the front, but close toward the wood, Captain Bachelle with his feet to the south, on one side of the tree, and the enlisted men in a trench dug with a battery hoe on the reverse side." The captain's dog was placed beside him.

Earl Rogers bitterly wrote that the dead of the Black Hat Brigade were quickly "carried to the trench and rot." "Lying close together in death, as they had stood elbow to elbow in the battle of life," said Gibbon, "they sleep their last sleep on the very spot consecrated by their blood." As each dead soldier was covered with dirt, Pvt. George Fink of the Sixth Wisconsin cut the man's name, company, and regiment into a "chestnut fence board" and placed it at the head of each body. Another Badger recorded in his diary that "Citizens by the thousands are wandering over the battlefield picking up souvenirs."[6]

On the second day after the fighting the Confederates were gone from the army's front, apparently headed back to Virginia. Gibbon's Brigade marched across the battlefield and bivouacked in a woods near the Potomac River west of Sharpsburg. It was a welcomed rest, but the duty was hard. For several days details were marched out to bury the Confederate dead. "This work was decidedly unpleasant," one Badger said, "as the weather was warm, and decomposition had set in." Another Wisconsin soldier noted, "The rebels did not take time to bury their dead, so hasty was their flight toward a safe refuge."[7]

It seemed every house, barn, shed, every shelter, straw stack, or rail fence—anywhere with shade—had been turned into a medical facility. "Operating tables everywhere," one volunteer said. "It was not an uncommon sight to see wagons drawing off loads of legs and arms to be buried from the temporary hospitals." Citizens from surrounding com-

munities arrived with their buggies and farm wagons to help carry the
wounded to nearby hospitals; some brought food. "The ladies do all
they can and as every large building is a hospital they have lotts to do,"
a wounded soldier wrote. One Wisconsin boy on a burial detail was
given a biscuit and he noted in his diary, "It was a tasty bite from
civilization. We have had nothing to eat for a long time except crackers
and water."

Hearing the approach of "a four-horse wagon of good things," one
wounded Sixth Wisconsin soldier limped out of the barn where he was
sheltered. The driver was a "Pennsylvania Dutch farmer," and the Sauk
County boy asked for something to eat. The farmer produced it, then
questioned whether the young soldier needed clothing. "Of course he
did—wanted shirt, underclothing, stockings, and most anything," a
comrade said. "The old man could not understand it until the boy
unbuttoned his coat and the old man discovered that all the boy had
was a hat, coat, pants and a pair of shoes, all worn, tattered dirty and
lousy. The tears started down the old man's cheeks as he helped him get
on the stuff he gave him, and the boy was never happier in his life than
just at the time.... Hundreds died for lack of attention but it would have
been much greater but for the great hearted, loyal people of southern
Pennsylvania and western Maryland the whole people of the north that
as soon as possible poured in supplies by the train load."[8]

One Wisconsin man was in a farm building where straw had been
scattered for bedding. "About 80 wounded were in this barn, and all of
them, except two or three, belonged to Gen. Gibbon's Brigade," he
recalled. The great need, said the soldier, "was clean clothes to take the
place of those saturated with blood. Many a poor fellow was obliged to
see maggots crawling about his wound, because he had no clean shirt to
put on. This state of affairs, however, did not last long. The sanitary
commission came and supplied their wants. Words cannot tell how
much some of these men suffered. Many were on the battle-field for
hours, with life's blood ebbing away, and no relief at hand."[9]

Pvt. William Harries of the Second Wisconsin, shot in the chest,
shared a blanket with Uriel Olin of La Crosse, a sergeant of his regiment.
During the long night, Dr. A. J. Ward came to the "little frame house"
and gave each some whiskey. But Olin was soon dead. "The wound he
received through the bowels gave him great pain early in the evening,
but for an hour or more before the final dissolution he made no com-
plaint and died without a struggle." Harries was told that "it was
considered quite probable that I could be buried in the morning with
Sergeant Olin as I was bleeding frequently from the mouth." The next

day Harries was moved to the barn, where Gibbon's wounded were housed. "Until the Sanitary Commission came along we were in horrible condition. I do not care to describe my own; suffice to say that I felt like a new creature when I got on a clean shirt."

In the same room was Jasper Chestnut, one of the boys who crossed the Mississippi River from Clayton, Iowa, to sign the Sixth Wisconsin roll the first days of the war. A bone in his forearm was splintered and he stubbornly refused amputation, finally agreeing only to an operation "whereby it was believed that if certain portions of the bone were removed he would get well." Chestnut consented with the understanding that under no circumstances was his arm to be amputated. To ensure it, he "arranged to have one of his comrades present with a revolver and instructed him to use it if the doctors undertook to cut off his arm." The operation lasted 20 minutes. But the arm did not mend and Chestnut again refused to have the festering limb removed. He died in a Frederick, Maryland, army hospital on January 22, 1863—a soldier more troubled over losing his arm than his life.[10]

Jerome Watrous of the Sixth Wisconsin went to visit wounded Andrew Deacon of his old company in the "little church hospital at Keedysville," where he found his friend "lying in a pew, white as a sheet, with his eyes closed." One arm was gone. "How are you feeling, Andy?" Watrous asked. Deacon's "black eyes opened" and he looked up. "All right; am sorry to lose this arm, but I am glad I was in that battle." The two talked for a while and then, as Watrous readied to leave, Deacon said, "I wish you would go out back the church and find my arm and bury it. I don't feel right to have that neglected. They threw it out of the window, but I think you can find it." Watrous went to the back of the church and "saw a sight that I shall never forget. There was a pile of legs and arms which would fill two of the largest wagons you can see in the city of Milwaukee. That was only one of twenty or thirty hospitals. There were at least three or four cords of those evidences of the horror of war. Of course, I could not find poor Deacon's lost arm, but I hurried around among the surgeons and attendants and got a promise that all of the arms and legs should be buried and went back and told my stricken comrade. There was a tremble on his lips and a tear in his eye when he said: 'May be I will find it in the great future, when we all come out of our graves.'"[11]

For reasons not explained to the men in ranks, the Army of the Potomac lingered at Sharpsburg. The hours stretched into days and the days into a week and more. News of South Mountain and Antietam was carried north, first in newspapers and then in letters from officers and soldiers to assure loved ones they were safe. "I often think our women were greater heroes than we were," a Wisconsin veteran said, "because when an engagement was over our anxiety was ended until the next one, while their suspense was of continual duration, and therefore, so much harder to bear."

An example was the headline in the *Milwaukee Sentinel* on the day before Antietam, September 16: "King's Division in the Recent Battles before Washington—Splendid conduct of the Wisconsin Troops—A GLORIOUS RECORD." Details of Second Bull Run and South Mountain were thin; more came in succeeding days. On September 20, there were lists of the Wisconsin wounded from the army hospitals, and four days later came the news that shuttered homes and dimmed lights: "The following is a list of killed and wounded in Gibbon's Brigade."

Newspapers also carried soldier dispatches. In the *Mauston Star* of October 1, 1862, was a letter from Lyman Upham of the Sixth Wisconsin under the headline, "CAMP CORRESPONDENCE—THE KILLED AND WOUNDED." "Knowing the anxiety felt in your community regarding the fate of the two companies, K and I, raised in the vicinity of Mauston," Upham had written, "I append a full list of casualties in said companies to this date, together with some incidents connected with their participation in the various battles in which our regiment has been recently engaged."

The list was seemingly endless: In Company I, killed at the battle of Gainesville, Henry Didiot of Hillsboro, Charles Barnbaum of Jefferson, Frank Ellsworth of Whitestown; August 31, "while on picket," Rudolph Fine of Hillsboro; September 14, at the battle of South Mountain, William Lawrence of De Soto; September 17, at the battle of Sharpsburg, George Douglass of Hillsboro, George Atwood of Whitestown. In Company K, killed, August 30 at the battle of Bull Run, Levi Gardner of Fountain; September 14, at the battle of South Mountain, George Chamberlain of Mauston, Reuben Huntley of Necedah; September 17, at the battle of Sharpsburg, Charles Abbot of Summit, Daniel Cummings of Sparta. "In this battle, William P. Harrison [of Lindina] was mortally wounded. Private Wm. Lawrence Co. I, afterwards killed at the battle of South Mountain, was personally complemented for coolness and bravery by Brig. Gen. Gibbon on the battle-field of Bull Run. Company I opened the battle of Sharpsburg, being together with Co. C, thrown forward as skirmishers in front of the Brigade. They drove in the rebel skirmishers following them up until they met and received the fire of an entire rebel brigade. . . ."[12]

The letters home were often heartbreaking. Pvt. George McDill of

Company I, Sixth Wisconsin, in a letter to his mother, responded to "inquiries sent by Mr. and Mrs. Lawrence" regarding the death of their son at South Mountain. Their son had been ill for a time, McDill wrote, but returned to the company in early August. "You can tell Mr. and Mrs. Lawrence that . . . William often talked to me of his friends and home and frequently on the arrival of mail expressed surprise and regret that he failed to receive letters from home. . . . You can tell Mr. and Mrs. Lawrence that William was too brave a boy to ever forget his Father and Mother. . . . He was buried in the field on the very ground we contested with the enemy. There is five others in our regiment and one of the Sixteenth Ill. Cavalry in the same grave. They lay side by side with head boards at the head of each one plainly stating the name, reg't. and co. of each of the occupants. . . . William lays the second one from the left as you face the head of the grave. The first man on the left is the cavalry-man, easily distinguishable by his short jacket. They are buried between two large boulders. There is just sufficient room for the grave and on one of the rocks is an inscription, Viz. Wisconsin Dead. This was made by one of our boys with a bayonet broken for the purpose. . . . William was buried in the best manner possible under the circumstances."[13]

The word spread from cities to towns and villages and finally to the backwoods farms of Wisconsin. It brought joy and prayerful thanks to some homes and plunged others into tears and black mourning. On occasion, there were tragic mixups, as with two officers of the Sixth Wisconsin—Lt. Col. Edward Bragg and Capt. Edwin Brown. Bragg had been wounded and Brown killed at Antietam. On September 18 a message reached the Wisconsin State Telegraph Company office at Fond du Lac addressed to Mrs. Bragg—"Your husband was shot Yesterday. I will send him home by express." It was signed by a sergeant of the Sixth Wisconsin. The news spread from the homes to the business places and one of the women hurrying to Mrs. Bragg's side was Ruth Brown, the young wife of Edwin Brown. The two had been left to wait and worry when their husbands went off to war in "Bragg's Rifles." The townsfolk felt with sadness the loss of the energetic, slight lawyer and remembered how he had signed on for the war, raising a company of local boys and naming the organization after himself. Friends and business acquaintances gathered. There must be a memorial service, they decided, and they organized committees to make preparations. A delegate was sent to Chicago to bring Bragg's body to Fond du Lac.

The family of Edwin Brown was worried, but as there had been no word it was taken as a good sign. Unaware his son was dead, Isaac Brown sent a letter September 21: "I write to express to you how anx-

*Edwin A. Brown. Courtesy
of the Wisconsin Veterans
Museum. Used by
permission.*

iously we are waiting to hear the reports of casualties to our men in the late battles and yet are almost afraid to hear—our earnest prayer is that you have gone through the deadly contest safely." The news about Bragg was very sad, Isaac Brown wrote, adding that "strange to believe there seems to be a disposition to believe the report is a hoax, we all hope it may be, but it is almost hoping against hope."

There was more: "I notice in your last letter to Ruth that you complain of being worn down by hard service, and that unless you could rest soon you was fearful that you should give out &—I suppose that in times such as our army's are now experiencing it is difficult to get either a furlough or a resignation accepted. But my advice is to try to get the utmost—one or the other rather than sink under the loads of sheer exhaustion. I think you have by this time proved your courage and patriotism so well as to silence all imputations of cowardice that seems to apply but too well in the case of some that have volunteered with a flourish of trumpets."

The letter was no sooner posted when a message arrived from the

Fond du Lac representative in Chicago—"The body of Capt. E. A. Brown, instead of Bragg. Will be home tomorrow. Chicago Times reports Bragg wounded in arm." Another telegram was carried to the home of Isaac Brown—"E. A. Brown's body is here and will be on the first train." Again the news spread from home to home and business to business. Mrs. Bragg wept in joy and relief, gathering her children around her; Mrs. Brown wept in bitter sorrow. Two days later Col. Edward Bragg wrote Mrs. Brown, and it was a proud letter for a wife, but carried scant solace for a widow with three young children: "He was a good soldier, a brave and chivalrous gentleman and above all he cherished a fond love for his home, and the domesticities this cruel war has severed. Believe me Madam, the Regiment . . . deeply mourns his loss; and his brother officers will long cherish his memory, and through me, express to you, their kindest and heartfelt sympathies in your bereavement."

In the end the hero's burial prepared at Fond du Lac for Edward Bragg was given to Edwin Brown, who counted himself one of the "Republic's patriotic children." The "cruel war" had stilled his singing voice forever.[14]

22.
The Men Have Stood Like Iron

The soldiers of the Sixth Wisconsin, Gibbon's Brigade, and the rest of the Army of the Potomac always felt they had accomplished much on the bloody fields around Sharpsburg, Maryland. "I will say this," one Wisconsin officer wrote home, "that if Gibbon's Brigade had of been as strong on the morning of the 17th as we were two months ago, I believe we could have succeeded in driving the Rebels into the river, for I tell you the troops that relieved us did not fight as we did for we drove them until our ammunition gave out and then held our ground until we were relieved." So if Robert E. Lee's advance had been met and stopped along Antietam Creek, what that all meant was less sure, except to Gen. George Brinton McClellan. He was convinced he had won a great victory against great odds, thereby lifting the threat to Washington and Baltimore and, in fact, preserving the Republic. He also believed he was never given the credit due him.

In his reasoning was some truth. McClellan was the only general, North or South, who could have taken the shattered Federal brigades of Second Bull Run and got them organized, equipped, and on the road to fight two weeks later at South Mountain and then at Antietam —a significant accomplishment often overlooked in measuring the general's role in the Maryland campaign. But his efforts were always overshadowed by what might have been accomplished. McClellan did not press his attacks on September 18 and, by the following day, the opportunity passed and Lee's Army of Northern Virginia was gone from his front. The general did not organize a pursuit, explaining to Washington that his supply wagons were empty, his soldiers ill-equipped, and his command structures tangled.

"The regiment was now in a condition of exhaustion from the severity of its service and from its losses in battle," said Rufus Dawes of the

Sixth Wisconsin. The "weeks of inaction" following Antietam, Edward Bragg explained later, stemmed from "the shattered condition of the troops and their want of proper blankets and clothing, particularly trousers, shirts and shoes." But John Gibbon, who used the time to visit his family at Baltimore, came back to the army in an unsettled mood. Everywhere he had been asked when McClellan would advance. "So strong had become the feeling at the delay that I returned to the army impressed with the conviction that unless a move took place very soon, McClellan would be relieved from command and so I expressed myself to a prominent member of his staff." The response was troubling. "The most important reason supposed to be for delay was the lack of supplies and it is certain when the army did at last move on the Twenty-sixth of October the equipment of the men was not as complete as it should have been and might have been though Lee's army must necessarily have been worse off than we were."[1] There was some of the same feeling in ranks. "We are constantly speculating on the cause of this inaction," a Wisconsin private wrote home. "We are not as blood thirsty as we used to be that is we are not anxious for another fight, but want the ball kept in motion even if we have to take the brunt."[2]

But the rest was welcomed by the men and officers of the Sixth Wisconsin. The fighting at Antietam closed a campaign of 45 days that Dawes called "the first battle epoch" of his regiment. During that period, the "Calicos boys" fought four major engagements and were 11 days subject to "battle fire of the enemy." To his mother the day after Antietam the young major had written, "I have come safely through two more terrible engagements with the enemy, that at South Mountain and the great battle of yesterday. Our splendid regiment is almost destroyed. We have had nearly four hundred men killed and wounded in battles. Seven of our officers were shot and three killed in yesterday's battle and nearly one hundred and fifty men killed and wounded. All from less than three hundred engaged. The men have stood like iron." It was the first time he referred to the name won by Gibbon's men at South Mountain—"The Iron Brigade of the West."[3]

Other soldiers were also using the description "iron" in their letters. An officer of the Seventh Wisconsin reported to the home folk September 21 that "General McClellan has given us the name of the Iron Brigade," and five days later, a private in the same regiment explained, "Gen. McClellan calls us the Iron Brigade. By gaining this name, we have lost from the brigade seventeen hundred and fifty men. We have never turned our backs to the enemy in any engagement, although they have outnumbered us every fight we have had." The brigade adjutant,

Frank Haskell, in a letter home, described the war as "a horrid thing" and urged his family to "believe in Genl. McClellan." To a younger brother thinking about "coming to the war," he wrote, "No boy, you must not think of it,—you could not begin to stand it,—The losses by sickness, are far more than those by bullets. One must be made of iron to stand it—I am three fourths iron, and the rest is oak. . . ."[4]

The "Iron Brigade of the West" was a mighty war name, and even "Little Mac" took note with an endorsement to the governor of Wisconsin of his "great admiration" for the three Badger regiments of Gibbon's Brigade. "I have seen them under fire, acting in a manner that reflects the greatest possible credit and honor upon themselves and their state. They are equal to the best troops in any army in the world." A similar letter was sent to Indianapolis about the Nineteenth Indiana.[5] The general's remarks were read at the evening dress parades on October 8, and a Badger wrote in his diary, "Hooray for Wisconsin! We are very cheered and encouraged."

But there was a reverse side to being the "Iron Brigade of the West." More was expected of such soldiers; they had to march farther, shoot straighter, and stand firmer in a battle line when other men just as brave gave it up. Jerome Watrous of the Sixth Wisconsin wrote of Antietam that "the men fought more like demons than anything else until but 400 or 500 were left of the Brigade that had 2500 as good men as ever carried guns, but two months before. Judge for yourselves whether the brigade has seen hard times or not, with three times three for brave 'Little Mac,' the man we *all* love, I await further movements." A private in the Seventh Wisconsin observed that of "our 98 brave Waushara [County] boys, there is only eight here now fit for duty. There is not many sick at present. We have no stragglers like some companies, but still the men are gone. They have died the soldier's death or have been wounded on the field of battle. We haven't a coward in our company."[6]

From Washington those days came an important announcement of an "Emancipation Proclamation" issued by President Lincoln in response to the thin Union "victory" at Antietam. As of January 1, 1863, it said, slaves in states in rebellion would "be then, henceforward, and forever free." The document would later be recognized as a great turning point of the Civil War (one Wisconsin veteran called it "that great paper which will always be associated with the history of Mr. Lincoln's administration"), but the proclamation would accomplish little that was not already happening; the Federal army was, in fact, creating freedom in its wake. As a political statement, however, the document was far-reaching and important, and the announcement, as expected, received a mixed reception when it was printed and distributed in the camps of the Army of the Potomac. Some soldiers and officers hailed it; others did not know what to make of it or where it would lead, and a few feared it, including George McClellan. He and others claimed, with some truth, that the proclamation was beyond the original aims of the war; that it would stiffen the resistance of the Confederate soldier, and that it threatened any negotiated settlement leading to restoration of the Union.

In ranks, however, others took a practical view. "I don't no what effect the President's proclamation will have on the South," a Wisconsin officer wrote, "but there is one thing certain it is just what was wanted, and if they don't lay down their arms we will have to annihilate them, niggers, cotton and all. It will make hard times for a while but it will forever settle the everlasting slavery question." In another letter, he reported that "Old Abe's proclamation" takes "well with the army here. Now the Rebs will have to die dog or eat the hatchet." Rufus Dawes of the Sixth Wisconsin also expressed the soldier's view while on furlough to Marietta, Ohio, a few weeks later. He had been approached by civic leaders and asked to speak "in regard to the war, and the state of the country." Dawes's presentation ("delivered in a forcible and eloquent manner," the *Marietta Register* reported) gave "the highest satisfaction and was listened to with almost breathless interest."

If there "remains any one in the army, who does not like the Proclamation, he is careful to keep quiet about it," Dawes told the Ohio audience. "We are hailed everywhere by the negroes as their deliverers. They all know that 'Mass Linkum' has set them free, and I never saw one not disposed to take advantage of the fact. . . . Slavery is the chief source of wealth in the South, and the basis of their aristocracy, and my observation is that a blow at slavery hurts more than battalion volleys. It strikes at the vitals. It is foolish to talk about embittering the rebels any more than they are already embittered. We like the Proclamation because it hurts the rebels. We like the Proclamation because it lets the world know what the real issue is. . . . We like the Emancipation Proclamation because it is right, and because it is the edict of our Commander in Chief, the President of the United States."[7]

But all that was yet to come, and as the Army of the Potomac rested and reorganized and outfitted, September slipped away. Fifer Ludolph Longhenry of the Seventh Wisconsin left a record:

> September 23, Tuesday—Wonderful autumn weather. Last night a horse got loose and went galloping through camp, jumping over sleeping soldiers. No one was injured. However, the whole brigade

was awake and somewhat alarmed. There is nothing to do around here. Rations, crackers and beef, coffee and sugar. . . .

September 24, Wednesday—Newspapers report that the rebels lost 30,000 men in Maryland. Rumor had it that we should march again this morning, but nothing happened.

September 25, Thursday—Cold weather, nice cool nights, good bread, twenty-five cents.

September 26, Friday—Roasting of pancakes is the fashion of the day. All is quiet around here.

September 27, Saturday—Orders to clean all guns. Baking pancakes. Stages to Washington, D.C., left here this morning.

September 28, Sunday—Inspection of guns. . . .

September 29, Monday—Today we left Shepherdstown, near the Potomac, where the rebels crossed the Potomac River after the Antietam battle. Sharpsburg is about a mile from here. Our camp is on a stony hill with little drinking water.

October 1, Wednesday—Occasionally a sharp cannonade from Harper's Ferry and Williamsport. All is quiet along the front. Thunder shower about dusk. Overcast and warm. Camp rumor: Jeff Davis and General Lee are bringing a flag of truce. Strong cannonade from Harper's Ferry.

October 2, Thursday—This afternoon President Lincoln was to hold a review on the battlefield near Sharpsburg. We had to forget our lunch on account of it. We waited the whole afternoon from the arrivals of the President. At sundown there was no sight of him or his entourage. He did not arrive. We marched hungry and thirsty back to our camp.

President Lincoln (Edward Bragg, always the Democrat, made a sour reference in a letter home to the president's "long legs, & jack knife face") finally arrived the next day. The army was drawn up for a ceremonial inspection, but the welcome was cool, with resentment and distrust in the air—an unsettled feeling in ranks that Lincoln and others of his administration were bungling the war effort for political gain and that the soldiers were paying the price. It was an army much changed from the one reviewed by the president outside Washington several months earlier. The regiments were now "well seasoned" with "a record of many great battles," said a Wisconsin man. "What changes had taken place with that army since his review of it at Bailey's Cross Roads. At least 100,000 of his partners in that one army had been killed or wounded. His thin, pale face and look of deep sorrow told of his aching heart at the great loss." Another Badger observed, "Abraham looked well and took especial interest in the Iron Brigade which was pointed out to him." The line, said Dawes, "was formed in almost the position occupied by the army of General Lee at the opening of the battle. We had about two hundred and fifty men in our ranks at this review. Our battle flags were tattered, our clothing worn, and our appearance that of men who had been through the most trying service. . . . Mr. Lincoln was manifestly touched at the worn appearance of our men, and he, himself, looked serious and careworn. He bowed low in response to the salute of our tattered flags. As I sat upon my horse in front of the regiment, I caught a glimpse of Mr. Lincoln's face, which has remained photographed upon my memory. Compared with the small figure of General McClellan, who, with jaunty air and somewhat gaudy appearance, cantered along beside him, Mr. Lincoln seemed to tower as a giant."[8]

In those days of late September there was another matter especially troubling to the officers and men of the Sixth Wisconsin, and it concerned the regiment's flags, a national banner and a blue state color, and some broad claims by Lt. Col. Theodore Gates of the Twentieth New York State Militia. In his report on Antietam, the colonel had written how Maj. Jacob Hardenbergh advanced half the small regiment to the support of Battery B of the Fourth U.S. Artillery. The Sixth Wisconsin was forward and left of the Twentieth, he wrote, and was "in some disorder" and had to abandon its "battle-flag." One of his New Yorkers, Gates said, then shot a rebel colorbearer and the captured red flag was carried off the field by Hardenbergh "as was also the regimental colors of the Sixth Wisconsin, which they had been compelled to leave on the field. . . ."[9]

The report was filed at headquarters and John Gibbon, always jealous of his reputation and the reputation of his regiments, soon went to examine it. "I was at the Battery when the Sixth Wis. came back and helped the Major (Dawes) rally it on its colors, which were then with the Regiment," Gibbon said of the incident three decades afterward. "A half regiment (I think the Twentieth N.Y.) had been sent to aid in protecting the battery. It never went beyond the position occupied by the limbers of the guns. After the battle the Col. of that half regiment (I am not certain of his name or the number of his regiment) turned in a Rebel color which he claimed to have captured on the field, and on the paper accompanying the color stated that he had brought off the field the colors of the Sixth Wisconsin. During the fight one of our men (I suppose one of the Brigade) brought me in the Battery a rebel color and in the excitement of the fighting I yelled at him to throw down the flag and take his place in ranks. When the N.Y. Col. turned in his rebel flag I *suspected* it was the one this man had brought to me as I knew the Col.

had never been in a place where he could have captured it, but when he said he had brought off the colors of the Sixth Wisconsin I knew that was not true, for I saw them come off the field myself."

Gibbon called in Gates to question him, and the explanation given, Gibbon wrote later, "was not very clear and was very weak, and I had not much difficulty in persuading him to omit all mention of the Sixth Wisconsin flag in his statement and I did not attempt to make any point out of his captured rebel flag."[10]

Edward Bragg of the Sixth Wisconsin answered the claim by the New Yorkers with sharp words in his own report of the battle. His regiment, he wrote, "conducted itself during the fight so as to fully sustain its previous reputation; that it did not abandon its colors on the field; that every color-bearer and every member of the guard was disabled and compelled to leave; that the state color fell into other keeping, tempo-rarily, in rear of the regiment, because its bearer had fallen, but it was immediately reclaimed and, under its folds, few but undaunted, the regiment rallied to the support of the battery." The color lance of the Sixth's national color "is pierced with five balls and both colors bear multitudes of testimony that they were in the thickest of the fighting."[11]

Many years later, Bragg wrote of the incident to an Antietam histo-rian. The Confederate flag, Bragg said, "fell or was thrown down or dropped in the last struggle of the Sixth Wis., and was picked up as trophy by a man of the Sixth who was carrying it, with one of the flags of the Sixth to the rear, when Gen. Gibbon, who was in the battery directing its fire, called to him, 'Put down the flags and come to the battery,' or something of that sort. . . . The man did as commanded, and both flags there laid down were picked up by the stragglers belong to Colonel Gates's command supporting the battery. There are the facts of the 'so-called' capture and rescue."[12]

The truth may never be determined. John Gibbon's story that he ordered an enlisted man to put down the flags has the ring of truth. The black hat soldier apparently left the flags and they were picked up by men of the Twentieth New York. When Rufus Dawes came out of the fighting in the cornfield, he may have found the Wisconsin flag in the hands of a New Yorker. "At the bottom of the hill, I took the blue color of the state of Wisconsin, and waving it, called a rally of Wisconsin men," Dawes wrote in one account of Antietam. In a second description of the fighting, he reported: "Here, at the bottom of the hill, I took the blue color of the state of Wisconsin, and called a rally of Wisconsin men."[13] In both cases, Dawes "took the blue color," but did not identify the soldier carrying it or how it came into his hands. No officer was more careful about claiming more than was due him than Dawes, and no officer was more careful giving credit where deserved. If it had been a soldier of his brigade, Dawes probably would have recorded it. Since it was a soldier from another organization, and an Eastern unit at that, Dawes may have simply omitted it, embarrassed that the Wisconsin flag had fallen into the care of a stranger.

How the Twentieth New York took the rebel flag is also obscure. Despite Bragg's claim the flag "captured" by the New Yorkers was the one carried from the cornfield by a Sixth Wisconsin man, several Confederate banners were taken that day.[14] It was a very confusing few minutes, and Bragg at the time was in the rear being treated for his wound. In his report, he claimed the Sixth Wisconsin captured two stands of colors which were "sent to the rear in charge of a wounded soldier and have become lost or fallen into the possession of someone desirous of military *eclat* without incurring personal danger, so that they cannot be reclaimed by the captors." To his wife, Bragg had written: "My regiment took a stand of colors, but it was sent to the rear by a wounded man & lost at the Hospital, and somebody else will claim it, I suppose. Who cares! We took it, and many witnesses can prove it, if disputed."[15]

That there were angry words over the incident should be of little surprise—the regimental banners from the very first were as much a part of the organizations as the soldiers themselves. "We are the color company of the Sixth Regiment, and carry the regimental colors," W. H. Druen of Rockville wrote with pride on August 1, 1861, "and I feel safe in saying in behalf of Company 'C' that the splendid flag entrusted to our care, shall not be dishonored by any act of ours. We shall bring it back unsullied by traitors' hands." The bright silk flags—one national, the other state—came to represent home, duty, and cause to the volunteers. At the presentation of a flag to the Fifth Wisconsin Infantry, it was not considered unusual that an officer "commanded all his men to kneel down and swear to fight for that flag as long as a drop of blood remained in their veins, which was enthusiastically complied with."[16] The flags were always with them, on the drill field, during march, and in battle, carried in the very center of the regiment in line of battle. It was the movement of the flags more than the commands of the officers (often lost in the din) that directed the men. The banners served to lead a charge or rally a broken regiment. It was not chance Pvt. Frank Deleglise of the Sixth Wisconsin would single out rebels carrying flags for careful aim or that Lt. Frank Haskell would come on the gallop when the Sixth's flag fell at Second Bull Run. If the flags advanced, so did the line; if the flag fell back, so did the men. The sole responsibility of the color guards—a picked detail of corporals— was to protect the unit's flags. It was the most perilous duty. And it was not surprising, given the sentimentalism of those days, that a popular war song called Union men to "Rally around the flag, boys, rally once again." In returning his regiment's state flag a few months after Antietam, Bragg noted: "When we received it, its folds, like our ranks, were ample and full; still emblematical of our condition, we return it, tattered and torn in the shock of battle. . . . The regiment, boasting not of deeds done, or to be done, sends this voiceless witness to be deposited in the archives of our State. History will tell how Wisconsin honor has been vindicated by her soldiery, and what lessons in Northern courage they have given Southern chivalry." Another Wisconsin speaker called the flags "sacred colors" and "priceless relics"—symbols of sacrifice and bravery as well as Wisconsin's "power and grandeur."[17]

But Jerome Watrous, who served his four years in the Sixth Wisconsin, was the most eloquent. He spoke for all the Badger veterans when he was called on to make the dedication address for a new Grand Army of the Republic Hall in the state capitol building where the soiled, shot-torn banners were displayed. "Through our dim eyes, we can see these old flags as they appeared in our camps of instruction, as they went with us upon great reviews, as they went with us in long marches, as they went into battles with us, and were a constant inspiration," he told the gathering. "It was in those days when we were boys or young men that we first began to understand what those flags, what our beautiful national emblem, means. It was in those early days in our experience in the war that we learned to love the stars and stripes, all of the stars, all of the stripes—everything about the dear old flag of our regiment; our flag, wherever it might be. There was a thrill whenever we saw it; it was a great part of us when the war ended."

Watrous went on: "We were not vain, yet we had learned much in those four years of awful struggle—American against American—to preserve the Republic made possible by the services and sacrifices of Washington and the men who followed in the war of the Revolution. I say we were not vain, we are not vain now, yet we realized after Appomattox that the lives of the thousands of our comrades who had died on battle fields had in a way been woven into our colors. Then we realized that it was equally true that we had been woven into the colors. We felt, as we wended our way homeward, that it was not only our flag, the flag of our country, but that we were a part of it. We had helped to cleanse it; we had given the new-born nation—for it was reborn at Appomattox—a new and clean flag; and that is what all these old, faded, torn, furled flags that we here to-day rededicate are—sacred remnants of the new-born nation's untarnished emblem. . . . "

The old soldiers "love the old flags," Watrous said. "We followed them in victory and in defeat; we were with them in great demonstrations; we marched under them after the great victory had been won."[18]

23.
May God Bless Us

As the Army of the Potomac rested in the Sharpsburg camps for a month, there were developments affecting Gibbon's Brigade. With Gen. Joseph Hooker in Washington recovering from his Antietam wound (and scheming for promotion), West Pointer John Reynolds, a soldier of some reputation, was promoted to command the First Corps. He was an officer of ability and it was an association that would prove valuable.

But it was the arrival of the Twenty-fourth Michigan Volunteer Infantry on October 9 that created the biggest stir. The Western unit, as promised by McClellan, was attached to Gibbon's Brigade, and the Wisconsin and Indiana men watched as the "new regiment, clad in clean, bright uniforms, a thousand strong, the band playing, went into camp near the remanent of the four regiments that had fought together since August, 1861...." Gibbon's Brigade "had been so reduced by shot, shell and disease" that the four regiments "did not number as many as 200 of this one regiment, fresh from the chief city of Michigan," said Jerome Watrous of the Sixth Wisconsin. It was a sight not seen since the Washington camps of the previous year—the full ranks, new uniforms, brass band, and unsoiled flags. "They are a splendid looking body of men, entirely new to the service," Rufus Dawes wrote home. "Their ranks are full now, and they are, as we were, crazy to fight." Another Badger noticed the "very good brass band" and how, from the "stony hill" where his regiment bivouacked, he could see the Michigan men camped "in a small valley." One of the band's selections was "Towards God We Are Mounting," he wrote. "It is beautifully done." John Gibbon also looked over his new organization. "From its bearing," he wrote home, "I have no doubt it will not be long before it will be a worthy member of the 'Black Hats.'"

But the Badgers and Hoosier veterans were cold and distant, coming down to the Michigan camp to stand a few rods off in small groups, hands in pockets, looking over the new men. Later, after Fredericksburg, Chancellorsville, and Gettysburg, the Michigan soldiers would be welcomed as full-fledged brigade members, but that acceptance was still a great distance off. At first the Twenty-fourth was just "the big regiment" (it numbered more than the other four combined), but later the Wolverines became the "Featherbeds"—a camp name given because they were slow to sign on for the war. "They knew the record of the balance of our brigade had made," one Badger said, "and realized that if they were to rank with their brethren from Wisconsin and Indiana, no time must be lost in preparing for the serious work which was to come. Early in the morning, companies and squads were put through a rigid course of drill, and during the day there were company and battalion drills . . . those hard Wolverines had to learn how to live upon army rations; that the first duty of a soldier was to obey all lawful orders; what was expected of them."[1]

The stand-off attitude was nowhere more evident than during an early drill. "Our regimental inspection over, we were drawn up in front of the rest of the brigade, whom we almost outnumbered," a Michigan soldier recalled. "Our suits were new; their's were army-worn. Our Colonel [Henry Morrow] extolled our qualities, but the brigade was silent. Not a cheer. A pretty cool reception, we thought. We had come out to reinforce them, and supposed they would be glad to see us." But, he admitted, the brigade "had already won envious fame . . . and had a right to know before accepting our full fellowship if we, too, had the mettle to sustain the honor of the brigade."[2] And there was more to the "cool reception" than organizational pride. A camp whisper had reached the Western bivouac that the Michigan soldiers were "bounty men"— recruits paid a bonus to enlist. To the "Boys of '61" that separated them from the men in the new regiment by a wide gulf. The Wisconsin and Indiana men enlisted because of "pure patriotism," one Badger explained. "There were no large bounties or donations as incentives to a service to the country. It was clearly a patriotic feeling of a desire for the maintenance of the Union and the preservation of our free institutions." The Michigan men were jeered as "bounty-bought" and told in loud voices "the Government could have secured mules much cheaper." Those Wolverines with their new uniforms, caps, fat wallets full of bounty money, and green ways, the Black Hats decided with solemn nods, could not be counted on in a pinch.

In fact, the story was simply not true. The new regiment had its start in July 1862 following a war meeting in Detroit to promote enlistments under Lincoln's call for 300,000 men. The rally, disrupted by rowdies and Confederate sympathizers, broke up in confusion. "To wipe out the unexpected insult, a second war meeting was held," one Michigan volunteer said, "which resolved to raise immediately an entire regiment—the Twenty-fourth—in Wayne County alone, *in addition to its regular quota. . . .*" Within a month, the new regiment was filled. "Not a man of us received a cent of State or county bounty. Each man, however, did receive, in advance, one month's pay and $25 of the regular $100 government bounty promised to all soldiers enlisting for two years; 673 of the men who were credited to Detroit received sums varying from $25 to $50 a piece as a gratuity from patriotic friends, while the remaining 354 of us never received a cent."[3]

The Michigan men had not been caught up in drums and flags. The war was in its second year and there were no illusions of glorious charges and grand marches. The volunteers of the Twenty-fourth Michigan knew what they were getting into, and the ranks included steady and serious men, such as John Tait, the fourth corporal in Capt. William Owen's Company G.

A native of England, Tait was living in Cherry Hill, Canton Township, Wayne County, Michigan, with his wife and five children; the youngest was Grace, born that January 10; the oldest, Elizabeth, was just nine. The 36-year-old blacksmith enlisted in the first call for the new Twenty-fourth Michigan. Tait was exactly the kind of recruit who needed a dollar or two for his family while he was off protecting the Union. He collected his $25 upon enlistment. But, in the final tally, there was no bounty large enough to cover his service to his adopted country—Tait would be killed in his second battle less than a year after he left home.[4]

But all that was to come, and in the camp around Sharpsburg the veterans made "unmerciful sport" of the new volunteers. Of course there were soldier pranks, one concerning several sheep "poached" while the Michigan volunteers had been on sentry duty. The animals had been "killed and dressed in fine style. . . ." The officer of the day was a Second Wisconsin man and the "Raggies," coveting the fresh meat, soon agreed on a plan. A short time later, in his full regimentals, the Wisconsin officer went down to the Michigan camp to read "a rather severe order" against foraging. There was some grumbling, but the Wolverines delivered the sheep. "It is hardly necessary to say that the Second boys had a fine breakfast of mutton," said a Badger, "and that the Twenty-fourth boys were hopping mad when they discovered how the trick had been played. They ever after held the captain in perfect contempt."[5]

On October 20, the five regiments broke camp and tramped seven miles to Bakersfield, Maryland. Ten days later the long columns again pushed into Virginia ("that hot bed of secession the soldier despises above all other places on earth," one Badger said), and Rufus Dawes reported, "At last the Army of the Potomac is moving and we are once more upon the sacred soil." His Sixth Wisconsin had been hard used, he said, and "the feathers in our hats were drooping and the white leggings, which, as a protection to the feet and ankles, were now more useful than ornamental, had become badly soiled."

It was the Twenty-fourth Michigan's first experience with active campaigning, and the pontoon bridges left an impression. "These bridges are strong enough to hold our heaviest wagon trains," a Wolverine wrote home. "It is very unpleasant walking on them. They keep in constant motion, making one walk like a drunken man. He soon gets to feel drunk or seasick—very uncomfortable at least." The march "was a long, hard and trying one," a veteran said. "When it did not rain and the roads were not heavy with Virginia mud, it snowed and froze." The Wolverines soon took to life on the march. "The soldiers from the Michigan Twenty-fourth Regiment plundered the nearby farmhouses," a Badger wrote in his diary. The column was halted at Warrenton, Virginia, by a snowstorm—"Ice half an inch thick was to be seen every where this morning. Stealing chickens. Snow fell all day long." Dawes wrote home, "It is cold, and exceedingly disagreeable campaigning now."

The marching was very hard, but the "weary patriots of McClellan," a Badger said, "waded through mud and water up to their knees without a murmur, believing that our gallant leader does all things for the best." The haversacks of the Wisconsin, Indiana, and Michigan men were empty. "To-day the regiment is without a cracker to eat, but our men bear it without a murmur," Dawes reported. "No regiment in the army endures privations more patiently. The new regiment, (Twenty-fourth Michigan) do not take it so easily. They have been shouting 'Bread! Bread!' at the top of their voices all day."[6] It was heavy going for veteran or recruit. "I am a fighting man no longer. The last battle was enough for me," a Second Wisconsin man wrote, while a Michigan soldier explained, "You folks there at home may read in the papers about the great battles and the hard marches . . . but you don't know nothing about it nor never will until you have been down here and carried a knapsack and gun 60 rounds of catriges and haversack with 3 days rations and march all day and then lay on the ground all night and perhaps in the rain at that and then march off again to go out on pickett and stand all night and then march off again in the morning. I tel you what thats what will take the patriotism away from a fellow." Another Wolverine was troubled by the hard attitude of the veterans, and he complained in a letter to his sister, "On drill or review, if they halt to rest a minute, they have out their cards, playing poker."[7]

John Gibbon was lifted by the spectacle of the Army of the Potomac's march into Virginia. His regiments crossed at Berlin October 30 and halted at Purcellsville. While there, George McClellan passed through the camp and Gibbon joined the general's party. "I shall never forget the magnificent appearance presented by the vast columns of troops moving along the foot of the mountain where a great many had already reached their camps for the night, the men being busy unloading their wagons, building fires and cooking rations," Gibbon said. "No sooner did our cavalcade make its appearance than the men along the road dropped everything and rushed to the fence, commenced cheering loudly for McClellan. The marching columns, catching sight of him, took up the cheering and he reached Snickersville in the midst of a grand ovation. McClellan's manner of receiving such applause added, I think, greatly to the enthusiasm. He also seemed to appreciate so highly these demonstrations, waving his cap and smiling in every direction as he rapidly rode along, that the men appeared to think that he enjoyed the thing as much as they did. Such a feeling between the Commanding General and the men in the ranks is an immense element of strength in war and certainly McClellan possessed the confidence of his men and excited their enthusiasm in a higher degree than any commander the Army of the Potomac every had." One of the new Michigan soldiers got a look at the general, then wrote home: "You would know him anywhere. His pictures are true—he is no ways remarkable in appearance—answering his descriptions exactly."[8]

It was during those first days of November that Gibbon was called to the headquarters and offered the command of a division. "My first feeling was one of regret at the idea of being separated from my gallant brigade and some of this was allowed to appear," he recalled. But by the night of November 4 his decision was made and he was saying his good-byes to the regimental officers "for the next morning I was to be separated, not only from my gallant little brigade, but from my own battery which usually accompanied the brigade into battle." There was an added concern—he would leave the brigade in the hands of "a perfectly new colonel who had never been in battle and did not yet know how to command a regiment." The commission of Henry Morrow of the Twenty-fourth Michigan was senior to that of Lt. Col. Lucius Fairchild of the Second Wisconsin, and Col. Lysander Cutler of the Sixth Wisconsin had yet to return to the army. "Under these circumstances feeling as averse as if trusting a cherished child in the hands of a strange and inexperienced nurse," Gibbon said, "I sent for Col. Morrow and tried to prevail on him to waive his rank and allow the command to go to Fairchild, but although a young soldier I found him disposed to cling as tenaciously as an old one to the rights of his rank, and he declined to yield." Frustrated, Gibbon appealed to headquarters, but the result was the same. The next morning he sat his horse by the roadside and watched his "gallant little brigade move from the last time from my command." One Wisconsin officer complained that the unit "shall never more be called 'Gibbon's Brigade,' but will be called by the name of his successor . . . and all the battles we have fought have been under him. . . ." Rufus Dawes wrote home: "We are sorry to lose him, for a brave and true man, tested as he has been, is a jewel here."[9]

Happily for the Wisconsin and Indiana veterans at least, Morrow's advancement lasted less than a week. On November 9, Lysander Cutler returned and assumed command of the regiments. But the old colonel was still hobbled by his Brawner farm wound.

"He is really unfit for duty," Dawes wrote.

24.

The Government Has Gone Mad

It was in November 1862 that the war effort took a hard turn touching the very foundation of the United States. It began with Abraham Lincoln's unexpected removal of George McClellan as commander of the Army of the Potomac. It was a decision the president had not reached easily. Frustrated over the army's inactivity, embarrassed by election reverses and whispers of McClellan's presidential ambitions, Lincoln sacked "Little Mac" and put Ambrose Burnside in his place.[1]

The news hit the Federal camps like a "thunderclap," said John Gibbon, the word quickly spreading from headquarters to regimental and company campfires. "There is but one opinion upon this subject among the troops and that is the Government has gone mad," Gibbon said of the army's reaction. "It is the worst possible thing that could have been done. . . . Every one feels gloomy and sad that a man who has done so much for his country, should be treated in this manner." In the tents of some officers there were angry words and talk of taking the army to Washington to end this government interference with the war effort once and for all.

The news reached the Sixth Wisconsin just as the men were pitching tents at the close of a hard march. Many of the young officers were McClellan partisans, and Dawes recalled "considerable expression of feeling" over the general's removal. Loyd Harris of Prairie du Chien, then a young captain, said the line officers, the captains and lieutenants of the various companies, "on the impulse of the moment assembled and signed a paper resigning their commissions. We took this to our Colonel, Lysander Cutler, afterwards a general. He begged us to with-draw it, as such action would have a very marked effect among the men, and if disaffection started among the officers of the Iron Brigade, no one could tell where it would stop." The officers withdrew to talk the matter over. "There was a general inclination to let those who opposed McClellan get through the war the best way they could, but finally we came to the conclusion that we were fighting for the country, and not for any individual, and withdrew our resignations." Harris concluded: "The Iron Brigade served loyally throughout the remainder of the war, but the old enthusiasm was never seen after the retirement of McClellan from the command, and the spontaneous cheers that greeted him whenever he appeared were never afterwards heard."

Some men in ranks would later deny the incident had occurred. After Harris talked with a St. Louis newspaper reporter in 1887, editor Jerome Watrous of the *Milwaukee Sunday Telegraph* (in 1862 a noncommissioned officer in the Sixth Wisconsin) reprinted the interview under the headline "Rather Sensational." Watrous, saying he was unaware of any such confrontation, contended the resignation threat was overstated and Harris was obviously "misrepresented." But in 1890, with the publication of his memoirs, Rufus Dawes credited Cutler's "known determination of character" as the "restraining influence" in preventing the mass resignation of the veteran line officers of the Iron Brigade.

The turmoil of the Wisconsin officers was typical. Following McClellan's removal, rumors swept the camps—from wild tales of soldiers throwing down their arms and declaring they would fight no longer to an unconfirmed story of a high-ranking officer telling McClellan, "Lead us to Washington, General. We will follow you there." Gibbon wrote he saw "nothing of this kind, myself, but I heard a good deal of talk calculated to produce apprehensions of the gravest character." Jerome Watrous of the Sixth Wisconsin recalled "whispers that there was a move set in motion by some of the officers . . . to reorganize the army according to their own notion, march to Washington and demand the restoration of McClellan." A "lieutenant colonel then in the Iron Brigade," said Watrous, was "approached with a view of getting his cooperation. His emphatic answer may have had a good deal to do with the abandonment of the revolutionary scheme."

Lewis Kent of Beloit, who rose from ranks to be the final commander of the Sixth Wisconsin, never believed it. "I was an enlisted man at the time and was as hot as any one at the removal of Little Mac, and if our officers intended to resign they took previous good care not to let the men know of their purposes," Kent wrote later with some anger. "We would have made their exit from 'the old Sixth' one that they would have remembered all their lives." A veteran of the Second Wisconsin said he saw veteran soldiers "look depressed, and express dissatisfaction, who never did so before." He concluded: "Whether McClellan had been as successful as he should have been or not, he had the confidence and admiration of the best soldiers in the army to a remarkable degree. His name was referred to with an enthusiasm, and even brave men shed tears on the occasion of his leaving." A Twenty-fourth Michigan soldier wrote home at the time of what he called the "great sensation." Although the army, he explained, "has great confidence in B. [Burnside], still Mc has the hearts of the army. They saw the army utterly demoralized and beaten under Pope. They saw Mc take the army, reorganize it and in two weeks from the time of its defeat [at Second Bull Run in August] utterly rout the victorious Rebel army in Md. . . . [T]he removal has knocked the heart out of the men. Still I hope for the best."[2]

Perhaps the officers were ready to take their regiments and brigades and march on Washington with McClellan at their head to seize the government; perhaps not. Certainly such an action by the common soldier in ranks was less likely. But it could be that at no time in the nation's history was the Republic so threatened by a military takeover. In the excitement and anger and debate, George McClellan typically stayed distant; perhaps any quick and decisive action was beyond his temperament. "Little Mac" accepted his removal with proper dignity, urged all to support Burnside, and quietly left the army never to return. "Of course, it was out of the question for McClellan not have heard some of the discontent expressed so freely, but his bearing was admirable," said Gibbon. "He checked imprudent expressions, when he heard them, assuring every one about him in a cheerful tone that everything would come out right in the end." Jerome Watrous wrote his hometown newspaper that it "was with feelings of deepest sorrow mingled with disgust that the men heard of the displacement of Gen'l McClellan. . . . The general query is, why was he taken from us at such a time, if at all? The prevailing opinion among the officers and men is that the Administration is awfully inefficient, beside having no inclination to do that which will tend to hasten the termination of the war." On November 10, Watrous wrote: "Little Mac commenced his farewell visit to his army. All day as he came in sight the air was rent with the heartiest cheers. Monday will long be remembered by this shamefully abused army. The last time Abraham [Lincoln] visited his children, they gave him a very cool reception, but I venture the next will be more so." Col. Edward Bragg of the Sixth Wisconsin expressed the feeling of most of the soldiers—"Little Mac is gone, and my heart and hopes have gone with him."[3]

In any light the decision to remove McClellan was first and foremost an attempt by Lincoln to hasten an end to the war. But he also understood it carried far-reaching political implications. The president, a Republican, and the general, a Democrat, were at odds over very fundamental questions. Lincoln had radically expanded the war by attacking slavery directly with his Emancipation Proclamation, while McClellan clung to the notion of compromise to restore the Union, even if it meant keeping slavery. It was as if the two men had switched roles—the general trying to dictate political policy, the president driving the war effort. McClellan always feared that a smashing Federal victory might prevent the negotiated peace and restoration of the Union. What he and other officers never grasped was that such decisions were not theirs to make. That was clearly shown by statements voiced freely at headquarters that the army must somehow be protected against the very government that created it, even to the point of military action. When such grumbling reached Washington and Lincoln was forced to sack a minor officer for careless statements that had became public, for example, McClellan promptly issued a general order reminding the soldiers of the necessity for military subordination to civil authority. The remedy for "political errors," McClellan explained, "is to be found only in the action of the people at the polls." That the order was released and published in the newspapers just before pending elections was a smug attempt by the general commanding the nation's most important army to influence a political outcome.

If all the talk smelled of treason, McClellan and others in the Army of the Potomac would have been astonished by such accusation. They believed, by their service and patriotism, they had earned a voice in the conduct of the war. It was that very feeling that would create a formidable obstacle in coming months because the young officers trained by "Little Mac" in the Washington camps were never quite able to shake off his spell. Even U. S. Grant found he had to handle the Army of the Potomac with kid gloves when he was brought east in 1864 to fashion the hard and decisive victory sought by Lincoln.

What happened those troubled hours in the Army of the Potomac was a turning point in the American story. Taking just the view from headquarters, or from Washington, it would be easy to dismiss the threat, but the letters and the journals and the diaries from the camps told a different story—the volunteers had come face to face with a military takeover of the elected government of the United States and looked away. All the death and suffering and hardship had come to a crossroads just as significant as Charleston Harbor and Fort Sumter or the green at Lexington, and that it had reached that point at all was due to the European military tradition embraced by McClellan with his bright uniforms, retinue of aides, and grand pronouncements. The Army of the Potomac created by "Little Mac" was always a strange mix of European *élan* and American pluck; no other American army—before, then, or since—has been quite like it.

The young soldiers desperately admired the little general the newspapers hailed as "the young Napoleon," but from the earliest days of the Republic Americans had looked ahead, not back. The new nation was fashioned in the image of farmer-soldiers rushing from their fields to win independence against the finest professional army in the world. It was a place where backwoods Wisconsin boys living in the Lemonweir River valley would not find it out of place to call themselves "Minute Men" or immigrant Germans at Milwaukee a "Citizens' Corps." The men risking lives to restore the Union recognized intuitively what the new nation represented and that a professional army of influence had no place in it. In the Old World what was suggested would be less threatening, but citizen-volunteers were hesitant to relinquish freedoms to someone even as admired as McClellan. The "Republic's patriotic children" (as the fallen Edwin Brown styled his comrades) would have a government that was servant not master. It was in those camps—amid angry words and hot emotions—the soldiers made the decision that, despite more suffering and death to come, there would be no turning back. It was in those camps time seemingly stood still as the soldiers decided between the limited war of "Little Mac" and the total war of Lincoln. It was in those camps the citizen-volunteers turned "McClellan's Army" into "Mr. Lincoln's Army"—a truly *national* army. And it was in those camps the "Boys of '61" abandoned their hero worship of George Brinton McClellan and accepted the nation being forged in the vision of Abraham Lincoln. No longer would it be just a war to restore the Union as it was but also a war to purge the United States of slavery and to fashion what Lincoln a few months later at a place called Gettysburg would call a "new birth of freedom."

That it was a birth sanctified by soldier blood was always understood. After Antietam, wounded George Fairfield of the Sixth Wisconsin wrote his sister, "I am just as ardent, and my hope of crushing the rebellion just as strong as ever. I have enlisted in the cause and without any compulsion or dissention I will go to the bitter end if I know that every pace was so much nearer the jaws of death. . . . I never want to see the North succomb." Edward Bragg used hard words in a letter to his wife: "The 'Iron Brigade' is sound to the core. We . . . will fight Copperheads at home, & Secesh across the lines. . . . We have no sympathy for treason anywhere, and but mighty little faith in the gilded stay at home, and talking patriotism. There can be but one peace, and that the result of victory over the Rebellious States, that will satisfy us. Compromise meets no favor here. 'Subjugation or Submission' is the doctrine, and we are ready to fight for it, as long as we have a musket & a cartridge." Rufus Dawes, writing to his uncle, Ohio Congressman William Cutler, had the clearest view: "For myself, I see much that is encouraging in the long continuance of the war. The more I come in contact with Southern ideas and institutions, the more firmly I become convinced that there can be no understanding between us so long as a vestige of their accursed institution of slavery remains. I expect no peace until its destruction is accomplished. Two years of bloody and unsuccessful war have brought our people to a point that they could have reached in no other way. They are willing to give us the men and the money, the power, and I say, do not let us stop short of our destiny, the entire destruction of slavery."

In ranks, said Lewis Kent of the Sixth Wisconsin, the men fought "for principles far higher than the love embodied in the person of their favorite commander." The soldiers of not only the Iron Brigade but also the rest of the Army of the Potomac, Bragg would observe later, thinking of those grim days of McClellan's removal, had reached that point where they would "march by night and fight by day, undismayed, unfaltering. No matter whether their choice of leadership was respected, no lisp of disloyalty ever arose from their ranks. But they pushed on through the shot and the shell, across the march and the swamp, up the mountain side and against fortifications, always certain, like true fatalists that the end would come, if not to-day, then to-morrow; and if not to-morrow, some other day, and the Government would be restored."[4]

By mid-November, the army was again marching with a new general in command, and Dawes wrote his uncle, "There will be another bloody battle. Nothing less will appease our valiant 'stay-at-home rangers.'. . . Wait and see how much better Burnside does, before 'rejoicing' over the removal of McClellan."[5] Haversacks were again empty. "While making so many changes the powers that be seemed to forget that the men could not live without rations," a Sixth Wisconsin soldier grumbled. "We reached the point of starvation before rations were furnished us." The

Sauk County boys subsisted on a sheep foraged by Amos Johnson of Baraboo and, they said to one another with a smile, "It was mutton or nothing." A few weeks before, as the army returned to Virginia, a weary Badger wrote in his diary that it was the second time his brigade had crossed the Potomac: "May God bless us in making this the last time and that this war will soon come to an end."[6]

But that day was still far off.

Somewhere ahead for the Wisconsin men were such grim places as Fredericksburg, FitzHugh Crossing, Gettysburg, Hatcher's Run, and Appomattox Court House. Then, finally, the dark road started so long ago in 1861 would spread out to Milwaukee and Ontario and Mauston and Prairie du Chien and all the places they called home.

NOTES

⊥. Gettysburg

1. In his July 19, 1863, report to Wisconsin Adj. Gen. Augustus Gaylord, Dawes put his regimental loss at 165. The breakdown included two officers killed and six wounded, 27 enlisted men killed and 105 wounded, and 25 men missing. Records, Sixth Wisconsin Infantry, State Historical Society of Wisconsin.

2. Lance J. Herdegen and William J. K. Beaudot, *In the Bloody Railroad Cut at Gettysburg* (Dayton, Ohio, 1990).

3. Rufus R. Dawes, *Service with the Sixth Wisconsin Volunteers* (Marietta, Ohio, 1890), p. 159.

4. Jerome A. Watrous, "Of One Day's Work," *Milwaukee Telegraph*, October 28, 1893. Of the Twenty-fourth Michigan, Watrous wrote, "It was not until the battle of Gettysburg that the boys of the Twenty-fourth were adopted into the family of the Iron Brigade." The Twenty-fourth Michigan had not joined the Western unit until October 8, 1862.

5. John W. Busey and David G. Martin, *Regimental Strengths and Losses at Gettysburg* (Hightown, N.J., 1986), pp. 265–266. The authors cite lower numbers but rank the Twenty-fourth Michigan as the Union regiment with the greatest total loss at Gettysburg (363), the greatest number killed (67), and the greatest number wounded (210).

6. Dawes, *Service*, p. 184; Alan T. Nolan, *The Iron Brigade* (New York, 1961), pp. 256, 365–366 n. 68; William W. Dudley, *The Iron Brigade at Gettysburg, 1878, Official Report of the Part Borne by the 1st Brigade, 1st Division, 1st Army Corps* (Cincinnati, 1879); William F. Fox, *Regimental Losses in the American Civil War* (Albany, N.Y., 1889), p. 117.

7. Dawes, *Service*, pp. 172–173, 182.

8. John A. Kress, "At Gettysburg," *Missouri Republican*, St. Louis, December 4, 1886. Kress was an officer with the Ninety-fourth New York Infantry.

9. George W. Downing, diary, July 4, 1863, private collection. Downing enlisted February 26, 1862, in Company H and was transferred to Company K on February 28, 1864. He was mustered out with the Sixth Wisconsin on July 14, 1865.

10. Charles Dow, *Portage Register*, August 1, 1863; Charles Walker, diary, July 4, 1863, private collection. Dow enlisted in the Portage Light Guard, Company G, Second Wisconsin Infantry. After the war he returned to Portage, where he served a term as postmaster. He died at Everett, Wash., in 1907. Walker, a native of Heptonstall, Yorkshire, England, came to America in 1858 and settled in Reedsburg, Wis. He served in Company B, Seventh Wisconsin. He died in 1902.

11. Dawes, *Service*, p. 179.

12. George Fairfield, diary, July 4, 1863, George Fairfield Papers, State Historical Society of Wisconsin. Fairfield, of DeSoto, Wis., enlisted in the "Prairie du Chien Volunteers," which became Company C, Sixth Wisconsin. He sur-

vived the war and later wrote several accounts of his experiences for various veteran newspapers. In the preface to his diary, he wrote: "This book is not written for public perusal. It is written for the perusal of friends and for my own meditation hereafter if I should live to see this wretched war close. But it is to be expected that many others will examine its pages, who are not acquainted with a soldier's life in the field and consequently not ready or unwilling to believe such unexpected and almost impossible things to be true as must be related in the following about the movements of a vast army. . . . I shall tell nothing but what is strictly true and that I shall do as genteel as possible. I do not now know what I shall write but it will be an every day account of whatever passed. Respectfully to the reader, George Fairfield."

13. Jerome A. Watrous, letter to Rufus Dawes, December 27, 1894, Rufus Dawes Papers, State Historical Society of Wisconsin. Watrous wrote: "You, as a soldier, through and through, as a patriot; as a Christian gentleman, as a man who never set anything but good example to the soldiers, did more than [Lysander] Cutler, [Edward] Bragg, [Frank] Haskell and [John] Gibbon to make the Sixth Wisconsin what it was, the noblest band of patriots that ever marched and fought."

14. Jerome A. Watrous, *Richard Epps and Other Stories* (Milwaukee, 1906), p. 102.

15. James P. Sullivan, "The Iron Brigade at Gettysburg," *Milwaukee Sunday Telegraph,* December 28, 1884.

16. Dawes, *Service,* pp. 154, 159–161; Rufus Dawes, letter to Mary Beman Gates, July 4, 1863.

17. Mary Frances (Dawes) Beech, "Mary Beman Gates Dawes," in Mary Walton Ferris, compiler, *Dawes-Gates Ancestral Lines, A Memorial Volume Containing the American Ancestry of Mary Beman Gates-Dawes,* vol. 2 (privately printed, 1931).

18. Dawes, *Service,* pp. 140–141; Beech, "Mary Beman Gates Dawes," p. 4.

19. Mary Beman Gates, letters to Rufus Dawes, July 4 and July 7, 1863; Dawes, *Service,* pp. 162–163.

20. Jerome A. Watrous, untitled manuscript, Jerome A. Watrous Papers, State Historical Society of Wisconsin. A fifer in the Seventh Wisconsin, Ludolph Longhenry, described it as "a serenade of pretty music." Ludolph Longhenry, diary, July 4, 1863, private collection.

2. Marching Day and Night

1. Longhenry, diary, July 5, 1863.

2. Fairfield, diary, July 5, 1863.

3. Frederick Neff manuscript, cited in Donald L. Smith, *The Twenty- fourth Michigan of the Iron Brigade* (Harrisburg, Pa., 1962), p. 184.

4. Downing, diary, July 6, 1863; Rufus R. Dawes, letter to Mary Beman Gates, July 6, 1863; Dawes, *Service,* p. 161.

5. Fairfield, diary, July 7–8, 1863. George Downing, diary, July 7- 8, 1863; George H. Otis, *The Second Wisconsin Infantry,* ed. Alan D. Gaff (Dayton, Ohio, 1984), p. 88 (the Otis history of his regiment appeared in 1880 editions of *The Milwaukee Sunday Telegraph*); *War of the Rebellion, Official Records of the Union and Confederate Armies,* series 1, vol. 27, part 1, pp. 80, 84; Meade to Maj. Gen. H. W. Halleck, July 8, 1863—2 P.M.

6. Rufus R. Dawes, letter to Mary Beman Gates, July 9, 1863; Dawes, *Service,* p. 184.

7. Dawes added: "One thing will appear, that the Army of the Potomac

saved Pennsylvania and the North. Not one shot was fired at Gettysburg by the Pennsylvania militia."

8. Longhenry, diary, July 14, 1863; Rufus Dawes, letter to Mary Beman Gates, July 12, 1863; Dawes, *Service,* p. 186.

9. John Hay, *Lincoln and the Civil War Letters and Dairies of John Hay,* ed. Tyler Dennett (New York, 1939), p. 667.

10. Dawes, *Service,* p. 182; Dawes, letter to Mary Beman Gates, July 27, 1863. Twenty-five years afterward, Dawes wrote: "There has been discussion upon the question whether General Meade should have attacked the rebel army in its position near Williamsport, Maryland, on the thirteenth of July. It is my belief that our army would have been repulsed if they had attacked the enemy in this entrenched position." Dawes, *Service,* p. 187. In 1886, John A. Kress, who had served on the staff of First Division commander James Wadsworth, reached the same conclusion: "After three days' fighting, marching and indescribably hard and exhausting work for the whole army, reserves included, it seemed as if we had just about reached the limit of human endurance and must have rest." He added, perhaps with faded memory of those weary hours: "I do believe, however, that if [Generals U.S.] Grant or [Phil] Sheridan had commanded our army at Gettysburg, Gen. Lee's army would never have recrossed the Potomac." John A. Kress, *Missouri Republican,* December 4, 1886.

11. Robert K. Beecham, "Adventures of an Iron Brigade Man" (paste-up of a series of articles appearing in *The National Tribune*), Washington, D.C., 1902. Beecham was exchanged. He was discharged December 15, 1863, to accept promotion as lieutenant of the Twenty-third U.S. Colored Troops.

12. George Fink, letter to his brother, printed in *The Milwaukee Sentinel,* July 20, 1863.

13. Watrous, *Richard Epps,* p. 9.

14. Charles Dow, letter, July 17, 1863; *Portage Register,* August 1, 1863.

3. Greenhorn Patriots

1. Of Rufus's middle initial, a family biographer said one other rendition was discovered but by "what process of reasoning is unknown." In the Library of Congress catalog, Dawes's *Service with the Sixth Wisconsin Volunteers* was originally credited to "Rufus Robinson Dawes," but the family successfully petitioned to have it changed to "Rufus R. Dawes." *A Memoir, Rufus R. Dawes* (New York, 1900), pp. 11–31; Rev. William E. Roe, "Brigadier General Rufus R. Dawes," in *Dawes-Gates Ancestral Lines,* vol. 1 (privately printed, 1943), p. 3.

2. Dawes, *Service,* p. 47; Orin Grant Libby, *Significance of the Lead and Shot Trade in Early Wisconsin History* (Madison, 1895), pp. 293-334; La Vern J. Rippley, *The Immigrant Experience in Wisconsin* (Boston, 1985), p. 1; Frank L. Klement, *Wisconsin and the Civil War* (Madison, 1963), pp. 4–10; Richard Current, *The History of Wisconsin: The Civil War Era* (Madison, 1976), pp. 81, 428–429; James P. Sullivan, *Milwaukee Sunday Telegraph,* May 9, 1886.

3. For a description of the raising of the companies of the Sixth Wisconsin, see Herdegen and Beaudot, *Railroad Cut,* pp. 43–71; Michael H. Fitch, *Echoes of the Civil War as I Hear Them* (New York, 1905), pp. 18- 19; Michael H. Fitch, "Old Company B," *Milwaukee Sunday Telegraph,* March 24, 1889.

4. James P. Sullivan, "Old Company K," *Milwaukee Sunday Telegraph,* May 16, 1886.

5. Ibid., March 18, 1883; [Loyd G. Harris], "Army Music," *Milwaukee Sunday*

Telegraph, November 12, 1882; I. F. Kelly, letter to Rufus Dawes, August 2, 1892, Dawes Papers, SHSW.

6. John Davidson, letter to George Fairfield, August 28, 1864.

7. Fitch, *Echoes*, p. 37. "The record of the Sixth Wisconsin in the war was one of exceptional merit. When it came into actual service in the field, it proved to be one of the finest volunteer regiments."

8. The field officers and staff of the Sixth Wisconsin Infantry upon muster into Federal service included Lysander Cutler, colonel, Milwaukee; Julius Atwood, lieutenant colonel, Madison; Benjamin Sweet, major, Chilton; and Frank A. Haskell, adjutant, Madison. The companies and home counties were: A—Sauk County Rifles, Sauk County; B—Prescott Guards, Pierce County; C—Prairie du Chien Volunteers, Crawford County; D—Montgomery Guards, Milwaukee County; E—Bragg's Rifles, Fond du Lac, Outagamie, and Shawano counties; F—Citizens' Corps, Milwaukee County; G—Beloit Star Rifles, Rock County; H—Buffalo County Rifles, Buffalo and Trempealeau counties; I—Anderson Guards, Juneau and Dane counties, and K—Lemonweir Minute Men, Juneau County. Of the 14,903 soldiers of Wisconsin's first 13 regiments, 10,334 were American; 2,178 from the German states, including Switzerland and Holland, of whom 90 percent were German; 677 Irish; 239 Norwegians and Swedes; 487 English, Canadians, Welsh, and Scotch; and 97 of other nationalities. *Annual Reports of the Adjutant General of the State of Wisconsin for the Years 1860, 1861, 1862, 1863, 1864* (Madison, 1912), p. 83.

9. Jerome Watrous, "Appleton Contribution," manuscript, Watrous Papers, SHSW.

10. H. W. Rood, *Company E and the Twelfth Wisconsin in the War for the Union* (Milwaukee, 1893), pp. 50–51; Dan Webster and Don Cameron, *Story of the First Wisconsin Battery* (Washington, D.C., 1907), p. 7; Ethel Alice Hurn, *Wisconsin Women in the War between the States* (Madison, 1911), p. 6.

11. [Jerome Watrous], "Long Ago Interesting Event," manuscript, Watrous Papers, SHSW. Writing 45 years afterward, Watrous questioned: "I wonder how many of the Milwaukeeans who watched the Sixth as it paraded there are still living? I wonder if any of those charming waiters have read this article and recall that pleasant event and those exciting days." *The Milwaukee Sentinel* on July 29, 1861, gave details of the route: "The Regiment will march from the depot through Second street to Fowler, up Fowler to Third through Third to Clybourn. Line to be formed on Clybourn, right resting on West Water Street. As soon as the line is formed the Regiment will march across Huron Street bridge to Main, up Main to Mason, up Mason to Jackson, up Jackson to Division, down Division to Main, down Main to Oneida, across Oneida street bridge up Wells to Fourth, down Fourth to Clybourn, down Clybourn to West Water. The Public are requested to give the military use of Clybourn street while the line is being formed. . . ."

12. [Jerome Watrous], "Some Good Stories," *Milwaukee Sunday Telegraph*, April 8, 1883; Sullivan, "Old Company K."

13. F. H. Magdeburg, "The Women of the North—1861–1865," in *War Papers Read before the Commandery of the State of Wisconsin, Military Order of the Loyal Legion of the United States*, vol. 2 (Milwaukee, 1896), p. 199; Hurn, *Wisconsin Women*, pp. 80–81.

4. The Volunteer Army of 1861

1. Jerome Watrous, *Appleton Crescent*, August 20, 1861; Jerome Watrous,

"Old Days in Washington," *Milwaukee Telegraph*, January 14, 1890; J. H. Stine, *History of the Army of the Potomac* (Philadelphia, 1892), p. 100; Dawes, *Service*, pp. 19–20; *Milwaukee Sentinel*, August 26, 1861. Stine served in the Nineteenth Indiana Infantry.

2. Dawes, *Service*, p. 30; *Milwaukee Sentinel*, August 26, 1861; Jerome Watrous, manuscript, Jerome A. Watrous Papers, State Historical Society of Wisconsin.

3. "Daughters of the Regiment" were often found in European armies, particularly the French. Often soldiers' wives or relatives, the women acted as nurses or sutlers and were respected. Mark M. Boatner, *Civil War Dictionary* (New York, 1959), p. 880; *Green Bay Advocate*, September 5, 1861; Hurn, *Wisconsin Women*, pp. 100–102; *State Journal*, Madison, September 4, 1861; *Green Bay Advocate*, October 3, 1861. One soldier correspondent said Miss Wilson sometimes appeared "in full uniform, consisting of red Zouave jacket, short skirt, Turkish trousers, neatly fitting boots and jaunty hat; but her usual costume is a water-proof tweed dress of the same pattern. Her father is a man of some wealth . . . and provides her with means so that she maintains herself entirely independent of the Regiment, messing at the field officers' table, and living in a tent of her own, with a female companion. Of course you will ask what sweetheart she is following to the wars, but of that I cannot tell you. She tells me that one of the companies here is made up entirely from her own neighborhood, and equipped to some extent by her father, and that she has come here to see to their welfare mainly, and in some sort of love for this gypsy and adventurous life. I am sure that she is liked by all, and is as safe here as if under her own father's roof." She was with the Fifth Wisconsin as late as January 1862, when it was noted by a soldier correspondent she was quite ill, "which elicited much sympathy."

4. Watrous, *Appleton Crescent*, August 20, 1861.

5. Nolan, *Iron Brigade*, pp. 20–21; James P. Sullivan, "Charge of the Iron Brigade at Fitzhugh's Crossing," *Milwaukee Sunday Telegraph*, September 30, 1883; *Green Bay Advocate*, October 3, 1861.

6. Jerome Watrous, "Heroes of Undying Fame," *Milwaukee Telegraph*, September 26, 1896; *The State Journal*, Madison, September 4, 1861; Ezra J. Warner, *Generals in Blue: Lives of Union Commanders* (Baton Rouge, La., 1964); *Dictionary of Wisconsin Biography* (Madison, 1961), p. 207; Dawes, *Service*, p. 27. King would resign his commission in 1863 because of ill health. He took his post as minister to the Papal States, serving until 1867. He spent the rest of his life in New York City, where he died October 13, 1876. Rufus King Papers, Carroll College, Waukesha, Wis.

7. *Green Bay Advocate*, September 19, 1861; John Marsh, "Early Days of the War," *Milwaukee Sunday Telegraph*, December 6, 1886; *Roster of Wisconsin Volunteers, War of the Rebellion, 1861–1865*, vol. 1 (Madison, 1886), pp. 49, 500; Dawes, *Service*, p. 25 n.; Herdegen and Beaudot, *Railroad Cut*, pp. 119–124; Edwin A. Brown, letter to his wife, December 15, 1861. The officer mentioned by Marsh was never identified, although two captains and six lieutenants of the Sixth Wisconsin resigned at about the time indicated. The wartime letters of Edwin Brown are held in two private collections.

5. Alas, It Was a Dream

1. Longhenry, diary, February 26, 1862; Julius Murray, letter, undated, Julius Murray Papers, State Historical Society of Wisconsin.

2. The volunteer infantry regiment was made up of 10 companies each consisting of 97 men and three officers. There were usually four regiments to a brigade and four brigades to a division.

3. Watrous, *Telegraph*, September 26, 1896.

4. Levi B. Raymond, diary, October 4, 1861, private collection; *Appleton Crescent*, October, 19, 1861; *Green Bay Advocate*, October 10, 1861; Edwin A. Brown, letter to his wife, October 2, 1861, private collection.

5. *Annual Report of the Adjutant General*, p. 51; [Loyd G. Harris], "Music in the Army," *Milwaukee Sunday Telegraph*, March 11, 1883.

6. Watrous, *Appleton Crescent*, August 20, 1861; Edward Bragg, letter to Earl Rogers, April 3, 1900; O[rson] B. Curtis, *History of the Twenty-fourth Michigan of the Iron Brigade* (Detroit, 1891), p. 455. The unattributed quotation is from a speech by Phil Cheek, Company A, Sixth Wisconsin, to a group of Michigan veterans.

7. Charles King, "Gainesville, 1862," in *War Papers*, vol. 3, (Milwaukee, 1903), p. 271. King was the son of Rufus King.

8. Nolan, *Iron Brigade*, pp. 9–10. The Second Wisconsin's first colonel was S. Park Coon of Milwaukee. No sooner had the regiment reached Washington than the officers called on the colonel and requested his resignation. Coon refused, but remained in Washington when the Second marched off under command of Lt. Col. Henry W. Peck of Green County, who had some military training at West Point although he was not a graduate of the U.S. Military Academy. Coon rejoined the regiment on the eve of Bull Run. To avoid a command problem, Brig. Gen. William T. Sherman named Coon to his personal staff and wrote later he "rendered good service." Coon resigned July 30, 1861. Peck and Maj. Duncan McDonald of Milwaukee, a former Wisconsin militia colonel, were criticized in the press for their conduct at Bull Run. Both resigned several weeks after the battle. Shortly after the Sixth Wisconsin's arrival at Washington, Lt. Edwin Brown wrote: "Col. Coon though not in command of the Second Wis. Reg. behaved like a hero while the man (Peck) who was placed in his place made extraordinary time for the long bridge [to Washington]. Col. Coon was acting as aid to Genl. Sherman and rallied the Second Twice while in full retreat and under fire. . . . The secessionists call it [First Bull Run] *Yankees Run*. . . ." Edwin A. Brown, letter to his parents, undated.

9. Edwin A. Brown, letter to his father, August 28, 1861.

10. Edward Bragg, letter to his wife, undated; *Green Bay Advocate,* August 29, 1861.

11. *Columbus Weekly Journal,* January 22, 1862.

12. [Loyd G. Harris], "A Celebrated Case," *Milwaukee Sunday Telegraph,* August 5, 1883; [Jerome A. Watrous], "The Old Brigade," *Milwaukee Sunday Telegraph,* September 27, 1885; Hurn, *Wisconsin Women,* p. 105; "General Bragg," *Milwaukee Telegraph,* February 25, 1899; Curtis, *Twenty-fourth,* p. 466; [Loyd G. Harris], *Milwaukee Sunday Telegraph,* March 11, 1883. The nickname "Hungry Second," Watrous wrote, stemmed from an incident early in the war before the brigade was organized. A visitor inquired where he would find the Second Wisconsin and was "told that if he went to the front, and out beyond where the Union army found it dangerous to move, then climbed the tallest tree in the neighborhood, he would probably see the boys he was after away off in some cornfield in front helping themselves." Capt. Gabriel Bouck of Oshkosh was the son of a New York governor and nephew of a congressman. He was remembered as "the bachelor captain, eccentric in his ways and manner of dress, yet decidedly popular; a safe man to follow." Bouck served as Wisconsin attorney general and a member of the state legislature before the war. He was promoted

to colonel of the 18th Wisconsin on April 29, 1862. Otis, *Second Wisconsin*, pp. 30, 40. The Otis history appeared in 1880 editions of *The Milwaukee Sunday Telegraph.*

13. Hurn, *Wisconsin Women*, p. 105; *Milwaukee Sentinel*, October 4, 1861; *Fox Lake Gazette*, January 23, 1862; Longhenry, diary, October 6, 1861; *Columbus Weekly Journal*, January 10, 1862.

14. Watrous, *Telegraph*, September 26, 1896; [Harris], *Telegraph*, March 11, 1883; Longhenry, diary, December 25, 1861; *Janesville Daily Gazette*, July 10, 1862.

15. Longhenry, diary, February 8, 1862; Edwin A. Brown, letter to his father, November 24, 1861; Julius A. Murray, letter to his brother, John, September 24, 1861, Murray Papers, SHSW. Murray and his wife had five children; the oldest, Mary, was 14 in 1853 when the family moved to Wisconsin from Indiana. Murray's son, Lucius, who served with him in the Sixth Wisconsin, was shot in the back and killed by a drunken soldier near the end of the war. He was buried in Woodland Cemetery in Shawano.

16. Stephen Vesper, letter to his sister, Clarissa, November 15, 1861, as quoted in Rena M. Knight, "The Civil War Letters of Stephen Vesper," *North-South Trader*, May–June 1989, pp. 31–32.

17. Marsh, *Telegraph*, December 6, 1886; Edwin Brown, letter to his parents, February 9, 1862; Dawes, *Service*, pp. 34–35; [John Kellogg], *Mauston Star*, November 20, 1861; Philip Cheek and Mair Pointon, *History of the Sauk County Riflemen, Known as Company "A," Sixth Wisconsin Veteran Volunteer Infantry, 1861–1865* (1909), p. 22; Sullivan, *Telegraph*, May 23, 1886.

18. Dawes, *Service*, pp. 23, 39; James M. Perry, diary, March 11, 1862. Perry served with Company A, Seventh Wisconsin. He enlisted June 12, 1861, from Kilbourn City, later Wisconsin Dells, and was detached to serve as an ambulance driver. James M. Perry Papers, State Historical Society of Wisconsin.

19. Dawes, *Service*, pp. 32–33. "One great reason that there is so much gambling in camp is that the soldiers have no other way of spending their time," one soldier said.

20. John H. Cook, "Cook's Time in the Army," manuscript, August 9, 1865, p. 1. John H. Cook Papers, State Historical Society of Wisconsin.

21. John H. Cook, "The Tough One Again," *Milwaukee Sunday Telegraph*, April 8, 1883.

22. [Charles Robinson], *Green Bay Advocate*, January 2, 1862. Robinson served as brigade quartermaster. He was editor of the *Advocate* before the war.

23. Louis Blenker, a leading member of the 1848 revolutionary government in Bavaria, emigrated to the United States in 1849. A farmer and New York City businessman, he was commissioned colonel of the 8th New York and saw limited service in the First Battle of Bull Run. Blenker was discharged in March 1863 and died October 31, 1863, of injuries received in a fall from his horse earlier in the war. Boatner, *Civil War Dictionary*, pp. 69–70.

24. *Milwaukee Sentinel*, November 20, 1861.

25. Longhenry, diary, September 17, 1861; Edwin A. Brown, letter to his wife, undated. A resident of Fond du Lac, Brown married Ruth R. Pier on November 14, 1853. The couple had two sons, Louie and Edwin Pier, and a daughter, Hattie. Brown left his law practice to enlist in "Bragg's Rifles," Company E, Sixth Wisconsin, in May 1861 and was promoted to captain on September 18, 1861. "He was formerly a student of Lawrence University, and a young man of more than ordinary ability. He left a good law business at home to serve his country, and all who knew him as a soldier and officer, knew him but to honor and respect," a comrade wrote of Brown during the war. Joseph Marston, *Appleton Crescent*, October 25, 1862, Brown Papers.

26. [Harris], *Telegraph*, November 12, 1882; [Jerome Watrous], *Milwaukee Sunday Telegraph*, August 24, 1884. The description is from Watrous.

27. Edwin A. Brown, letter to his wife, February 2, 1862.

28. Wallace Henton, letter, undated; Edwin A. Brown, letter to his wife, March 1, 1862. Henton was one of five brothers to serve in the Union army—three in Company A, Seventh Wisconsin. He enlisted at Otsego on January 15, 1862.

29. Longhenry, diary, January 16 and 24, 1862. On February 15, 1862, Longhenry noted: "Miss A. L. is not married, though she is engaged."

30. Vesper, quoted in Knight, "Civil War Letters," pp. 32–34.

6. Little Mac

1. Almost rounded up was Lt. Edwin Brown of the Sixth Wisconsin. "I was in front of the National Hotel, up comes about fifty men with an officer at the head of them, who stepped up to me in the Gas light and wanted to see my pass," he wrote home. "I told him I had none . . . and he said it made no difference to him, he was ordered to arrest every one running at large. . . . [A]bout that time a Pennsylvania Officer was passing by a little tight and in arresting him there was a little confusion. I slipped into the Hotel, engaged a room and got to bed as quick as I could. They made search for me, but the landlord covered my back." Edwin A. Brown, letter to his wife, August 9, 1861.

2. Stephen W. Sears, *George B. McClellan: The Young Napoleon* (New York, 1988).

3. *Mauston Star*, October 23, 1861.

4. Dawes, *Service*, p. 21.

5. Edwin Brown, letter to his parents, November 24, 1861; Edwin Brown, letter to his wife, November 23, 1861; Edward S. Bragg, letter to his wife, November 21, 1861.

6. Jerome A. Watrous, manuscript, Watrous Papers, SHSW.

7. Dawes, *Service*, p. 29.

8. Fitch, *Echoes*, p. 331.

9. Edwin A. Brown, letter to his wife, October 13, 1861.

10. Otis, *Second Wisconsin*, pp. 65, 83–84; William H. Harries, "In the Ranks at Antietam," in Otis, *Second Wisconsin*, p. 270 (typed manuscript is also in the Jerome A. Watrous Papers, SHSW); Fitch, *Echoes*, p. 304.

11. Edward Bragg, speech to an Army of the Potomac reunion at Chicago, date uncertain; the copy of the address was not dated. Edward Bragg Papers, State Historical Society of Wisconsin.

12. John Marsh, "Early Days of the War," *Milwaukee Sunday Telegraph*, December 12, 1886. One Second Wisconsin officer, Thomas Allen, writing long afterward, stated: "I cannot refrain from saying that, in my humble opinion, Gen. McDowell was among the most capable of our army officers. His failure at Bull Run, however, aroused the ghouls of the press to charge him with incapacity, with disloyalty, and with drunkenness—three as baseless charges as were ever aimed at the reputation of a capable, loyal and temperate man. But for these vile slanders he might have had command of the Army of the Potomac, which under him would not have fought only to be repulsed or defeated through all its campaigns until it held its own at Gettysburg." Thomas S. Allen, "The Second Wisconsin at the First Battle of Bull Run," in Otis, *Second Wisconsin*, p. 230.

13. Stine, *Army of the Potomac*, pp. 103–104.

14. John Kellogg and Edwin Brown were classmates at Lawrence College at Appleton, Wisconsin, in 1852.

15. Julius Murray, letter, undated. His father, Capt. Elias Murray, was commissioned as superintendent of the Indians of the Northwest Territory and, in 1851, was the first agent to the Menominees. Born in the East, Captain Murray and family moved to Huntington, Indiana, in 1829. He remained there until 1850, when he moved to Wisconsin.

16. Edwin A. Brown, letter to his wife, September 8, 1861.

7. The Fair Miss Peters

1. Adj. Frank Haskell to Capt. William Lindwurm, October 8, 1861. William Lindwurm Papers, Milwaukee County Historical Society.

2. [Jerome Watrous], "Sleeping on Picket," *Milwaukee Sunday Telegraph*, January 1, 1885.

3. *Milwaukee Sentinel*, December 19, 1861.

4. Hugh Perkins, letter, January 9, 1862, in "Letters of a Civil War Soldier," ed. Marilyn Gardner, prepared for syndication, April 9, 1983, *Christian Science Monitor*. The letter was to Herbert Frisbie, great-grandfather of Gardner.

5. Longhenry, diary, October 7, 1861.

6. Edwin Brown, letter to his wife, December 15, 1861.

7. *Green Bay Advocate*, January 2, 1862.

8. Hugh Perkins, letter, March 1, 1862; Dawes, *Service*, p. 36.

9. Julius Murray, letter, March 17, 1862.

10. Sears, *McClellan*, p. 160.

11. Jerome Watrous, *Appleton Crescent*, June 28, 1862.

12. Dawes, *Service*, pp. 39–40.

13. [Loyd G. Harris], *Milwaukee Sunday Telegraph*, February 13, 1881.

14. Frank A. Haskell, letter to his brothers and sisters, September 22, 1862, Frank Haskell Papers, State Historical Society of Wisconsin; [Albert V. Young], "His Pilgrimage," *Milwaukee Sunday Telegraph*, July 1, 1888 (Young served with Company E); Julius Murray, letter, May 7, 1862.

15. Lucius Murray, letter to his sister, August 1, 1862, Julius A. Murray Papers, State Historical Society of Wisconsin; Horace E. Emerson, letter to his sister, October 9, 1861, private collection; Downing, diary, January 1, 1863; Edward Bragg, letter to his wife, April 15, 1862, Edward Bragg Papers, SHSW. Emerson served in the "Portage Light Guard," Company G, Second Wisconsin. He was born in North Bridgeton, Maine, and moved with the family to Boston some time in the 1850s, and later to Wisconsin. After the war, he settled in St. Paul, Minn.

16. Cheek and Pointon, *Sauk County*, p. 26; Jerome Watrous, *Appleton Crescent*, May 31, 1862; Edward P. Kellogg, "Another Regiment," *Milwaukee Sunday Telegraph*, September 28, 1879.

17. [Loyd G. Harris], "The Fair Miss Peters," *Milwaukee Sunday Telegraph*, January 1, 1883. In the old soldier yarn written for his former comrades, Harris thinly disguised himself as "Grayson," his middle name. The name of the young lady was not Peters, Harris wrote, "but it sounded like that, of a family who lived on the Potomac river, below Belle Plain, Virginia, during the late war." The soldiers were Jesse Adams of Prairie du Chien; John H. Beoman of Madison, who would die in the Confederate prison in Andersonville, Ga., after being captured June 22, 1864; and Alfred R. Withrow of Albany, Ill., *Roster of Wisconsin Volunteers*, vol. 1, pp. 505, 508.

8. Massa Linkum's Men

1. *Green Bay Advocate*, July 10, 1862.

2. James M. Perry, diary, April 22, 1862; Horace Emerson, letter to his sister, May 21, 1862; Edwin Brown, letter to his parents, undated.

3. [Jerome Watrous], *Appleton Crescent*, December 21, 1861.

4. *Green Bay Advocate*, December 19, 1861.

5. *Milwaukee Sentinel*, May 12, 1862.

6. [Loyd G. Harris], "Old Matt. Bernard (Colored)," *Milwaukee Sunday Telegraph*, April 8, 1883.

7. Earl M. Rogers, ed., *Memoirs of Vernon County* (Madison, Wisconsin, 1907), p. 21; Sullivan, *Telegraph*, October 21, 1883.

8. Edward Bragg, letter, June 13, 1863. Bragg was in Washington recovering from a kick from a horse that left him lame and bruised. The badge referred to the red felt disc of the First Army Corps; Horace E. Emerson, letter to his sister Maria, May 21, 1862. Emerson added: ". . . if Wendell Phillips, Horace Greely and the other big guns of that party should show them selves here I would not ans. for thair safety and if seen on a battle field would be shot as quick as a Rebel and it would serve them right. Excuse this Sis if it does not agree with you but I have seen so much of them I get mad every time I think of it." He referred to abolitionist Wendell Phillips, who was active in the American Anti-Slavery Society, and Horace Greeley, editor of the *New York Tribune*.

9. Dawes, *Service*, p. 48.

10. Dawes, *Service*, pp. 121–122. Dawes said the owner of the plantation, whom he said was a refined and cultured man, was a Dr. "Jacob" or "James" Smith. The lady was identified only as "Mrs. Brockenbrough," and, Dawes noted, it was said her husband was a colonel in the Confederate army.

11. Edward P. Kellogg, *Telegraph*, September 28, 1879.

12. [Albert Young], "His Pilgrimage," *Milwaukee Sunday Telegraph*, July 1, 1888.

13. Rufus Dawes, letter, April 26, 1862; Dawes, *Service*, p. 41. Nine months later, Dawes—after the bloody battles of Second Bull Run, South Mountain, Antietam, and Fredericksburg—wrote: "For myself, I see much that is encouraging in the long continuance of the war. The more I come in contact with Southern ideas and institutions, the more firmly I become convinced that there can be no understanding between us so long as a vestige of their accursed institution of slavery remains. I expected no peace until its destruction is accomplished. Two years of bloody and unsuccessful war have brought our people to a point that they could have reached in no other way. They are willing to give us the men and the money, the power, and I say, do not let us stop short of our destiny, the entire destruction of slavery." Rufus R. Dawes, letter to W. P. Cutler, February 24, 1863; Dawes, *Service*, p. 123.

9. The Boss Soldier

1. Levi B. Raymond, diary, March 20, 1862.

2. Augustus Buell, *The Cannoneer: Recollections of Service in the Army of the Potomac* (Washington, D.C., 1897), pp. 12, 17; John Cook, "A Tough One," *Milwaukee Sunday Telegraph*, March 11, 1883. Buell's account has been questioned. Milton W. Hamilton, "Augustus C. Buell, Fraudulent Historian," *Pennsylvania Magazine of History and Biography* 80 (1956), pp. 478–492, documented

that Buell, in fact, did not enlist until August 21, 1863, six weeks after Gettysburg, and then joined the Twentieth New York Cavalry. Author Silas Felton has since demonstrated that Buell's account included solid information and was supported by veterans who were there. Felton concluded Buell's articles were probably based on extensive oral interviews with three Battery B veterans. In addition, Buell's story was published in the major old soldier newspaper of the day, *The National Tribune*, and later reprinted in book form, certainly a path of publication that would be avoided by an author putting together a bogus record. Obscure Wisconsin sources also confirm minor details of Buell's account. Silas Felton, "Pursuing the Elusive 'Cannoneer,'" *Gettysburg Magazine*, no. 9 (July 1993), pp. 33–39.

3. Cook, "Army," p. 4.

4. Buell, *Cannoneer*, pp. 24–25; Jerome Watrous, *Milwaukee Sunday Telegraph*, September 7, 1884.

5. John Gibbon, *Personal Recollections of the Civil War* (New York, 1928), pp. 12–14, 27–28; Buell, *Cannoneer*, pp. 24–26.

6. Cook, "Army," p. 5.

7. [Young], *Telegraph*, July 1, 1888.

8. Jerome Watrous, "Tribute to Adjutant Haskell," in Frank Aretas Haskell, *The Battle of Gettysburg*, 2d ed. (Madison, 1910), pp. xxi–xxviii. Watrous concluded: "As a subsequent adjutant of the Sixth Wisconsin, I am glad of an opportunity to pay tribute to our first adjutant. He was as perfect a soldier as I ever knew—an officer who ought to have been a corps commander immediately after his great achievement at Gettysburg."

9. Haskell, *Gettysburg*, pp. xi–xxiii; Frank L. Byrne and Andrew T. Weaver, eds., *Haskell of Gettysburg* (Madison, 1971), pp. 241–250; [Jerome A. Watrous], "About the Boy Patriots," *Milwaukee Telegraph*, November 27, 1897; Dawes, *Service*, pp. 20–21; *Milwaukee Sentinel*, November 11, 1861.

10. [Jerome Watrous], "Gen. John Gibbon," *Milwaukee Sunday Telegraph*, December 7, 1879; J. O. Johnson, "Army Reminiscences," *Milwaukee Sunday Telegraph*, November 30, 1884.

11. Gibbon, *Recollections*, pp. 27–28.

12. [Watrous], *Telegraph*, September 26, 1896.

13. First Brigade Order Book, Circular, May 13, 1862, National Archives.

14. Gibbon, *Recollections*, p. 37.

15. Edwin Brown, letter to his parents, September 1, 1861. "Our Reg. have also rec'd new blue uniforms so that any grey fatigue suit will be useless, and I shall have to get another fatigue suit or wear my best every day rain or shine."

16. For a description of the distinctive apparel of the brigade, see Howard Michael Madaus, "The Uniform of the Iron Brigade at Gettysburg, July 1, 1863," in Herdegen and Beaudot, *Railroad Cut*, appendix 3, pp. 301–367.

17. Dawes, *Service*, p. 44; Cheek and Pointon, *Sauk County*, p. 27; Fitch, *Echoes*, p. 39. "The next morning after the issue, General Gibbons found the legs of his horse ornamented with white leggings. This was a silent protest against those leggings," wrote Fitch. There was another story, told after the war, by a Second man. Gibbon got even, and it came during a reunion at Boscobel, Wis. Gibbon, in civilian clothing, was passing through the town, heard of the gathering, and stopped off, inquiring if there were any members of the Iron Brigade present. "They brought him one of the old boys of whom the general inquired if he was a member of the Iron Brigade and he said he was." Gibbon smiled. "Well, I am looking for the man." "What man?" questioned the old veteran. "Why the man who put the leggings on my horse when we were opposite Fredericksburg."

"Geewilikins," said the old soldier, and motioning to a group of veterans standing a short distance away, he called, "Come over here, boys, quick, here's Johnny, the War Horse." Harries, "Antietam," p. 557.

18. Dawes, *Service*, p. 45.

19. *Mineral Point Tribune,* October 22, 1861; Jerome Watrous, manuscript, Watrous Papers; *Appleton Crescent,* August 9, 1862.

20. King, in *War Papers*, vol. 2, p. 271.

21. Gibbon, *Recollections*, p. 37.

22. Fitch, *Echoes*, p. 330. Fitch, who left the regiment in July 1862 to become an officer in the Twenty-first Wisconsin, also noted: "The regiment became finely drilled before I left it. But of course that did not foreshadow its fighting qualities. Its real efficiency depended upon the way it was handled under fire by its officers. Its death list of officers tells the real tale of how the men were held under fire in many battles. It was one of the nineteen volunteer regiments in service that lost sixteen or more officers killed or mortally wounded. It is the only Wisconsin regiment which lost as many as sixteen" (pp. 38–39). The figure of 16 officers killed is from Fox, *Regimental Losses*, p. 39.

23. Dawes, *Service*, p. 43.

10. Hindquarters in the Saddle

1. Dawes, *Service*, p. 44; Horace E. Emerson, letter to his sister, Maria, April 19, 1862.

2. Edwin A. Brown, letter to his father, June 15, 1862.

3. Julius Murray, letter, July 5, 1862.

4. Edward P. Kellogg, *Telegraph*, September 28, 1879. Kellogg served with Company C, Second Wisconsin, and was not related to John A. Kellogg of the Sixth Wisconsin. The quotation in the *Telegraph* was from a letter Edward wrote May 24, 1862.

5. *War of the Rebellion, Official Records of the Union and Confederate Armies* (Washington, D.C., 1889–1900), series 1, vol. 1, part 3, pp. 473–474.

6. Dawes, *Service*, p. 51.

7. Mickey of Co. "K" [James Sullivan], "Ready, Aim, Aim Low, Fire," *Milwaukee Sunday Telegraph*, November 4, 1883. Pope denied he used the phrase: "A good deal of cheap wit has been expended upon a fanciful story that I published an order or wrote a letter or made a remark that my 'headquarters would be in the saddle.' It is an expression harmless and innocent enough, but it is even stated that it furnished General Lee with the basis for the only joke of his life. I think it due to army tradition, and to be the comfort of those who have so often repeated the ancient joke in the days long before the civil war, that these later wits should not be allowed with impunity to poach on this well-tilled manor. This venerable joke I first heard when a cadet at West Point . . . and I presume it could be easily traced back to the Crusades and beyond. Certainly I never used this expression or wrote or dictated it, nor does any such expression occur in any order of mine; and as it has perhaps served its time and effected its purpose, it ought to be retired." John Pope, "The Second Battle of Bull Run," in Robert U. Johnson and Clarence C. Buel, eds., *Battles and Leaders of the Civil War*, vol. 2, pp. 493–494.

8. Rufus Dawes wrote later that McDowell had said of the brigade: "Many times I have shown them to foreign officers of distinction, as specimens of American Volunteer soldiers, and asked them if they had ever anywhere seen even among the picked soldiers of royal and imperial guards, a more splendid

body of men, and I have never had an affirmative answer." Dawes himself noted: "The brigade was not excelled in the precision and accuracy of their movement by any other body of troops I have ever seen, not excepting the cadets at West Point. Beyond a doubt, it was this year of preparation that brought the 'Iron Brigade' to its high standard of efficiency for battle service." Dawes, *Service*, p. 45.

9. Alan Gaff's careful study put the strength of Gibbon's Brigade at 1,937. He credited the Second Wisconsin with 430; Sixth Wisconsin, 504; Seventh Wisconsin, 580; and Nineteenth Indiana, 433. Alan D. Gaff, *Brave Men's Tears: The Iron Brigade at Brawner Farm* (Dayton, Ohio, 1985), p. 157 n. 8; Johnson, *Telegraph*, November 30, 1884; Edward P. Kellogg, *Telegraph*, September 26, 1879; Charles Dow, "Wartime Letters of Charles C. Dow, Company G, 2d Wisconsin," in Otis, *Second Wisconsin*, p. 146 (originally in *Wisconsin State Register*, July 5, 1862); Edwin R. Hancock, *Columbus Weekly Journal*, January 22, 1862.

10. Therron W. Haight, "King's Division: Fredericksburg to Manassas," in *War Papers*, vol. 2 (Milwaukee, 1896), p. 348; Johnson, *Telegraph*, November 30, 1884; Edward Bragg, letter to Earl Rogers, April 3, 1900; Edwin Brown, letter to his father, August 13, 1862; Gibbon, *Recollections*, p. 43; Cheek and Pointon, *Sauk County*, p. 30; Chester A. Wyman, letter, May 28, 1918, private collection. Haight, who was living in Wisconsin at the outbreak of the war, returned to his native New York State and served with the Twenty-fourth New York; he returned to Wisconsin after the war. In 1870, when his father-in-law, Dr. H. A. Youmans of Mukwonago, bought the *Freeman* at Waukesha, he was named to manage the newspaper. "Haight was the best editor the *Freeman* had yet known, and the paper became influential under him," the newspaper said in a recent history of its operations (*Waukesha Freeman*, June 30, 1992).

11. Otis, *Second Wisconsin*, p. 54; John Marsh, *Milwaukee Sunday Telegraph*, January 16, 1881; Edwin E. Bryant, *History of the Third Regiment Wisconsin Veteran Volunteer Infantry, 1861–1865* (Madison, 1891), pp. 75–97; Julian Wisner Hinkley, *Service with the Third Wisconsin Infantry* (Madison, 1912), pp. 32–38.

12. Edwin A. Brown, letter to his father, August 13, 1862. In the first portion of his letter, Brown wrote: "Our division arrived at this point [Cedar Mountain] *just after the battle.* We made a forced marched to get here at that. Before that we had been out on an expedition to Frederick Hall Station on the Va. Central Rail Road. The Sixth Wis., did all that was done. The balance of the expedition failed. We tore up the track for miles and blowed up two Culverts, burned the Depot, and destroyed the commissary stores & other confederate property, including 1,400 sacks of flour. The day that one did this, we made a forced march of *39 miles* crossing the branch of the Pamunkey, *which was not fordable going 10 miles beyond the Bridge over it.* And only left a guard of 100 men who were tired out to guard it. On our retreat we burned the Bridge which was a wooden structure 150 long & 70 feet above the water. We think we did a big thing. We marched *102 miles in 3 1/2 days,* accomplishing a good deal. As above stated, had no support within 30 miles hardly slept or eat during the time, rested one night & half a day, were ordered peremptorily to march here. . . ."

13. Johnson, *Telegraph*, November 30, 1884. Kelly would be wounded at Laurel Hill, Va., and died June 23, 1864. He was buried at Arlington. *Roster of Wisconsin Volunteers*, vol. 1, p. 526.

14. Cheek and Pointon, *Sauk County*, p. 31.

15. Dawes, *Service*, p. 56; Hugh Perkins, letter, August 17, 1863.

16. Longhenry, diary, August 11, 16, 1862.

17. Sullivan, *Telegraph,* November 4, 1883.

18. Pope, in Johnson and Buel, *Battles and Leaders,* vol. 2, p. 460; Cheek and Pointon, *Sauk County,* p. 36; Cook, *Telegraph,* April 8, 1883.

19. Johnson, *Telegraph,* November 30, 1884; Gibbon, *Recollections,* p. 45.

20. Dawes, *Service,* p. 46 (the account contains the quotation from Riley's journal); James P. Sullivan, "How We Lost Our Cook," *Milwaukee Sunday Telegraph,* October 21, 1882.

21. Dawes, *Service,* pp. 56–57.

22. The brigade was commanded by Brig. Gen. Marsena R. Patrick and contained the Twenty-first, Twenty-third, Thirty-fifth, and Twentieth New York State Militia [Eightieth New York Infantry], supported by Battery I, First New York Artillery. A graduate of West Point in 1835, Patrick resigned his commission in 1850 after service in the infantry, including a brevet for staff work during the Mexican War. At the start of the Civil War, he was president of the New York State Agricultural College.

23. Dawes, *Service,* p. 57; Edwin Brown, letter to his father, September 5, 1862.

24. Sullivan, *Telegraph,* October 21, 1882.

25. Dawes, *Service,* pp. 57–58. In writing their own record of their company, two of the Sauk County men used a long quotation from the Dawes passage but added that "the experience was valuable in showing the men that artillery fire was not so dangerous as they *(or the officers)* had anticipated." Cheek and Pointon, *Sauk County,* p. 35.

26. Frank A. Haskell, letter to his brothers and sisters, September 22, 1862; Byrne and Weaver, *Haskell of Gettysburg,* p. 43. This letter was also printed in the *Wisconsin State Register* at Portage, October 4, 1862.

27. *Soldiers' and Citizens' Album of Biographical Record,* vol. 2 (Chicago, 1892), p. 722. The account was that of Francis Deleglise of Company E, Sixth Wisconsin.

28. Cheek and Pointon, *Sauk County,* p. 32. Mair Pointon of Company A, who belonged to the headquarters guard, wrote that his squad "put up in a tent away from the wagons and the men had gone to bed or were just going when the first shots were fired; some of the bullets struck the tent; the light was kicked out in a hurry and every one tried to get into his clothes as fast as he could." One Confederate was killed and two captured. After the shooting, E. H. Richmond of Baraboo was missing, apparently "captured at the tent," Pointon said.

29. [Jerome Watrous], "Fitzhugh Lee's Close Call," *Milwaukee Sunday Telegraph,* December 3, 1882. Kellner, of Milwaukee, would be wounded at South Mountain and taken prisoner at Gettysburg. He mustered out February 18, 1865, at the end of his enlistment. *Roster of Wisconsin Volunteers,* vol. 1, p. 518.

30. Dawes, *Service,* pp. 58–59. In a footnote, Dawes added: "Our Brigade park of twenty-one wagons, was a short distance from the headquarters wagon train of General Pope. General Pope's wagons, and all others in the vicinity, excepting those of our brigade, were captured and destroyed by Stuart's cavalry. But Lieutenant [Arthur C.] Ellis [of Aurora, Illinois, Company B. 'himself disabled from marching'] rallied the crippled and sick men from our brigade, and directing them to lie on the ground under the wagons successfully defended, and saved from capture our train."

31. Sullivan, *Telegraph,* November 4, 1883.

32. Gibbon, *Recollections,* pp. 47–48. Gibbon said the exchange between Meade and Pope demonstrated Pope was "lacking in that sort of independence of character which not only prompts but enables an army commander to do on the spot that which he knows the exigencies require, independent of orders received from superiors at a distance and ignorant of the situation."

33. Gibbon, *Recollections*, pp. 47–48; Dawes, *Service*, pp. 58–59; Sullivan, *Telegraph*, November 4, 1884; Longhenry, diary, August 18, 1862.

34. John Marsh, "The War's First Days," *Milwaukee Sunday Telegraph*, January 16, 1881; Edwin Brown, letter to his father, August 19, 1862; Sullivan, *Telegraph*, November 4, 1884.

11. Come On, God Damn You!

1. Douglas S. Freeman, *Lee's Lieutenants*, vol. 2 (New York, 1943), pp. 102–107; Gaff, *Brave Men's Tears*, pp. 43–54; Nolan, *Iron Brigade*, pp. 72–79.

2. For a discussion of King's illness, see Gaff, *Brave Men's Tears*, pp. 33, 55–56; Gibbon, *Recollections*, pp. 49–50, 56; Dawes, journal, undated; Dawes, *Service*, pp. 46–47, 59. ". . . We learned afterwards that the enemy had fired upon Reynolds' Division, which was leading, killing and wounding several of his men," wrote John Gibbon. Of the brigade's march from Washington to Fredericksburg in late May, Dawes said the men "had been required to carry each an overcoat, an extra pair of shoes, and an extra pair of pants. These superfluous articles added to the necessary hundred rounds of ball cartridges, shelter tent, gum and woolen blankets, haversack full of rations, canteen full of water, musket and accouterments, were a load beyond the strength of ordinary men. Our young boys were broken down by the needless overtaxing of their strength. . . . Vast numbers of new overcoats, and many knapsacks were flung away by the exhausted men on this march."

3. Gibbon, *Recollections*, p. 56.

4. Edward Bragg, letter to Earl Rogers, April 3, 1900, Bragg Papers, SHSW (Rogers served on Bragg's staff during the war); Fairfield, diary, August 28, 1862; Cheek and Pointon, *Sauk County*, p. 37. Confederate reports refer to the engagement of August 28, 1862, as the battle of Groveton, while Federals called it the battle of Gainesville. Alan Nolan correctly located the fighting at "Brawner Farm"; Nolan, *Iron Brigade*, pp. 315–316.

5. Dawes, *Service*, p. 60; A. R. Bushnell, "How the Iron Brigade Won Its Name," *Grant County Herald*, undated clipping, Watrous Papers, State Historical Society of Wisconsin; *Dictionary of Wisconsin Biography*, p. 61; Edwin Brown, letter to his father, September 5, 1862; Cheek and Pointon, *Sauk County*, p. 37; Sullivan, *Telegraph*, November 4, 1884; Gibbon, *Recollections*, p. 51; [Watrous], *Telegraph*, September 7, 1884. A native of Hartford, Ohio, Bushnell moved to Wisconsin in 1854, settling in Plattesville, where he studied law and set up a practice in 1857. In 1860 he was elected district attorney of Grant County but resigned to serve with the Seventh Wisconsin. He rose to the rank of captain. Bushnell resigned in 1863 and returned to Wisconsin, where he became the first mayor of Lancaster. He also served one year in Congress. These details were presented in a speech made by Gibbon to the Iron Brigade Association at Lancaster, Wis., in 1884.

6. Gibbon, *Recollections*, pp. 51–52; [Young], *Telegraph*, May 6, 1888; Harries, in Otis, *Second Wisconsin*, p. 250; Cheek and Pointon, *Sauk County*, pp. 37–38; [Watrous], *Telegraph*, September 7, 1884. "When this shelling commenced I realized that the enemy in search of whom we had been marching for days and days, were right there, and somebody ought to have known it," said Gibbon.

7. Gilbert Woodward, letter to Charles King, May 3, 1913, Gilbert Woodward Papers, State Historical Society of Wisconsin; Dawes, *Service*, p. 60; Cheek and Pointon, *Sauk County*, p. 38; [Watrous], *Telegraph*, September 7, 1884.

8. Earl Rogers Papers, Wisconsin Veterans' Museum, Madison; King, in *War Papers*, vol. 2, p. 212; [Harris], *Telegraph*, April 8, 1883; *OR*, series 1, vol. 12, part 2, p. 378 (this is Gibbon's first report); [Watrous], *Telegraph*, September 7, 1884.

Farther up the turnpike, a watching soldier from Hatch's Brigade recalled Battery B of the Fourth U.S. "planted a shell among the rebels before they had time to fire. A yell of laughter came from our lines at the way the enemy fell on their faces and scattered themselves about. . . ." Theron W. Haight, "Gainesville, Groveton and Bull Run," in *War Papers*, vol. 2, p. 361.

9. Bushnell, *Herald*, undated; Cheek and Pointon, *Sauk County*, p. 38; Sullivan, *Telegraph*, November 4, 1883; Cornelius Wheeler, journal, August 28, 1862, Cornelius Wheeler Papers, Milwaukee County Historical Society; King, in *War Papers*, p. 271. Wheeler, a Second Wisconsin man, noted: "The regiment . . . advanced in line of battle at double quick time upon the battery and soon met a heavy body of the enemy's infantry; here for nearly twenty minutes, until succored by the other regiments of the brigade, the Second Regiment alone sustained and checked the whole of 'Stonewall' Jackson's division, under one of the most intensely concentrated fires of musketry probably ever experienced by any troops in this or any other war."

10. Dawes, *Service*, p. 60; [Watrous], *Telegraph*, September 4, 1884; Gibbon, *Recollections*, pp. 53–54.

11. [Watrous], *Telegraph*, quoting John Gibbon, September 4, 1884.

12. Harries, in Otis, *Second Wisconsin*, p. 251; [Watrous], *Telegraph*, September 4, 1884; Thomas Allen, letter, September 4, 1862; *Civil War Times Illustrated*, November 1962, pp. 32–33; Haight, in *War Papers*, p. 361.

13. O'Connor graduated from the U.S. Military Academy in 1854. The superintendent at the time was Robert E. Lee. In his class were Lee's eldest son, Custis Lee, John Pegram, and J.E.B. Stuart, all to become Confederate generals, and Oliver Howard and Stephen H. Weld, who would become Union generals. A Nineteenth Indiana soldier recalled seeing O'Connor at Brawner farm: "I thought I never saw a handsomer man." Stine, *Army of the Potomac*, p. 132.

14. *The State Journal*, Madison, September 4, 1861. A soldier correspondent wrote: "Col. O'Connor has late assumed command [of the Second Wisconsin], and is steadily at work in drill and discipline though laboring under a bronchial difficulty, which has so affected his voice, that it is feared he may yet have to give up the command. . . . O'Connor by the way has just received his commission as Colonel and taken the fullest oath of allegiance. I mention this particularly, as there have been unfavorable things said as to his sympathies in this conflict. He is sound in every respect." The dispatch was written August 29, 1861, and signed by "F.H.," probably Frank A. Haskell.

15. King, in *War Papers*, p. 273.

16. Gibbon said later: "That action in throwing the brigade into position under those circumstances has been criticized. Well, I presume it is open to fair criticism, but fortunately the reports of the rebel officers have come out since that time written before they know anything of our side of the question, and this fact is developed: Jackson had got his troops into position and he proposed to stay there. His main point was to keep his right flank (his troops then facing to the south) open and protected, so that the main force of Lee's army coming in should join on to his right. We interfered with that. He made preparations for attack. The principal part of his force was on the right flank, including his own brigade. When he saw our troops marching along the turnpike and ordered an attack on them, his picket line was out, when to his astonishment this brigade was hurled into the force of the assault. What was the effect? They made no attack: they stood and received ours, and after we got into a certain place we staid [sic] there and received theirs, and staid there until the fight was over, and in one hour and fifty minutes one-third of his command lay dead and wounded on the ground." [Watrous], *Telegraph*, September 4, 1884.

12. I Would Not Like to Hear It Again

1. Gaff, *Brave Men's Tears*, p. 73; Cheek and Pointon, *Sauk County*, p. 38; Marsh, *Telegraph*, January 16, 1886; Fairfield, diary, August 28, 1862; *OR*, series 1, vol. 12, part 2, p. 382. Burus would die May 7, 1864, of wounds received at the Wilderness; Dunn was mustered out at the end of his three year enlistment; and Campbell would resign his commission as first lieutenant October 11, 1864. *Roster of Wisconsin Volunteers*, vol. 1, pp. 513–514, 533; Sullivan, *Telegraph*, November 4, 1884.

2. Dawes, *Service*, p. 61; Rufus Dawes, journal, undated, Rufus R. Dawes Papers, State Historical Society of Wisconsin. Dawes noted in pencil that he wrote the journal in late 1862 or early 1863.

3. [Young], *Telegraph*, May 6, 1888.

4. Sullivan, *Telegraph*, November 4, 1884.

5. Cheek and Pointon, *Sauk County*, p. 38. The first Sauk County man wounded was Cpl. Philip Hoefer of Freedom. He would be discharged as disabled January 2, 1863; Dawes, *Service*, p. 61.

6. [Young], *Telegraph*, May 6, 1888.

7. Johnson, *Telegraph*, November 30, 1884.

8. Dawes, journal, undated; Cheek and Pointon, *Sauk County*, p. 39; Dawes, *Service*, pp. 61–62; Chester Wyman, letter, May 28, 1918, private collection.

9. Marsh, *Telegraph*, January 16, 1886.

10. Frank Haskell, letter, September 22, 1862; Byrne and Weaver, *Haskell of Gettysburg*, p. 44.

11. *Beaver Dam Home League*, October 18, 1862; Dawes, journal, undated; Rufus R. Dawes, "Skirmishes of the Rappahannock and Battle of Gainesville," T. C. H. Smith Papers, Ohio Historical Society, Columbus; Bushnell, *Herald*, undated; Stine, *Army of the Potomac*, pp. 131–132.

12. Gibbon, *Recollections*, p. 54.

13. Johnson, *Telegraph*, November 30, 1884; Bushnell, *Herald*, undated; Edwin A. Brown, letter to his father, September 5, 1862; Edward Bragg, letter to Earl Rogers, April 3, 1900; Earl Rogers, *Milwaukee Sunday Telegraph*, August 29, 1884; Dawes, journal, undated. Warham's arm was amputated and he was discharged as disabled December 31, 1862; *Roster of Wisconsin Volunteers*, vol. 1, p. 532.

14. John St. Claire, letter to his parents, September 6, 1862, John St. Claire Papers, State Historical Society of Wisconsin; Cheek and Pointon, *Sauk County*, p. 39; Fairfield, diary, August 28, 1862; Sullivan, *Telegraph*, November 4, 1884; [Jerome Watrous], *Milwaukee Sunday Telegraph*, September 4, 1884; Bushnell, *Herald*, undated.

15. Dawes, *Service*, pp. 62–63; Dawes, journal, undated; [Young], *Telegraph*, May 6, 1888; Fairfield, diary, August 28, 1862; Johnson, *Telegraph*, November 30, 1884. One Confederate wrote: ". . . [I]t was a stand-up combat, dogged and unflinching. . . . There were no wounds from spent balls; the confronting lines looked into each other's faces at deadly ranges, less than one hundred yards apart, and they stood as immovable as the painted heroes in a battle-piece. There was cover of woods not very far in rear of the lines on both sides, and brave men—with that instinct of self-preservation which is exhibited in the veteran soldier, who seizes every advantage of ground or obstacle—might have been justified in slowly seeking this shelter from the iron hail that smote them; but out in the sunlight, in the dying daylight, and under the stars, they stood, and although they could not advance, they would not retire. There was some discipline in this, but there was much more of true valor." W. B. Taliaferro,

"Jackson's Raid around Pope," in Robert U. Johnson and Clarence C. Buel, *Battles and Leaders of the Civil War,* vol. 2, p. 510.

13. Devil Take the Hindmost

1. Frank A. Haskell, letter to his brothers and sisters, September 22, 1862; Dawes, *Service,* pp. 63, 70.

2. Patrick said he declined to put his brigade in on Gibbon's left because he disapproved of Gibbon's making the attack without more consideration and knowledge of the strength of the enemy. Stine, *Army of the Potomac,* p. 132.

3. Gibbon, *Recollections,* pp. 55–57. In ranks there was anger over the decision to leave the battlefield. Rufus Dawes, mistaking King's illness and critical of McDowell, wrote in his journal: "It would not do for Gen. McDowell's troops to have had a *battle* when he was not *there.* Or to have found any Confederate force of the enemy where according to his theory of the situation there was only a reconnoiter party. It might look as though he didn't know where the enemy were. Neither would it do for a division General (King) to have his troops fight a *battle* at the beginning of which he was almost dead drunk, and in which he did not show his precious head. Nor is he anxious to have any thing particular said about the matter of his withdrawing his division without orders, ill natured folks would say *hurriedly,* to Manassas." Cornelius Wheeler of the Second Wisconsin noted in his journal: "Then our division commander, Brigadier General Rufus King, orders a retreat, the first and only command he is known to have given since the opening of the battle, and we march by the Bethlehem road to Manassas Junction, arriving there about sunrise." Cornelius Wheeler, journal, August 28, 1862. See also John J. Hennessy, *Return to Bull Run: The Campaign and Battle of Second Manassas* (New York, 1993), p. 193.

4. Cheek and Pointon, *Sauk County,* p. 40; Harries, in Otis, *Second Wisconsin,* p. 253; *Beaver Dam Home League,* October 18, 1862; Dawes, *Service,* pp. 63–64; Edward S. Bragg, letter to his wife, September 13, 1862; Chester Wyman, letter, May 28, 1918. Bragg said the Sixth Wisconsin engaged the Twelfth Georgia supported by the Twenty-first North Carolina, two regiments in the Confederate brigade commanded by Isaac R. Trimble. Chester Wyman wrote later: "With no one to care for us all the care we had was from some of the wounded that could walk. They would bring us water. I did not have as much to eat in the 10 days as I now eat in one day. Our men were fighting in sight and hearing of me for 5 days. . . . While our men were fighting the wounded were added to our numbers until there were about 500. With no . . . help it was every man for himself. Many died there. One man that was near me died and he had a blanket. I did not. After he died I took his blanket and spread over myself and was more comfortable than I had been for it kept me warm after 10 days. Our men came with a flag of Truce and carried us to Washington some 40 miles from there. The city of Washington contributed carriages to bring in the wounded but the suffering we endured on that night over the rough roads can be imagined but not told. When we arrived there a number of dead were removed from the carriages and at least one third of the wounded died within 2 weeks after we were in the hospital." Wyman was soon discharged and sent home.

5. Sullivan, *Telegraph,* October 21, 1883; Edwin A. Brown, letter to his father, September 5, 1862. The reference was to Confederate generals Thomas J. Jackson and Richard Ewell. Ewell was shot in the leg while in front of the Sixth Wisconsin line. It was subsequently amputated. He was fitted with a wooden leg and returned to the field in May 1863.

6. John Marsh, "Army Life Incidents," *Milwaukee Sunday Telegraph,* January 16, 1881.

7. Dawes, *Service,* p. 64; Edwin Brown, letter to his father, September 5, 1862. Brown noted: "Lieut. Johnson & 12 men of my Co. was wounded and John Weymier was taken prisoner. The Lieut. is badly wounded in the groin." Johnson, of Fond du Lac, had risen from ranks and received his commission in September 1861. Johnson resigned December 27, 1862. *Roster of Wisconsin Volunteers,* vol. 1, p. 513.

8. Thompson Jones was one of five brothers who served with Company A of the Sixth Wisconsin. A future Jones brother-in-law, Daniel Odell, served in the same company. Thompson Jones died of disease in 1864. The others were Horatio D. Jones, who served his original term and later enlisted in the First Wisconsin Heavy Artillery; George Jones, discharged May 22, 1862; Reuben Jones, wounded at Antietam and discharged December 18, 1862; and Bodley Jones, killed in action July 1, 1863, at Gettysburg. Odell, who married Agnes Eleanor Jones following the war, was wounded at South Mountain and discharged December 15, 1862. Two other brothers were David Jones, who served with Company L, Third Wisconsin Cavalry, and Charles Jones, who enlisted in Company E, Forty- ninth Wisconsin Infantry, and died September 16, 1864, of cholera at Benton Barracks, Mo. The Jones family moved to Wisconsin from Virginia via Indiana sometime before 1850. They settled in Excelsior Township. The father, Horatio Jones, despite his Virginia birth, was "intensely loyal" to the Union. Jones family records; Cheek and Pointon, *Sauk County,* p. 11.

9. Cheek and Pointon, *Sauk County,* pp. 40–41; Longhenry, diary, August 27–29, 1862.

10. Frank Haskell, letter to brothers and sisters, September 22, 1862; Sullivan, *Telegraph,* October 21, 1883; Fairfield, diary, August 28, 1862.

11. Marsh, *Telegraph,* January 16, 1881.

12. Dawes, *Service,* p. 64.

13. Harries, in Otis, *Second Wisconsin,* p. 255.

14. Gibbon, *Recollections,* p. 58.

15. Sullivan's assumption his brigade received no assistance was contested in the November 11, 1883, *Milwaukee Sunday Telegraph.* The dispatch was signed "Orderly," and likely written by Charles King, son of Division Commander Rufus King. The dispatch noted: "Mickey says that except Gibbon's brigade and Battery B, he has 'no knowledge of a shot being fired by any of King's division.' More than that he says 'although the rest of the division lay there in sight and hearing, not a shot was fired nor a man sent forward to our assistance.' Here Mickey is in error. When the fight began[,] [Gen. John Porter] Hatch's brigade was sent out of sight a mile ahead. [Gen. Marsena R.] Patrick's brigade was over a mile behind. [Gen. Abner] Doubleday's was the only one close at hand, and that Doubleday's brigade was speedily ordered in to support Gibbon, and that the Fifty-sixth Pennsylvania and the seventh-sixth New York pushed right forward on the same line with the Sixth Wisconsin wherein Mickey was blazing away for all he was worth, is attested by the reports of General Doubleday and Colonels [J. William Hoffmann] Hoffman and [Charles B.] Wainwright, and by the fact that right there on that line the fifty-sixth lost their colonel, four captains, two lieutenants and 55 enlisted men, shot down and the seventh-sixth 10 killed, 72 wounded (including five officers) and 18 missing. The Ninety-fifth was sent to the right in support of old Battery B, and did not get into the heavy fire. Mickey is hardly to blame for his lack of information on this point as it was quite the custom to speak of it as Gibbon's fight as though no other brigade was engaged. In saying, too, that not until

midnight was General King aware that his division was attacked, and that that officer allowed our brigade to fight alone and unaided, Mickey does grave injustice to a man who yielded to none in his love and admiration for the Iron Brigade. It was General King who sent orders to Patrick to push in to Gibbon's support, to Hatch to hasten back, and to Doubleday to hurry forward, and though it was barely dark by the time Hatch and his men did return and though Patrick's orders failed to reach him in time, it was no fault of General King. More than this, at nine o'clock at night King wrote to [Gen. William] Ricketts, telling him to come to his support as Jackson was there in full force, and that hour, 9 o'clock, Hatch, Gibbon and Doubleday were there with King talking over the situation and 'Little Johnny Gibbon,' as Mickey affectionately calls him, was vehemently urging General King to fall back and push for Manassas— the very move that resulted in their wounded being left on the field."

16. Sullivan, *Telegraph*, October 21, 1883.

17. Frank A. Haskell, letter to brothers and sisters, September 22, 1862.

18. [Watrous], *Telegraph*, December 7, 1879.

19. Gaff, *Brave Men's Tears*, pp. 156–158; Stine, *Army of the Potomac*, p. 132; Dawes, journal, undated; Thomas Allen, letter, September 4, 1862; Wheeler, journal, August 30, 1862.

20. There was a controversy over Rufus King's decision to march to Manassas Junction instead of holding his division at Gainesville. Pope claimed later in print he had directed orders to King to "hold his ground at all costs." In a defense of his father, Charles King responded to Pope's claim: "No order or message of any kind, sort, or description reached General King that night from General Pope or any other superior officer; no staff-officer of General King saw or heard from General Pope that night." He also quoted from a letter of May 7, 1863, from John Gibbon to King in which Gibbon wrote, "I deem it not out of place to say that that retreat was suggested and urged by myself as a necessary military measure. . . . I do not hesitate to say, and it is susceptible of proof, that of the two courses which I considered open to you, of obeying your orders to march to Centreville or treat on Manassas on your own responsibility, the one you adopted was the proper one." Charles King, "In Vindication of General Rufus King," in Johnson and Buel, *Battles and Leaders*, vol. 2, p. 495. For a discussion of King's decision, see Gaff, *Brave Men's Tears*, pp. 164–169.

21. Sullivan, *Telegraph*, May 16, 1884; Longhenry, diary, August 29–30, 1862; Dawes, *Service*, pp. 68–69. "Fitz-John Porter's corps from the army of the Potomac passed as we lay along the road. We felt good thinking we would be reinforced by the Army of the Potomac," two Sauk County men wrote long afterward. Cheek and Pointon, *Sauk County*, p. 42.

22. Longhenry, diary, August 29–30, 1862.

23. Dawes, *Service*, pp. 69–70; Sullivan, *Telegraph*, May 16, 1884; Gibbon, *Recollections*, p. 61.

24. Dawes, *Service*, p. 68. The "lost in the woods" was a reference to McDowell's explanation he was unable to direct King's Division because he had lost his way in the woods. A court of inquiry found McDowell "separated himself from his command at a critical time, without any orders from his superior officer and without any imperative necessity." *OR*, series 1, vol. 12, part 1, pp. 328–331. In a letter, John Hall of the Sixth praised Dawes's account: "I suppose there is good reason why this battle has been ignored or slightly referred to as the 'affair at Gainesville' by the general officers in command from Pope down to McDowell and King. Naturally they did not want to furnish themselves the shameful dark background to the glorious picture of

Gainesville. They had to be-little it to save themselves from disgrace." Dr. John
Hall, letter to Rufus Dawes, December 3, 1890, Dawes Papers, SHSW.

25. Cheek and Pointon, *Sauk County*, p. 42; Sullivan, *Telegraph*, May 16, 1884.

14. The Little Colonel

1. [Jerome Watrous], *Milwaukee Telegraph*, December 10, 1898; *Milwaukee
Sentinel*, October 4, 1861; Dawes, *Service*, p. 19; Julius Murray, letter, June 22,
1861; Jerome Watrous, "An Appleton Contribution," manuscript.

2. Edwin Brown, letter to his wife, August 13, 1861.

3. Jerome A. Watrous, "Famous Iron Brigade," *Milwaukee Telegraph*, March
27, 1896; Jerome Watrous, *The Old Captain*, pamphlet, undated; Watrous, *Telegraph*, December 10, 1898; James P. Sullivan, *Milwaukee SundayTelegraph*, May
16, 1884.

4. Watrous, *Telegraph*, March 27, 1896.

5. Sullivan, *Telegraph*, May 16, 1884; Dawes, journal, undated; Fairfield,
diary, August 30, 1862; Gibbon, *Recollections*, p. 62.

6. Gibbon, *Recollections*, pp. 62–63.

7. Quaw, of Friendship in Bad Ax (Vernon) County, enlisted as a private May
10, 1861. He rose from noncommissioned ranks to become second and then first
lieutenant of Company K. He gained the captaincy June 24, 1862, but resigned
in October. *Roster of Wisconsin Volunteers*, vol. 1, p. 533. Gardner was the first
man of Company K to be killed in battle. Dawes, in a letter to a reunion of
Company K veterans, wrote: "He was a gentleman of intelligence and education. He was a willing and faithful soldier, and earnest in his patriotic feeling.
He went forward to his death with unflinching bravery. He was mourned as a
friend to every man of Company K. Let the boys stand with uncovered heads
to recall the member of the first man who fell dead in battle from the ranks of
Company K." Rufus R. Dawes, letter to J. T. Hanson, November 23, 1884, as
printed in *Mauston Star*, January 8, 1885.

8. Dawes, journal, undated; Sullivan, *Telegraph*, May 16, 1884; Dawes, *Service*, pp. 71–72. John Johnson of the Sixth said the skirmishers received "such a
withering fire that they came running back inside of three minutes, with half
their numbers lost. Johnson, *Telegraph*, November 30, 1884.

9. Sullivan, *Telegraph*, May 16, 1884; Fairfield, diary, August 30, 1862; Dawes,
Service, p. 72.

10. [Young], *Telegraph*, June 3, 1888. Years later, Young asked his old captain
if he ever felt fear; Bragg's reply, "Never, until I was wounded [at Antietam],
and after that every bullet I heard seemed to hit me."

11. Dawes, journal, undated; Dawes, *Service*, p. 72; Edwin Brown, letter to his
father, September 5, 1862. Petit would be discharged February 25, 1863. Miller,
of Cassville, was wounded at Gettysburg and was sick and absent when the
regiment mustered out in 1865. Bickelhaupt died in Washington October 22,
1862. *Roster of Wisconsin Volunteers*, vol. 1, pp. 507, 519, 517. Brown said the
Sixth killed two rebel sharpshooters carrying the target rifles.

12. Johnson, *Telegraph*, November 30, 1884.

13. Jerome Watrous, manuscript, undated, Watrous Papers, SHSW.

14. Gibbon, *Recollections*, p. 63; Edward Bragg, letter to Earl Rogers, April 3,
1900.

15. Jerome Watrous, manuscript, Watrous Papers, SHSW; Brown, letter to his
father, September 5, 1862.

16. Sullivan, *Telegraph,* May 16, 1884; Dawes, *Service,* p. 73.

17. Johnson, *Telegraph,* November 30, 1884; Cheek and Pointon, *Sauk County,* p. 43; Sullivan, *Telegraph,* May 16, 1884. Edward Simmon of Marion enlisted May 10, 1861. He was wounded at South Mountain in 1862 and again at Petersburg in 1865. He veteranized in late 1864 but was absent wounded when the Sixth was mustered from service in July 1865. *Roster of Wisconsin Volunteers,* vol. 1, p. 353.

18. The bay horse Tartar entered the service at Fort Leavenworth, Kan., in July 1857, just before Battery B started on the Utah expedition. He was then four years of age. The horse was abandoned at Green River, Utah, a short time later when taken sick with distemper. The following spring, two Indians brought him back to the battery. The shell at Second Bull Run carried away Tartar's tail and wounded him in both flanks. When the army retreated the next day, Stewart left Tartar behind, turning him out into a small pasture. The next morning, Tartar was again found with the battery horses, having jumped the fence. Sometime later in the war, during a review attended by President Lincoln, Tartar again attracted attention. As the battery passed the reviewing stand, Lincoln made one of his small jokes, remarking to the generals standing about him, "This reminds me of a tale." Lincoln's son Tad, who had accompanied his father, was much taken with Tartar. Tad was mounted on a pony and followed the battery while pestering Stewart to trade horses. "I told him I could not do that, but he persisted in telling me that his papa was the President, and would give me any horse I wanted in trade for Tarter. I had a hard time to get away from the little fellow," Stewart later related. Tartar was wounded again at Fredericksburg in late 1862 and again left behind, only to show up on a Federal cavalry picket line a month later. Stewart said when he was promoted and transferred to the Eighteenth Infantry in 1866, Tartar was still in harness with Battery B, in the 10th year of "his honorable and distinguished service." James Stewart, letter, December 8, 1889, quoted in Buell, *Cannoneer,* pp. 30–31.

19. Sullivan, *Telegraph,* May 16, 1884; Dawes, *Service,* p. 73.

20. Johnson, *Telegraph,* November 30, 1884.

21. Edward S. Bragg, letter to Rufus Dawes, December 21, 1890, Dawes Papers, SHSW; Cheek and Pointon, *Sauk County,* p. 43.

22. Curtis, *Twenty-fourth Michigan,* p. 466; Cheek and Pointon, *Sauk County,* p. 43.

15. The Army Ran Like Sheep

1. Dawes, *Service,* p. 74.

2. Johnson, *Telegraph,* November 30, 1884; Cheek and Pointon, *Sauk County,* p. 44; Curtis, *Twenty-fourth Michigan,* p. 466. The quotation is from Phil Cheek of the Sixth Wisconsin to a postwar veterans' meeting.

3. Sullivan, *Telegraph,* May 16, 1884.

4. Dawes, *Service,* p. 74; Gibbon, *Recollections,* pp. 64–65.

5. In the aftermath of Second Bull Run, several units claimed being the rear guard of the army. Joseph Mills Hanson, *Bull Run Remembers* (Manassas, Va., 1953), pp. 131–132. Lt. Frank Haskell of the Sixth Wisconsin, then serving on John Gibbon's staff, wrote home: "On the night of the Thirtieth after the battle the army fell back to Centreville, and Gibbon's Brigade, with Campbell's (formerly Gibbon's) Battery, Co "B" Fourth Artillery, was the rear guard of the whole army. This is no small honor, and you may set it down as a fact, the lying newspapers to the contrary notwithstanding." Frank A. Haskell, letter to brothers and sisters, September 22, 1862; Byrne and Weaver, *Haskell of Gettysburg,* p. 45.

6. Gibbon, *Recollections*, pp. 64–65; Sullivan, *Telegraph*, May 16, 1884.

7. Kearny had a distinguished record of service. He was an observer with the French cavalry in the Algerian war of 1840, lost his left arm in the capture of Mexico City during the Mexican War, and fought with the French in Italy, winning the Legion of Honor at Solferino. During the Peninsular campaign, he distinguished himself at Williamsburg and Seven Pines and was appointed a major general of volunteers. Boatner, *Civil War Dictionary*, p. 449.

8. Dawes, *Service*, p. 75; Gibbon, *Recollections*, p. 69. Reno would be killed at South Mountain on September 14, 1862.

9. Sullivan, *Telegraph*, May 16, 1884. The reference to the mock campfires is in Dawes, *Service*, p. 75. The regiment's loss at Second Bull Run totaled 47 killed, wounded, and missing. Dawes, *Service*, p. 74.

10. Gibbon, *Recollections*, p. 69; Cheek and Pointon, *Sauk County*, p.44.

11. Jerome Watrous, manuscript, Watrous Papers, SHSW.

12. Edward Bragg, letter to Earl Rogers, April 3, 1900; Dawes, *Service*, p. 75. Fine enlisted from Hillsboro on May 10, 1861. *Roster of Wisconsin Volunteers*, vol. 1, p. 531.

13. Gibbon, *Recollections*, p. 69.

14. Cheek and Pointon, *Sauk County*, p. 45; Earl Rogers Papers, Wisconsin Veterans' Museum, Madison; Dawes, *Service*, pp. 75–76.

15. The battle of Chantilly is considered the last of the fighting in the Second Bull Run campaign. Fought September 1, 1862, it took the lives of two Union divisional commanders—Isaac I. Stevens as well as Philip Kearny.

16. Gibbon, *Recollections*, p. 70.

17. Edward Bragg, letter to Earl Rogers, April 3, 1900; Dawes, *Service*, pp. 75–76.

18. Frank Haskell, letter to "Dear brothers and Sisters," September 22, 1862, from "Battlefield, Sharpsburg [Maryland]"; Edward Bragg, letter to his wife, September 13, 1862; Watrous, manuscript, undated, Watrous Papers, SHSW; Gibbon, *Recollections*, p. 70.

19. Edward Bragg, letter to Earl Rogers, April 3, 1900; Thomas Allen, letter, September 4, 1862; Frank Haskell, letter to his brother and sister, August 31, 1862.

20. Upton's Hill lay between the Potomac River and the Loudon & Hampshire Railroad near Arlington Heights, Va.

21. Smith, of Lemonweir, enlisted the same day as Sullivan. Smith became a first sergeant and was mustered out at the expiration of his three-year term on July 15, 1864. *Roster of Wisconsin Volunteers*, vol. 1, p. 536.

22. James P. Sullivan, "A Private's Story," *Milwaukee Sunday Telegraph,* May 13, 1888.

23. In November 1862, Porter was relieved of his command to face court-martial charges leveled by Pope for disobedience, disloyalty, and misconduct in the face of the enemy. The trial found Porter guilty and he was cashiered. After years of trying to clear his record, Porter was reappointed a colonel of infantry in 1886. *Dictionary of American Biography* (New York, 1946), vol. 15, p. 91.

24. Sullivan, *Telegraph,* May 16, 1884. Sullivan prefaced his statement with an unsubstantiated report passed in ranks those days: "A recent writer narrating how his company, after a fatiguing march (in dust so thick that one was unable to see the length of the company,) was turned out and worked all night constructing a bridge only to get orders as the last plank was laid at daylight, to destroy it, described that campaign as 'blunder,' and that is the only word that does justice to Pope's Bull Run campaign. It was said, but I did not see it, that Pope, McDowell and Sigel quarrelled on the battle-field, and that Sigel drew his

pistol to shoot Pope, calling him a cowardly ignoramus, who was not qualified to hold the rank of corporal." Sullivan concluded: "It is a mystery to the men who served in the late war why McDowell, who never won a battle, and Pope, who was continually defeated from the time the enemy appeared in his front until he took shelter in the defences of Washington, should hold high commands at this day. . . . "

25. Edwin Brown, letter to his father, September 5, 1862.

26. Dawes, *Service*, p. 78.

16. We Have Got a General Now

1. Cheek and Pointon, *Sauk County*, p. 46; Thomas Allen, letter, September 4, 1862; Longhenry, diary, September 3, 1862.

2. Jerome Watrous, "New Facts Touching a Long Ago Time," manuscript, Watrous Papers, SHSW. Watrous identified the soldier who told him the story as Oscar H. Pierce, a Milwaukeean who served with Company B of the Fifth Wisconsin. The orderly was George H. Cooper of Beloit, who served in the same company. Cooper, after being wounded in the Seven Days fighting outside Richmond, was transferred to various headquarters posts. *Roster of Wisconsin Volunteers*, vol. 1, pp. 442- 443.

3. Dawes, *Service*, pp. 76–78.

4. Cheek and Pointon, *Sauk County*, pp. 45–56.

5. John O. Johnson, "Recollections of Soldier life, read on the Meeting of the GAR Post 186 by J.O.J.," undated, Bragg Papers, SHSW. Johnson was promoted to second lieutenant of Company H, Forty-fifth Wisconsin, on September 17, 1864. *Roster of Wisconsin Volunteers*, vol. 1, p. 526.

6. Cheek and Pointon, *Sauk County*, p. 46.

7. Longhenry, diary, September 7, 1862.

8. Longhenry, diary, September 8–12, 1862.

9. Edwin A. Brown, letter to his wife, September 13, 1862.

10. Gibbon, *Recollections*, pp. 71–73.

11. Dawes, *Service*, p. 78.

12. Longhenry, diary, September 14, 1862; Zebulon Russell, *Columbus Republican*, August 24, 1895.

13. Dawes, *Service*, p. 79; Longhenry, diary, September 14, 1862; Russell, *Columbus Republican*, August 24, 1895.

14. Gibbon, *Recollections*, pp. 74–75.

15. Russell, *Columbus Republican*, August 24, 1895.

16. Gibbon, *Recollections*, pp. 74–75.

17. *Milwaukee Sunday Telegraph*, July 9, 1882; Cheek and Pointon, *Sauk County*, pp. 212–213. Cheek and Pointon told this story: "While in camp at Arlington in the winter of 1862, Adjutant Haskell was trying to get the company details for guard into line so as to hold 'Guard Mount,' but one fellow down the line persisted in remaining so his breast was back of the line Haskell was trying to establish. Several times he told the men to dress on the line, but it was no use, there was a sag in the line—finally becoming out of patience, he stepped a pace to the front, where he could see every man in line and said: 'No. 6, move up into line.' No. 6 was totally ignorant that he was the sixth man from the head of the line, and did not move. Haskell could stand it no longer and he yells out: 'I mean that man with a plow coulter for a nose.' Bill Palmer of Company A immediate stepped up in line. Palmer was named a First lieutenant, a promotion dated August 28, 1862, for his behavior in the battle at Gainesville."

18. Johnson, "Recollections."

19. Dawes, *Service*, pp. 78–80.

20. Cheek and Pointon, *Sauk County*, pp. 46–47. The writers added: "This incident is related here because four other just such predictions were made by members of the company at various times and all came as predicted when there was apparently nothing to suggest the possibility when the prediction was made. These premonitions, as they are called, often occurred, but who can explain the phenomena that produces the same—not the writers of this."

21. Russell, *Columbus Republican,* August 24, 1895; Sullivan, *Telegraph,* May 13, 1888.

17. The Iron Brigade of the West

1. "Gen. Gibbon's brigade was detached from Hatch's division by Gen. Burnside, for the purpose of making a demonstration on the enemy's centre, up the main road, as soon as the movements on the right and left had sufficiently progressed." George B. McClellan, *McClellan's Own Story* (Philadelphia, 1887), pp. 579–580.

2. Johnson, "Recollections."; Haskell, manuscript, September 22, 1862; Byrne and Weaver, *Haskell of Gettysburg,* pp. 35, 32.

3. Cheek and Pointon, *Sauk County,* p. 48; Gibbon, *Recollections,* p. 76.

4. *The Milwaukee Sentinel,* October 31, 1862. The correspondent added, "I give the story as it is told here by Wisconsin men. If it is true, the cowardly assassin who wrote such a letter to the Governor, derogatory of the bravery of such a man as Captain Colwell, may have the gratification of feeling that his malice, or envy perhaps, has succeeded in destroying one of the bravest and noblest men that Wisconsin has sent to the field. For the sake of humanity, I trust that what everybody believes may not prove true, and that there is no craven-hearted coward among the troops from the Badger State, who has been thus guilty." Colwell was born in Pennsylvania and moved before the war to La Crosse, where he became a banker. At Fort Sumter in 1861, Colwell was the newly elected mayor of La Crosse and he was soon elected captain of the La Crosse Light Guard, which became Company B of the Second Wisconsin. Alan Gaff, *If This Is War* (Dayton, Ohio, 1991), p. 37; Dawes, *Service,* p. 81; [Harries], *Telegraph,* September 9, 1883; Frank Haskell, manuscript, September 22, 1862; Bryne and Weaver, *Haskell of Gettysburg,* p. 37. Haskell described Colwell as a "brave and accomplished officer." *OR,* series 1, vol. 19, part 1, p. 254. On September 22, 1862, *The Milwaukee Sentinel* carried a dispatch of the *Chicago Times* from the previous day: "Among the killed was Capt. Wilson Colwell of Company B, Second Wisconsin, who was formerly Mayor of La Crosse. His body was enclosed in a metallic coffin and brought here [Chicago], but was so much decomposed on its arrival that the process of embalming was found to be impossible."

5. Rufus R. Dawes, *Mauston Star,* January 8, 1885; *Milwaukee Sunday Telegraph,* August 24, 1884.

6. Sullivan, *Telegraph,* May 13, 1888.

7. Dawes, *Service,* p. 81.

8. Russell, *Columbus Republican,* August 24, 1895; Haskell, manuscript, September 22, 1862; Byrne and Weaver, *Haskell of Gettysburg,* pp. 35–36.

9. McClellan wrote: "The brigade advanced steadily, driving the enemy from his positions in the woods and behind stone walls, until they reached a point well up towards the top of the pass, when the enemy, having been

reinforced by three regiments, opened a heavy fire on the front and on both flanks. The fight continued until nine o'clock, the enemy being entirely repulsed; and the brigade after having suffered severely, and having expended all its ammunition, including even the cartridges of the dead and wounded, continued to hold the ground it had so gallantly won until twelve o'clock, when it was relieved by Gen. Gorman's brigade, of Sedgwick's division, Sumner's corps (except the Sixth Wis., which remained on the field all night). Gen. Gibbon, in this delicate movement, handled his brigade with as much precision and coolness as if upon parade, and the bravery of his troops could not be excelled." McClellan, *Own Story*, p. 582.

10. An example was a statement by John O. Johnson of the Sixth Wisconsin to a veterans' meeting: "That evening [at South Mountain] we were baptized, and received the name of the 'Iron Brigade.' Who it was that gave us the name, I have never learned. Some said it was McClellan, others that it was [General] Sumner." He closed his address with the observation his view was "from the ranks, where observation is limited." Johnson, "Recollections."

11. McClellan told the story to John Callis of the Seventh Wisconsin at a reception for the general October 8, 1868, at the Continental Hotel in Philadelphia. The version cited appeared in the program for the 1900 reunion of the Iron Brigade Association in Chicago at which President William McKinley was the featured guest. Also see *Indiana at Antietam*, Indiana Antietam Monument Commission (Indianapolis, 1911), p. 111. The account includes a letter from Callis describing the exchange as he was told it by McClellan.

12. Gibbon, *Recollections*, p. 77; "Heros of Undying Fame," *Milwaukee Telegraph*, September 12, 1898. The quotation was from Jerome Watrous, who was interviewed by the *Chicago Chronicle* before the 1898 Iron Brigade Association reunion at Baraboo, Wis. The dispatch was reprinted in the *Telegraph*. William H. Harries of the Second Wisconsin twice spoke of the origin of the name in speeches to the Loyal Legion of the Commandery of the State of Minnesota. On October 8, 1895, he said, "My own recollection is, that the name originated with a war correspondent of a New York paper, three or four days after this event [South Mountain]." William H. Harries, "The Iron Brigade in the First Day's Battle of Gettysburg," cited in Otis, *Second Wisconsin*, p. 272. In another address to the Minnesota Commandery on April 12, 1904, Harries said the name was first applied by a correspondent of the Cincinnati *Daily Commercial* from Keedysville, Md., while reporting a list of killed and wounded from Gibbon's Brigade. Harries said the reporter wrote: "The last terrible battle has reduced this brigade to a mere skeleton, there being scarcely enough members to form half a regiment. This brigade has done some of the hardest and best fighting in the service. It has been justly termed the Iron Brigade of the West." Harries, in Otis, *Second Wisconsin*, p. 256. Manuscript copies of both speeches can be found in Watrous Papers, SHSW. There is evidence the men themselves very early linked the name to McClellan. Capt. Aleck Gordon, Jr., wrote home September 21, 1862, "Gen. McClellan has given us the name of the Iron Brigade," and Pvt. Hugh Perkins of the same regiment wrote to a friend in Wisconsin on September 26, 1862, that "Gen. McClellan calls us the Iron Brigade." Wisconsin Newspaper Volumes, vol. 4, pp. 21–22; "Letters of a Civil War Soldier," ed. Marilyn Gardner, prepared for syndication for April 9, 1983, *Christian Science Monitor*. The name "Iron Brigade" was also used by some of the soldiers in Hatch's Brigade, which included the Second U.S. Sharpshooters, the Twenty-second, Twenty-fourth, Thirtieth, and Eighty-fourth New York [Fourteenth Brooklyn]. Fox, *Regimental Losses*, p. 117.

13. *OR,* series 1, vol. 19, part 1, p. 25; Cook, *Telegraph,* March 11, 1883.

14. [Harries], *Telegraph,* September 9, 1883; Russell, *Columbus Republican,* August 24, 1895; *Columbus Republican,* clipping, undated (the account was written by an unnamed soldier from Company B, Seventh Wisconsin); Dawes, *Service,* p. 81.

15. Sullivan, *Telegraph,* May 13, 1888.

16. *Columbus Republican,* clipping, undated; Cheek and Pointon, *Sauk County,* p. 48; Dawes, *Service,* p. 82; Longhenry, diary, September 14, 1862. The lesser wounds were probably a result of the Confederates' being armed with smooth-bore muskets; Russell, *Columbus Republican,* August 24, 1894.

17. Sullivan, *Telegraph,* May 13, 1888.

18. Russell, *Columbus Republican,* August 24, 1895.

19. Johnson, "Recollections"; Dawes, journal, September 14, 1862; Dawes, *Service,* p. 82.

20. Dawes, journal, September 15, 1862.

21. Johnson, "Recollections."

22. Fairfield, diary, September 14, 1862; Jerome A. Watrous, manuscript, undated; Johnson, "Recollections."

23. Dawes, journal, September 15, 1862; Dawes, *Service,* pp. 82–83; D. H. Hill, "The Battle of South Mountain or Boonsboro," in Johnson and Buel, *Battles and Leaders,* vol. 2, pp. 275–276; Cheek and Pointon, *Sauk County,* pp. 47–49. In his journal, young Dawes, with a proper sniff given his New England background, remarked on the words exchanged between the combatants: "Not very refined or moral but reflective of an anxious enmity loosened in a battle." Of Whitty's wounding, Cheek and Pointon added: "The ball that went into him was never removed and the after effects of this wound finally killed him in 1906. He was wounded in three other engagements, in one of which (the Wilderness) he lost a leg. Poor Jim! he was a great soldier." Whitty had previously suffered a minor wound August 28 at Gainesville. Of George Miles, Cheek and Pointon wrote: "A braver or better soldier never gave his life for his country."

24. John Gibbon's report, *OR,* series 1, vol. 12, part 2, p. 379. Gibbon wrote, "I take great pleasure in calling especial attention to the conduct of Pvt. William Lawrence of Co. I of the Sixth Wisconsin Volunteers, whose coolness and bravery under fire fell under my personal observance on the thirtieth."

25. Johnson, "Recollections"; George D. McDill, letter to his mother, October 8, 1862; *Roster of Wisconsin Volunteers,* vol. 1, pp. 529, 531; Dawes, *Service,* p. 83; Cheek and Pointon, *Sauk County,* p. 48.

26. Bragg's report, *OR,* series 1, vol. 19, part 1, p. 254; Cheek and Pointon, *Sauk County,* p. 48; Dawes, *Service,* p. 83.

27. Dawes, journal, September 15, 1862; Dawes, *Service,* p. 83; Bragg, Chicago speech; Johnson, "Recollections."

28. "General Bragg," *Milwaukee Telegraph,* February 25, 1899. Marston's statement came as a contingent of Iron Brigade veterans called on Bragg at his Fond du Lac home on the occasion of the general's 72nd birthday. Another Sixth Wisconsin veteran, Lewis A. Kent, wrote 25 years after South Mountain that the regiment had exhausted every cartridge; Lewis A. Kent, "Capt. Kent's Memory," *Milwaukee Sunday Telegraph,* September 25, 1887.

29. Dawes, *Service,* p. 84; Lawrence enlisted from DeSoto in southwestern Wisconsin. *Roster of Wisconsin Volunteers,* vol. 1, p. 531.

30. Boatner, *Civil War Dictionary,* p. 349; Dawes, *Service,* p. 84; Dawes, journal, September 15, 1862.

31. Cheek and Pointon, *Sauk County,* p. 49.

18. Sharpsburg, Maryland

1. Dawes, *Service*, p. 85; Dawes, journal, undated. The fighting at South Mountain pitted two Old Army friends against each other. John Gibbon and his Confederate brother, Lardner Gibbon, had been groomsmen in the prewar wedding of Daniel Hill, who was in command of the Confederate defenders of Turner's Gap. Hill later described Gibbon's regiments as a "choice brigade, strong in numbers and strong in the pluck of his men, all from the North-west where habitually good fighters are reared." Hill concluded: "The Western men had met in the . . . Georgia regiments men as brave as themselves and far more advantageously posted. . . . General Gibbon reports officially 318 men killed and wounded—a loss sustained almost entirely, I think at the stone-wall. The colonel of the Seventh Wisconsin reports a loss of 147 men in killed and wounded out of 375 muskets carried into action. This shows that he had brave men and that he encountered brave men." Hill, in Johnson and Buel, *Battles and Leaders*, pp. 275–276.

2. *OR*, series 1, vol. 19, part 1, p. 254; Johnson, "Recollections."

3. Longhenry, diary, September 15, 1862.

4. *Milwaukee Free Press*, September 22, 1912. The reporter noted "a huskiness came into his voice and a suspicious glisten in his eye."

5. Jerome Watrous, manuscript, Watrous Papers, SHSW.

6. Gibbon, *Recollections*, pp. 85–86. Unaware of Sumner's salute, Gibbon added, ". . . I know I was very much disappointed at the time that his order to his troops had not reached them until they had passed by."

7. Edward Bragg, letter to Rufus Dawes, December 21, 1890, Dawes Papers, SHSW; Watrous, manuscript, undated. Watrous added he had met Sumner's son long after the war. The son was a second lieutenant on his father's staff "when the old general and his corps saluted the brigade. Among other things he once said to me was: 'My father greatly admired the Iron Brigade.'" Bragg said the salute was given "in recognition of our sturdy fight of the night before."

8. Johnson, "Recollections"; Jerome Watrous, *Appleton Crescent*, September 27, 1862.

9. Theron W. Haight, "Among the Pontoons at Fitzhugh Crossing," in *War Papers*, vol. 1 (Milwaukee, 1896), p. 421. Haight served with Company K, Twenty-fourth New York. He later was the editor of the *Waukesha* (Wis.) *Freeman*. He said the Western organization was "known among us then as the Wisconsin Brigade, but afterwards renowned throughout the west as the Old Iron Brigade."

10. Gibbon, *Recollections*, pp. 78–79.

11. Dawes, *Service*, p. 93; Edward Bragg, letter to Rufus Dawes, December 21, 1890, Dawes Papers, SHSW. Von Bachelle was born in Hanover and immigrated to the United States in 1851, arriving in New York, where he filed an initial declaration for citizenship. At the outbreak of the war, he was living in Granville, Wisconsin (now Milwaukee) with William H. Lindwurm. With the firing on Fort Sumter, Lindwurm, Von Bachelle, and another immigrant, Frederick Schumacher, began organizing the "Citizen Corps' Milwaukee," which became Company F, Sixth Wisconsin. William J. K. Beaudot, "A Milwaukee Immigrant in the Civil War," *Milwaukee History, The Magazine of the Milwaukee County Historical Society*, vol. 7, no. 1 (Spring 1984), pp. 18–28.

12. Dawes, *Service*, pp. 85–86.

13. Longhenry, diary, September 16, 1862; Dawes, *Service*, p. 86.

14. Gibbon, *Recollections*, p. 80.

15. Dawes, *Service*, p. 87; Gibbon, *Recollections*, pp. 80–81.

16. Gibbon, *Recollections*, p. 81.

17. Dawes, *Service*, p. 92.

18. Dawes, *Star*, January 8, 1885. Huntley was the grandfather of pioneer television news commentator Chet Huntley. Reuben Huntley's wife, Sarah, lived the rest of her life in Necedah, Wis., dying April 20, 1898. She was buried in the Necedah Cemetery. Members of the Dawes and Huntley families moved to the Portage, Wisconsin, area in 1855. Rufus Dawes's father, Henry, moved to nearby Mauston shortly thereafter.

19. George Fairfield, letter to his sister, October 2, 1862, Fairfield Papers, SHSW. Fairchild served in Company C and referred to Alexander S. Hooe of Prairie du Chien, one of those officers capable in all ways but one—he was frozen by the danger of battle. He resigned his commission February 7, 1863.

20. Rufus Dawes, letter to Mary Gates, August 6, 1863; Dawes, *Service*, p. 197.

21. *Telegraph*, September 28, 1879. Kellogg recovered strength enough to return to Wisconsin, but died soon after.

19. The Cornfield

1. Edward S. Bragg, letter to Col. E. A. Carman of the Antietam Battlefield Commission, December 26, 1894, Bragg Papers, SHSW; Wheeler, journal, September 17, 1862; Dawes, journal, undated; Dawes, *Service*, p. 87; Pointon and Cheek, *Sauk County*, pp. 51, 215.

2. Hooker's nickname of "Fighting Joe" was derived from the "slug" line on a series of telegraphic news dispatches filed during the Seven Days' battles in which an unknown copyist headed them "Fighting-Joe Hooker." Newspapers all over the country simply removed the hyphen and used "Fighting Joe Hooker" as a subhead. The name was forever associated with him. Rufus Dawes left a measured assessment: "The Apollo like presence of General Hooker, his self-confident, even vain glorious manner, his haughty criticism of others and his sublime courage at the battle front have combined to make impressions upon the public judgement that obscure his most valuable traits of character and his best qualities as a commander." Boatner, *Civil War Dictionary*, p. 409; Harries, in Otis, *Second Wisconsin*, p. 261; Dawes, *Service*, p. 132.

3. Frank Haskell, letter to brothers and sisters, September 22, 1862; *Soldiers' and Citizens' Album*, vol. 1, p. 722; Gibbon, *Recollections*, p. 81; John Gibbon, "Antietam Eighteen Years After," *Milwaukee Sunday Telegraph*, December 5, 1880; Edward Bragg, letter to his wife, September 21, 1862; Dawes, *Service*, pp. 87–88. Haskell added: "He [Noyes] has had his right foot amputated, saving the heel and ankle joint, is doing well, and undoubtedly will recover." Gibbon added: "I had not yet learned the powers of discipline in that brigade, nor what extant of the tests it could take and successfully pass through."

4. Bragg's Report, *OR*, series 1, vol. 19, part 1, p. 255; Rufus R. Dawes, "On The Right at Antietam," *Sketches of War History*, Ohio Military Order of the Loyal Legion of the United States, vol. 3, pp. 252–263, as reprinted in Dawes, *Service*, pp. 333–334; Eugene Anderson, letter to his mother and father, September 22, 1862, private collection.

5. From a letter written by John P. Hart of Fond du Lac for Sgt. Andrew Deacon, dated Keedysville, Md., October 2, 1862. Deacon enlisted from Fond du Lac and was wounded at Antietam. His arm was subsequently amputated

and he was discharged as disabled December 10, 1862. The sergeant said Lucius Murray stayed with Brown until he died, the officer giving Murray "his revolver and he thinks his watch wishing them to be sent home to his wife." The letter concluded: "Company 'E' will long remember him. He was ever kind and noble and human man. It is a loss to the Company, deeply regretted by all. He had not a single enemy in the whole Regiment, and may he rest in peace is the wish of the whole company."

6. In a letter September 28, 1862, Bragg wrote his own wife: "Mrs. Capt. Brown, must feel the loss of her husband severely. I wrote her a letter of condolence, a day or two since, it was difficult for me to do, but I thought it would be something to her feelings and gratifying to the family. But, such duties, I do not like to perform they are not to my taste."

7. Dawes, journal, undated; Dawes, *Service*, pp. 88–89; Edward Bragg, letter to Ezra Carman, December 26, 1894; Gibbon, *Recollections*, p. 82. In his official report, Bragg wrote "the right of my line of skirmishers having failed to advance, either from a failure to hear or heed commands. [sic.]" The "[sic.]" was added, he wrote Carman, because Company C's Alexander Hooe "showed the white feather. . . ." *OR*, series 1, vol. 19, part 1, p. 250. Hooe, whose father of the same name was a hero in the Mexican War, organized the Prairie du Chien Volunteers, Company C of the Sixth. The elder Hooe (some records spell the name Hove) was a Virginian by birth and had moved west to Prairie du Chien in the 1830s. The editor of the Prairie du Chien newspaper in 1861 described the younger Hooe as a "patriotic and efficient officer who has a thorough knowledge of the duties of a soldier acquired at West Point. He is the most capable man in this part of the country to lead a company." Hooe was discharged from the Sixth Wisconsin February 7, 1863. *Prairie du Chien Courier*, May 2, 1861; *History of Crawford and Richland Counties*, Wisconsin (Springfield, Ill., 1884), pp. 497–499; *Roster of Wisconsin Volunteers*, vol. 1, p. 505.

8. Bragg probably saw one of the guns from Cutt's Battalion of the Confederate artillery reserve under Brig. Gen. William N. Pendleton. See Ezra A. Carman, manuscript, Manuscript Division, Library of Congress, p. 23. Carman was colonel of the Twelfth New Jersey Infantry at Antietam. He also served on the Antietam Battlefield Board after the war. His account was written following an extensive exchange of letters and conversations with officers serving at Antietam.

9. This force comprised Jones and Winder's Virginia brigades of Jackson's Division. Carman, manuscript, p. 24.

10. Bragg's report, *OR*, series 1, vol. 19, part 1, p. 255; Edward S. Bragg, letter to Rufus Dawes, December 21, 1890; Dawes, journal, undated; Edward Bragg, speech to Chicago reunion, undated; Gibbon, *Telegraph*, December 5, 1880; Carman, manuscript, p. 23.

11. Dawes, *Service*, p. 89; Dawes, journal, undated. In his war memoir, Dawes deleted reference to the fact it was Federal artillery which struck Bode and Ticknor. Bode enlisted May 10, 1861. He served as corporal and first sergeant before being commissioned July 16, 1862. *Roster of Wisconsin Volunteers*, vol. 1, pp. 517, 533; Eugene Anderson, letter to his parents, September 22, 1862.

12. Edward S. Bragg, letter to his wife, September 21, 1862.

13. Dawes, *Service*, p. 89; Dawes, journal, undated.

14. Edward Bragg, letter to his wife, September 21, 1862; [Jerome A. Watrous], "Old Man, are you Hurt?" *Milwaukee Telegraph*, December 10, 1898.

15. Dawes, *Service*, pp. 89–90.

16. *Milwaukee Free Press*, September 22, 1912.

17. Carman, manuscript, p. 27; Dawes, *Service*, pp. 90–91. The two Wisconsin

regiments faced the Twenty-sixth, Thirty-eighth, and Sixty-first Georgia of Lawton's Brigade. The distance between the two lines was about 200 yards.

18. *Soldiers' and Citizens' Album*, vol. 1, p. 722. Gaffney subsequently recovered, but was soon discharged as disabled. After the war, he was a farmer in the Town of Osceola, Fond du Lac County, where he served several terms as town clerk. [Jerome Watrous], "Bragg's Rifles," *Milwaukee Sunday Telegraph*, January 4, 1880.

19. Frank A. Haskell, letter to his brothers and sisters, September 22, 1862; Dawes, *Service*, pp. 93–94; *Soldiers' and Citizens' Album*, vol. 1, p. 722.

20. Frank A. Haskell, letter to his brothers and sisters, September 22, 1862.

21. Converse entered the war as a sergeant of the Prescott Guards, Company B of the Sixth, and became one of the best-loved officers of the regiment. Born in Lawrence County, New York, he was working as a clerk in Prescott in 1861. He was mortally wounded in the Battle of the Wilderness in 1864 and died before his 24th birthday; Dawes, *Mauston Star*, January 8, 1885. Gerlaugh and Black were found in the same grave at Keedysville, Md. The gravestone noted: "To the memory of Franklin Gerlaugh and Wm. P. Black, aged respectively nineteen years five months and twenty-one days. Killed at the Battle of Antietam, September 17, 1862. Rest Soldier." Doc Aubrey, *Echoes of the Marches of the Famous Iron Brigade, 1861–1865* (Milwaukee, 1900) pp. 66–67.

22. Carman, manuscript, p. 28; Dawes, journal, undated. The attacking line consisted of Starke's Louisiana Brigade and Taliaferro's Brigade of Alabama and Virginia regiments. Starke had about 650 men, Taliaferro about 500. Starke aimed his attack on the southwest corner of the cornfield where the Wisconsin men had made their appearance in pursuit of the three Georgia regiments. The Federals extending the Union line were from the Second U.S. Sharpshooters; Report of Marsena Patrick, *OR*, series 1, vol. 19, part 1, p. 235. Patrick said his brigade was "25 paces" behind the Wisconsin line when he ordered his men to lie down in the corn before moving up in support.

23. Dawes, *Service*, p. 90.

24. Dawes, journal, undated; Dawes, *Service*, pp. 214–215. Tomlinson, who enlisted from Diamond Bluff in the Prescott Guards, was later wounded at Gettysburg and captured at Haymarket, Va., a few months later. He died June 28, 1864, in the Confederate prison at Andersonville. *Roster of Wisconsin Volunteers*, vol. 1, p. 405.

25. Dawes, *Service*, pp. 214–215; Dawes, journal, September 17, 1862; Horace Emerson, letter to mother and sister, September 28, 1862. Emerson identified the soldier who was struck in the face as Gustav Elterman, and added: "He did not know what hit him. He was a good man and had never been hit before and had been in all the fights that the Regt had been in." Elterman, a native of Germany, was 18 when he enlisted at Portage April 19, 1861; Harries, in Otis, *Second Wisconsin*, p. 18; Emerson, letter to mother and sister, September 28, 1862. "It made a very bad wound and a very painful one," Emerson wrote of Hill's wound. Charles Dow of the Second Wisconsin wrote September 24, 1862: "I got a letter from Lieut. Hill the other day. He was wounded in the groin on the 17th. It is a bad wound, but not considered dangerous; he is doing well, and is going home (to his wife I suppose) as soon as he is able to ride." Dow, letter, September 24, 1862. Hill resigned June 1, 1863. *Roster of Wisconsin Volunteers*, vol. 1, p. 364.

26. Dawes, journal, undated.

27. Dawes, *Service*, pp. 90–91.

28. Dawes, journal, undated; Edward Bragg, letter to Ezra Carman, December 26, 1894.

29. Gibbon, *Telegraph*, December 5, 1880.

20. Give 'Em Hell!

1. Gibbon, *Telegraph*, December 5, 1880; Stewart's report, *OR*, series 1, vol. 19, part 1, p. 231. Stewart cited Meeds's "cheerful and very effective service." Meeds, of Perry, Wis., was a member of Company B. He was wounded at Chancellorsville in 1863 and was discharged on January 31, 1864, to enlist in the regular army. *Roster of Wisconsin Volunteers*, vol. 1, p. 503. A 12-pound Napoleon could be fired two or three times a minute depending on the proficiency of the crew; see Boatner, *Civil War Dictionary*, p. 120. ·

2. "John Cook, the Boy Gunner," in W. F. Beyer and O. F. Keydel, eds., *Deeds of Valor*, vol. 1 (Detroit, 1903), pp. 75–76; Gibbon, *Telegraph*, December 5, 1880. Cook, born August 10, 1847, enlisted when he was 14. Gibbon reported three cannoneers were killed and 11 wounded in the space of a few minutes. Bugler Cook was not related to John "Tough One" Cook of the Sixth Wisconsin. Both served with the battery at the same time.

3. Buell, *Cannoneer*, p. 34; Carman, manuscript, pp. 59–60. ·

4. Gibbon, *Telegraph*, December 5, 1880; Edward Bragg, letter to Ezra Carman, December 26, 1894; Gibbon, *Recollections*, pp. 83–84.

5. "John Cook," pp. 75–76.

6. A canister round was made up of a powder charge and a metallic container filled with cast-iron or lead balls or long slugs set in dry sawdust. The canister ruptured on firing, scattering the slugs much like a round fired from a modern-day shotgun. It was mainly used against infantry and had an effective range of between 100 and 400 yards. Occasionally, a gun would fire double or even triple canister. In these cases, the drill called for the powder container to be broken off the second round before loading. Boatner, *Civil War Dictionary*, p. 119.

7. Klinefelter enlisted in Company D, Seventh Wisconsin, in 1861 and served with that regiment until he was transferred to Battery B of the Fourth U.S. on March 7, 1862. He served with the battery until January 1864. He was wounded at the Wilderness in May 1864, and was mustered out on March 6, 1865. He subsequently accepted a commission with the Fifty-first Wisconsin Infantry, but the war ended before the regiment was readied for the war. *Roster of Wisconsin Volunteers*, vol. 1, p. 552.

8. Buell, *Cannoneer*, pp. 38–39. Ripley was transferred to Battery B September 12, 1862, and served with the guns until August 1864. He mustered out September 1, 1864, at the end of his enlistment. *Roster of Wisconsin Volunteers*, vol. 1, p. 547.

9. "John Cook," pp. 114–115; Gibbon, *Recollections*, p. 83; Gibbon, *Telegraph*, December 5, 1880; Buell, *Cannoneer*, pp. 34–35.

10. Buell, *Cannoneer*, p. 39; Gibbon, *Recollections*, pp. 83–84. William Harries of the Second Wisconsin later told the story about Gibbon to former Confederate Gen. Harry Heth, who had been a classmate of Gibbon's at the U.S. Military Academy. "John, did you leave your brigade during the fight and act as gunner of your old battery?" Heth asked. "Why, you should have been court-martialed for it." Gibbon replied, "Yes, I did do that. I knew the men of my old brigade would fight without me and just at that particular moment that gun needed looking after to make its fire effective." Harries said the exchange occurred in the Army and Navy Club room at Washington a few years before Gibbon's death in 1896. Harries, in Otis, *Second Wisconsin*, p. 262.

11. Buell, *Cannoneer*, p. 34; "John Cook," pp. 75–76.

12. Dawes, journal, undated; Dawes, "Sketches of War History," pp. 252–263; Gibbon, *Recollections*, pp. 82–84; John Gibbon, letter to James Stewart, August 4, 1893, National Archives, Antietam Studies; "John Cook," p. 76; Edward Bragg, letter to Ezra Carman, December 26, 1894; "Choice Reminiscences," *Milwaukee Sunday Telegraph*, March 4, 1883. It was Gibbon's recollection the 20th New York did not advance beyond the caissons of Battery B.

13. Dawes, *Service*, p. 91; Dawes, journal, undated; Edward Bragg, letter to Ezra Carman, December 26, 1894; William Dudley's report, *OR*, series 1, vol. 19, part 1, p. 252; Stine, *Army of the Potomac*, p. 193. The Confederate line on the brow of the hill south of the cornfield was made up of survivors of Ripley's Brigade; Carman, manuscript, pp. 59–60.

14. Carman, manuscript, pp. 60–62.

15. Gibbon, *Telegraph*, December 5, 1880.

16. *Telegraph*, March 4, 1883. Another incident often related at veterans' meetings supposedly occurred at the very height of the fighting. Nearby was a brigade chaplain, a pious man "always at hand when the boys were double shooting, sleeves rolled up, working their guns to the best." As he watched, one gunner stepped back before firing, telling his comrades, "Now, boys, give 'em hell." The chaplain stepped in to reprimand the gunner. "How do you expect to have the support of Divine Providence when you use such language!" The gunner, a man with his hands full at the moment, gave the chaplain a hard look. "To hell with the Divine Providence, the Iron Brigade supports us," he said, turning back to his gun—or at least that is how the story was told at the meetings. Cheek and Pointon, *Sauk County*, p. 214.

17. Gibbon, *Telegraph*, December 5, 1880; Edward Bragg, letter to Earl Rogers, April 5, 1900; Aubrey, *Echoes*, p. 51; Buell, *Cannoneer*, p. 35.

18. Dawes, journal, undated; Cheek and Pointon, *Sauk County*, pp. 51–52. Morris enlisted July 12, 1861. He was wounded May 12, 1864, and mustered out July 14, 1865. Pruyn was killed at Laurel Hill in 1864; Vanleuven and Klein mustered out at the end of their three-year enlistments; Pearson was killed at Gettysburg; and Saare and Keyes served their four years and went home. *Roster of Wisconsin Volunteers*, vol. 1, pp. 496, 500, 507.

19. Dawes, journal, undated; Dawes, *Service*, p. 92; Gibbon, *Recollections*, pp. 87–89. John Kellogg with Rufus Dawes helped organize the "Lemonweir Minute Men" at Mauston. He was a native of Bethany, Wayne County, Pennsylvania, the son of a tavernkeeper, stage proprietor, and contractor. His grandfather served in the Revolutionary War. The Kellogg family moved to the Wisconsin Territory about 1840. At the start of the war, Kellogg was district attorney of Juneau County. He resigned to go to war. Kellogg, one of the founders of the Republican Party, being a member of the Madison convention of September 5, 1855, died in 1883 at age 55. On the field following the repulse of the First Corps, Gibbon found Brig. Gen. George H. Gordon with Gordon's Brigade. "My attention was attracted to him and to his command first because he was a classmate and second because in talking with him, I learned that he had in his brigade a Wisconsin regiment (the 3rd) of whose conduct in battle he seemed as proud as I was of my three regiments from the same state," Gibbon wrote later. Gordon's Brigade had been involved in the second Federal assault on the cornfield.

20. [Watrous], *Telegraph*, December 10, 1898. Bartlett, of East Troy, was assistant surgeon from June 1861 until October 1862, when he was transferred to the Third Wisconsin. *Roster of Wisconsin Volunteers*, vol. 1, pp. 494–514.

21. Dawes, *Service*, pp. 92–93; Dawes, journal, undated; Edward Bragg, letter to Earl Rogers, April 3, 1900; [Watrous], *Telegraph*, September 26, 1896.

22. Edward Bragg, letter to Earl Rogers, April 3, 1900; [Watrous], *Telegraph,* September 26, 1896; Cook, *Telegraph,* March 11, 1883.

21. Too Horrible to Behold

1. *Milwaukee Free Press*, September 22, 1912; Dawes, *Service,* p. 94; Cheek and Pointon, *Sauk County*, p. 213. Moran escaped several close calls during his four years of service with the Sixth Wisconsin, mustering out with his regiment in July 1865. *Roster of Wisconsin Volunteers*, vol. 1, p. 511.

2. Nolan, *Iron Brigade*, pp. 142–143; [Lucius Fairchild], *Wisconsin Journal,* September 24, 1862; Buell, *Cannoneer*, pp. 24–25.

3. Dawes, *Service*, pp. 94–95; Edward Bragg, letter to wife, September 21, 1862; Longhenry, diary, September 18–20, 1862; Gibbon, *Recollections*, p. 91; Gibbon, *Telegraph*, December 8, 1880; Edward Bragg, letter to E. A. Carman, December 20, 1894. The Confederate was Matthew Dale, acting lieutenant colonel of the First Texas. *OR*, series 1, vol. 19, part 1, p. 923.

4. Hugh Perkins, letter to a friend, September 21, 1862; Wheeler, journal, September 19, 1862; Horace Emerson, letter to mother and sister, September 28, 1862; Julius Murray, letter to a daughter, September 27, 1862.

5. Julius Murray, letter to a daughter, September 27, 1862; Hugh Perkins, letter to "friend Herbert," September 21, 1862; Horace Emerson, letter to mother and sister, September 28, 1862.

6. *Milwaukee Free Press*, September 22, 1912; Edward Bragg, letter to Ezra Carman, December 26, 1894; Gibbon, *Telegraph*, December 5, 1880; Longhenry, diary, September 19, 1862; Earl Rogers, *Vernon County Censor*, November 21, 1906. Von Bachelle's body was later moved to the Antietam National Cemetery. It was placed in the officer's section and not with Wisconsin dead. Basel and Gotsch mustered out with the regiment in 1865; Mueller was discharged at the end of his three-year enlistment; Schilcke was discharged March 18, 1864, for wounds received at Gettysburg and Fitzhugh's Crossing; and Fink was discharged disabled January 9, 1865, for a wound suffered at Laurel Hill in 1864. *Roster of Wisconsin Volunteers*, vol. 1, pp. 516–519.

7. Wheeler, journal, September 19, 1862; Longhenry, diary, September 20, 1862.

8. Wheeler, journal, September 19, 1862; Horace Emerson, letter, September 28, 1862; Cheek and Pointon, *Sauk County*, pp. 52–53; Longhenry, diary, September 18, 1862.

9. [William Harries], "Hospital Experiences," *Milwaukee Sunday Telegraph,* November 8, 1885.

10. [Harries], *Telegraph,* November 29, 1885; [Harries], *Telegraph,* November 8, 1885; *Roster of Wisconsin Volunteers*, vol. 1, p. 505.

11. [Harries], *Telegraph,* November 8, 1885; [Jerome Watrous], *Milwaukee Sunday Telegraph,* October 5, 1890. Watrous also wrote the sight of those amputated arms and legs "would cause the generation that has grown up since the war some of whose members feel a little disposed to laugh at old soldiers and to place a slight estimation upon their services, to confess that the war cost was something." Edward Bragg wrote his wife September 21, 1862: "Poor Deacon I hear has lost his arm, but I do not know certainly. I shall try and get permission to go to the rear this afternoon and look him up. He is not dangerous and I hear is doing well. He was a brave boy, and never flinched. This was his fourth battle." Deacon was discharged as disabled December 10, 1862. *Roster of Wisconsin Volunteers*, vol. 1, p. 494.

12. Magdeburg, in *War Papers,* vol. 2, p. 197; Lyman Upham, *Mauston Star,* October 1, 1862.

13. George D. McDill, letter to his mother, October 8, 1862. McDill was promoted to Second Lt. Co. E, Thirty-seventh Wisconsin Infantry, March 7, 1864. *Roster of Wisconsin Volunteers,* vol. 1, p. 531.

14. Isaac Brown, letter to his son, September 21, 1862. To the *Appleton Crescent,* Joseph Marston of Brown's Company E wrote: "Captain E. A. Brown fell while leading his men on the field. He died nobly for his country, which he so much loved. I have often seen him point to the old starry banner and affirm that he would either live under its protecting folds or die in its defence. He was formerly a student of Lawrence University, and a young man of more than ordinary ability. He left a good law business at home to serve his country, and all who knew him as a soldier and officer, knew him but to honor and respect. Every man in his Company loved him, and his loss is deeply mourned by us all." Joseph Marston, *Appleton Crescent,* October 25, 1862. Edward Bragg wrote his wife September 21, 1862: "By the way have the information conveyed . . . I have the Capts sword. It was found by a New York man, in the field & I reclaimed it, & will have it sent home as soon as possible."

22. The Men Have Stood Like Iron

1. Sometime after October 26, 1862, the regiments of Doubleday's Division, including the Sixth Wisconsin, were inspected, with deficiencies and faults reported directly to McClellan's headquarters. The result for the Sixth Wisconsin was as follows:

Field officers present, one.
Line officers present, ten.

Co. A present effectives 46;	noneffectives, 5,	total 51.
" B, " " 32;	" 1,	" 33.
" C, " " 44;	" 3,	" 47.
" D, " " 33;	" 3,	" 36.
" E, " " 26;	" 0,	" 26.
" F, " " 21;	" 1,	" 22.
" G, " " 22;	" 0,	" 22.
" H, " " 14;	" 1,	" 15.
" I, " " 40;	" 5,	" 45.
" K, " " 35;	" 4,	" 39.
Effectives 313	noneffectives 23	total 336.

Dawes added: "There were 81 defective cartridge boxes in the regiment. There were no men without arms. The condition of arms was 'very good.' The absent were all accounted for. The condition of clothing was generally 'bad, and shoes very bad.' The tin magazines in the cartridge boxes were to keep the powder dry. In battle the men would often throw them away in order to more quickly and easily get at their cartridges; but the cartridge box was thus ruined for further service. It would no longer keep the cartridges dry. Instruction had been given to particularly examine all cartridge boxes. The inspect was very thorough and rigid, and it disclosed that the army was in a destitute and almost disorganized condition." Dawes, *Service,* p. 103.

2. Dawes, *Service,* p. 96; Edward Bragg, letter to Earl Rogers, April 3, 1900; Gibbon *Recollections,* p. 92; George D. McDill, letter to his mother, October 8, 1862.

3. Dawes, *Service*, p. 96; Rufus Dawes, letter to his mother, September 18, 1862, written "in line of battle near Sharpsburg, Maryland."

4. Aleck Gordon, Jr., letter, September 21, 1862, Wisconsin Newspaper Volumes, vol. 4, pp. 21–22, State Historical Society of Wisconsin; Hugh Perkins, letter to "Dear friend Herbert," September 26, 1862; Frank Haskell, letter to brothers and sisters, September 22, 1862.

5. Cheek and Pointon, *Sauk County*, p. 53; Nolan, *Iron Brigade*, p. 174. McClellan's letter to Indiana Gov. Oliver Morton was printed in the *Indianapolis Daily Journal*, October 13, 1862.

6. Longhenry, diary, October 8, 1862; Jerome Watrous, *Appleton Crescent*, September 27, 1862; Hugh Perkins, letter, September 21, 1862.

7. Harries, in Otis, *Second Wisconsin*, p. 268; letter of Henry F. Young, an officer of the Seventh Wisconsin, Wisconsin Veterans Museum, Madison; Dawes, *Service*, p. 126. Dawes's address was made March 19, 1863.

8. Edward Bragg, letter to his wife, October 3, 1862; Jerome Watrous, manuscript, Watrous Papers, SHSW; George D. McDill, letter to his mother, October 8, 1862; Dawes, *Service*, p. 100. Bragg, who was wounded, did not attend the review for Lincoln.

9. *OR*, series 1, vol. 19, part 1, pp. 246–247.

10. John Gibbon, letter to James Stewart, August 4, 1893, National Archives, Antietam Studies, Record Group 94. Gibbon was responding to a question by Stewart. The general admitted his recollections were "dim," adding the records would identify the regiment but it was his memory the "Regiment was the Twentieth N.Y. and the Col. or Lt. Col's name, Gates." Lt. John McEntee of the Twentieth New York wrote his father that the Sixth "broke and run, leaving their colors on the field, which our boys picked up and brought off, together with a rebel color, the bearer of which one of our men shot."

11. *OR*, series 1, vol. 19, part 1, pp. 254–256.

12. Edward Bragg, letter to E. A. Carman of the Antietam Battlefield Commission, December 26, 1894. "I cannot forbear saying that the report of this last named officer [Gates] relative to a flag of the Sixth Wis. (The Regiment had two flags) which was abandoned and rescued (?) by his command, and the capture also of a Confederate flag by his regiment, going into details, naming the sergeant who shot down the bearer, smacks of 'Munchausenism.'"

13. Dawes, *Service*, pp. 91, 339.

14. The Confederate flag credited to the Twentieth New York (War Department capture no. 33) is presently in the Museum of the Confederacy in Richmond. Attached is a card stating: "HdQrs., Doubleday's Div, Confederate Battle Flag captured at the Battle of Sharpsburg, Sept. Seventeenth 1862 by Privt. Isaac Thompson, Co. C, Twentieth N. York S.M. He shot the Rebel color Bearer, ran forward and brought off the colors. Theodore B. Gates Lt. Col. commanding." Civil War flag expert Howard Michael Madaus believes the flag "most likely belonged to one of the Georgia regiments of Evans' Brigade, which had arrived from the deep South just before the Second Manassas campaign, and which encountered the Second and the Sixth Wisconsin in the cornfield." Register of Captured Flags, 1861–65, Records of the Adjutant-General's Office (Record Group No. 94) National Archives; Howard Michael Madaus, letter to the author, December 12, 1992.

15. *OR*, series 1, vol. 13, part 1, pp. 255–256; Edward Bragg, letter to his wife, September 21, 1862.

16. Jerome Watrous, *Appleton Crescent*, July 27, 1861.

17. Howard Michael Madaus, "The Flags of the Iron Brigade," part 1, *Wisconsin Magazine of History*, vol. 69, no. 1 (Autumn 1985), pp. 3–35; Edward Bragg,

letter to the governor, April 4, 1863, cited Dawes, *Service,* p. 131. The speaker was Wisconsin Supreme Court Justice Orsamus Cole. He addressed the reception June 15, 1864, when the Second Wisconsin returned to Madison to be mustered out of service. In his address, Cole noted: "And now as Wisconsin received from the possession of this Regiment, these sacred colors intrusted to its charge, colors faded and torn by the smoke and shot of many battlefield, and folds them up and places them away with these other blood-stained and battle-scarred banners borne by her gallant sons on other fields—priceless relics—symbols of her power and grandeur—she well knows that not one among them all has been carried by braver men—not one has been in the hour of conflict more steadily or further advanced in the face of a haughty foe." Otis, *Second Wisconsin,* pp. 123–124.

18. Jerome Watrous, "Program for the Dedication of Grand Army Memorial Hall in the Capitol, Madison, Wisconsin, June 14, 1918," Wisconsin Veterans Museum, Madison.

23. May God Bless Us

1. Jerome Watrous, "Of One Day's Work," *Milwaukee Telegraph*, October 28, 1893; Dawes, *Service*, p. 101; Longhenry, diary, October 9, 1862, January 13, 1863; Lucius Shattuck, letter to his brother, October 17, 1862, University of Michigan Historical Library, Ann Arbor; Gibbon, *Recollections*, p. 92; Curtis, *Twenty-fourth*, p. 466

2. Curtis, *Twenty-fourth*, p. 65.

3. Otis, *Second Wisconsin*, p. 111; George E. Smith, "In the Ranks at Fredericksburg" [part 1], in Johnson and Buel, *Battles and Leaders*, vol. 3, p. 142; Orson B. Curtis, "In the Ranks at Fredericksburg" [part 2], in *Battles and Leaders*, vol. 3, p. 142. Smith served with the Second Wisconsin and Curtis the Twenty-fourth Michigan. "We made unmerciful sport of them, but never a joke or word of abuse did I hear after the Twenty-fourth had shown its mettle in the battle of Fredericksburg," said Smith. In reality, 428 men came from Detroit, 479 from Wayne County townships, and 120 from other Michigan counties. Curtis, *Twenty-fourth*, p. 45.

4. U.S. Pension Office, John Tait file, "Widow's Claim for Pension," July 10, 1863; *Detroit Free Press*, May 13, 1863; Curtis, *Twenty-fourth*, p. 336. Typical of the bounties offered by community leaders was the $100 for the first regimental colorbearer of the Twenty-fourth Michigan from Theodore H. Eaton, a retail druggist in Detroit. Eaton, in a letter to Col. H. A. Morrow of the Twenty-fourth Michigan, also pledged an additional $100 to the regiment's colorbearer at the close of the war "if the Colors shall not have been lost in battle." Eaton added: "You will particularly oblige me by not allowing the contents of this note to be published." The original letter is in a private collection.

5. Otis, *Second Wisconsin*, p. 63.

6. Rufus Dawes, letters, October 31, November 7, and November 9, 1862; Dawes, *Service*, pp. 104–105; Lucius Shattuck letter, cited Donald L. Smith, *The Twenty-fourth Michigan of the Iron Brigade* (Harrisburg, Pa., 1962), p. 47; Watrous, *Telegraph*, October 28, 1893; Jerome Watrous, *Appleton Crescent*, November 11, 1862; Longhenry, diary, October 30–31, November 7, 1862.

7. Lucius Shattuck, letter to his sister, November 10, 1863; Horace Emerson, letter to mother and sister, September 28, 1862; James Bartlett, letter to "Dear Brother and Sister," January 13, 1863, James Bartlett Papers, Plymouth Historical Society, Plymouth, Mich. Bartlett added: "I could endure it all well eoug

[enough] if I thought that the leaders were trying to setle the war. But I believe that the rebels is no nearer subdued now than they were 2 years ago. But if the officers on both sides who are working for had to take up with the same force . . . as we privates[,] I believe the thing would be settled in a hurry."

8. Lucius Shattuck, letter to his sister, Ellen, November 2, 1862; Gibbon, *Recollections*, p. 94.

9. Gibbon, *Recollections*, pp. 95–96; P. W. Plummer, letter, November 8, 1862, to the *Wisconsin State Journal*; Rufus Dawes, letter, November 7, 1862; Dawes, *Service*, p. 105. Morrow assumed temporary command of the brigade because Cols. Lysander Cutler of the Sixth Wisconsin, William Robinson of the Seventh Wisconsin, and Solomon Meredith of the Nineteenth Indiana were absent wounded and Morrow outranked Fairchild. Meredith was given command of the brigade November 25, 1862, and held the post until he was wounded at Gettysburg on July 1, 1863.

24. The Government Has Gone Mad

1. One of the "War" candidates defeated in the 1862 election was Lt. Col. Edward Bragg of the Sixth Wisconsin, who returned to Wisconsin to recover from his wound at Antietam and campaign for Congress. "It is manifest that the cowardly sneaks who stay at home intend to sell out the country," Rufus Dawes wrote home November 10, 1862; Dawes, *Service*, pp. 105–106.

2. [Jerome A. Watrous], "Rather Sensational," *Milwaukee Sunday Telegraph*, August 7, 1887; [Kent], *Telegraph*, September 26, 1887; George C. Gordon, letter to "my dear wife," November 12, 1862. Watrous used a long quotation taken from Harris's interview with the St. Louis newspaper, the *Globe Democrat*. The "lieutenant colonel" referred to was probably Edward Bragg of the Sixth Wisconsin. Gordon served as captain of Company I, Twenty-fourth Michigan; George Gordon Papers, State Archives of Michigan.

3. Gibbon, *Recollections*, p. 96; *Appleton Crescent*, November 11, 1862; Edward Bragg, letter to his wife, November 16, 1862.

4. George Fairfield, letter to his sister, October 2, 1862; Edward Bragg, letter to his wife, March 22, 1863; Rufus Dawes, letter to William Cutler, February 24, 1863; Dawes, *Service*, pp. 123, 126; [Kent], *Telegraph*, September 26, 1887; Edward Bragg, speech to reunion at Chicago, undated.

5. Rufus Dawes, letter to W. P. Cutler, November 30, 1862.

6. Cheek and Pointon, *Sauk County*, p. 54; Longhenry, diary, October 30, 1862.

BIBLIOGRAPHY

Books

Annual Report of the Adjutant General of the State of Wisconsin, Madison, William J. Park & Co., 1866.

Annual Reports of the Adjutant General of the State of Wisconsin for the Years 1860, 1861, 1862, 1863 and 1864, Madison, 1912.

Aubrey, Doc [Cullen B.], *Recollections of a Newsboy in the Army of the Potomac*, Milwaukee, 1900. [Contains the monograph *Echoes of the Marches of the Famous Iron Brigade, 1861–1865*.]

Beaudot, William J. K., and Lance J. Herdegen, *An Irishman in the Iron Brigade*, New York, Fordham University Press, 1993.

Beecham, R[obert] K., "Adventures of an Iron Brigade Man" [pasteup of a series of articles appearing in *The National Tribune*], 1902.

Beyer, W. F., and O. F. Keydel, eds., *Deeds of Valor*, 2 vols., Detroit, Perrien-Keydel Company, 1903, 1906.

Boatner, Mark M., *Civil War Dictionary*, New York, 1959.

Bryant, Edwin E., *History of the Third Regiment Wisconsin Veteran Volunteer Infantry, 1861–1865*, Madison, Veteran Association of the Regiment, 1891.

Buell, Augustus, *The Cannoneer: Recollections of Service in the Army of the Potomac*, Washington, D.C., National Tribune, 1897.

Byer, F. H., *A Compendium of the War of the Rebellion*, Des Moines, Iowa, 1908.

Byrne, Frank L., and Andrew T. Weaver, eds., *Haskell of Gettysburg, His Life and Civil War Papers*, Madison, State Historical Society of Wisconsin, 1970.

Cheek, Philip, and Mair Pointon, *History of the Sauk County Riflemen, Known as Company "A," Sixth Wisconsin Veteran Volunteer Infantry, 1861- 1865*, n.p., 1909.

Coddington, Edwin B., *The Gettysburg Campaign*, New York, Charles Scribner's Sons, 1968.

Cook, John H., "Cook's Time in the Army," manuscript, John H. Cook Papers, Madison, State Historical Society of Wisconsin.

Current, Richard N., *The History of Wisconsin: The Civil War Era, 1848–1873*, Madison, State Historical Society of Wisconsin, 1976.

Curtis, O[rson] B., *History of the Twenty-fourth Michigan of the Iron Brigade*, Detroit, Winn & Hammond, 1891.

Dawes, Rufus R., *Service with the Sixth Wisconsin Volunteers*, Marietta, Ohio, E. R. Alderman & Sons, 1890. [Reprinted Dayton, Ohio, Morningside House, 1984.]

Dawes, Rufus R., "Sketches of War History," Military Order of the Loyal Legion of the United States, Commandery of the State of Ohio, in *War Papers*, vol. 3. [Reprinted in Dawes, *Service with the Sixth Wisconsin Volunteers*, 1984.]

Dawes-Gates Ancestral Lines, A Memorial Volume Containing the American Ancestry of Mary Beman (Gates) Dawes, comp. Mary Walton Ferris, vol. 1, privately printed, 1943.

Dawes-Gates Ancestral Lines, A Memorial Volume Containing the American Ancestry of Rufus R. Dawes, comp. Mary Walton Ferris, vol. 2, privately printed, 1931.

Dennett, Tyler, ed., *John Hay, Lincoln and the Civil War Letters and Diaries of John Hay*, New York, Dodd, Mead & Company, 1939.

Dictionary of Wisconsin Biography, Madison, State Historical Society of Wisconsin, 1961.

Dudley, William W., *The Iron Brigade at Gettysburg, 1878, OfficialReport of the Part Borne by the 1st Brigade, 1st Division, 1st Army Corps*, Cincinnati, privately printed, 1879.

Dunn, Craig L., *Iron Men, Iron Will: The Nineteenth Indiana Regiment of the Iron Brigade*, Indianapolis, Guild Press of Indiana, Inc., 1995.

Fitch, Michael H., *Echoes of the Civil War as I Hear Them*, New York, 1905.

[Flower, Frank A.], *History of Milwaukee Wisconsin*, Chicago, Western Historical Co., 1881.

Freeman, Douglas S., *Lee's Lieutenants*, 3 vols., New York, Charles Scribner's Sons, 1942–1944.

Gaff, Alan D., *Brave Men's Tears: The Iron Brigade at Brawner Farm*, Dayton, Ohio, Morningside House, 1985.

Gaff, Alan D., *If This Is War*, Dayton, Ohio, Morningside House, 1991.

Gates, Betsey Shipman, *Grandma's Letters*, prepared by Mary Dawes Beach, Chicago, privately printed, 1926.

Gates, Theodore B., *The "Ulster Guard" [20th N.Y. State Militia] and the War of the Rebellion*, New York, Benj. H. Tyrrel, 1879.

Gibbon, John, *Personal Recollections of the Civil War*, New York, G. P. Putnam's Sons, 1928.

Gramm, Kent, *Gettysburg: A Meditation on War and Values*, Bloomington, Indiana University Press, 1994.

Haskell, Frank Aretas, *The Battle of Gettysburg*, second edition, Madison, Wisconsin History Commission, 1910.

Hennessy, John J., *Return to Bull Run: The Campaign and Battle of Second Manassas*, New York, Simon & Schuster, 1993.

Herdegen, Lance J., and William J. K. Beaudot, *In the Bloody Railroad Cut at Gettysburg*, Dayton, Ohio, Morningside House, 1990.

Hinkley, Julian Wisner, *Service with the Third Wisconsin Infantry*, Madison, Wisconsin History Commission, 1912.

History of Vernon County, Wisconsin, Springfield, Ill., Union Publishing Co., 1884.

Hurn, Ethel Alice, *Wisconsin Women in the War between the States*, Madison, Wisconsin History Commission, 1911.

Indiana at Antietam; Report of the Indiana Antietam Monument Commission and Ceremonies at the Dedication of the Monument, Indianapolis, Indiana Monument Commission, 1911.

Johnson, Robert U., and Clarence C. Buel, eds., *Battles and Leaders of the Civil War*, 4 vols., New York, Century Co., 1884–1887.

Kellogg, John A., *Capture and Escape: A Narrative of Army and Prison Life*, Madison, Wisconsin History Commission, 1908.

Klement, Frank L., *Wisconsin and the Civil War*, Madison, State Historical Society of Wisconsin, 1963. [Originally published in *Blue Book of the State of Wisconsin*, 1961.]

Libby, Orin Grant, *Significance of the Lead and Shot Trade in Early Wisconsin History*, Madison, 1895.

Linderman, Gerald F., *Embattled Courage: The Experience of Combat in the American Civil War*, New York, Free Press, 1987.

Long, E. B. and Barbara Long, *The Civil War Day by Day; An Almanac, 1861–1865*, Garden City, N.Y., Doubleday, 1971.

Love, William D., *Wisconsin in the War of the Rebellion*, Chicago, Church & Goodman, 1866.

McClellan, George B., *McClellan's Own Story*, Philadelphia, J. B. Lippincott & Co., 1887.

McPherson, James M., *Battle Cry of Freedom*, New York, Ballantine Books, 1989.

Mitchell, Reid. *Civil War Soldiers*, New York, Viking, 1988.

Nichols, Edward J., *Toward Gettysburg: A Biography of John F. Reynolds*, University Park, Pennsylvania State University Press, 1958.

Nolan, Alan T., *The Iron Brigade*, New York, Macmillan, 1961.

Otis, George H., *The Second Wisconsin Infantry*, with letters and recollections by other members of the regiment, ed. Alan D. Gaff, Dayton, Ohio, Morningside House, 1984. [Originally serialized in *The Milwaukee Sunday Telegraph* in 11 parts, July–December 1880.]

Quiner, E[dwin] B., *The Military History of Wisconsin*, Chicago, Clarke & Co., 1866.

Rogers, Earl M., ed., *Memoirs of Vernon County*, Madison, Western Historical Association, 1907.

Rood, H. W., *Company E and the Twelfth Wisconsin in the War for the Union*, Milwaukee, 1893.

Sears, Stephan W., *George B. McClellan: The Young Napoleon*, New York, Ticknor and Fields, 1988.

Shue, Richard S., *Morning at Willoughby Run: July 1, 1863*, Gettysburg, Pa., Thomas Publications, 1995.

Smith, Donald L., *The Twenty-fourth Michigan of the Iron Brigade*, Harrisburg, Pa., Stackpole Co., 1862.

Soldiers' and Citizens' Album of Biographical Record, 2 vols., Chicago, Grand Army Publishing Company, 1888, 1892.

Still, Bayrd, *Milwaukee, The History of a City*, Madison, State Historical Society of Wisconsin, 1948.

Stine, J. H., *History of the Army of the Potomac*, Philadelphia, J. B. Rogers Printing Co., 1892.

Swinton, William, *Campaigns of the Army of the Potomac*, New York, Charles B. Richardson, 1866.

Tucker, Glenn, *Hancock the Superb*, Indianapolis, Bobbs-Merrill, 1960.

War of the Rebellion, Official Records of the Union and Confederate Armies, Washington, D.C., United States Government Printing Office, 1889–1900.

War Papers Read before the Commandery of the State of Wisconsin, Military Order of the Loyal Legion of the United States, vols. 1 and 2, Milwaukee, 1896; vol. 3, Milwaukee, 1903.

Warner, Ezra J., *Generals in Blue: Lives of Union Commanders*, Baton Rouge, 1964.

Washburn, William H., "Jerome A. Watrous: The Civil War Years," manuscript, Madison, Wisconsin Veterans Museum.

Watrous, J[erome] A., *Richard Epps and Other Stories*, Milwaukee, 1906.

Webster, Dan, and Don Cameron, *Story of the First Wisconsin Battery*, Washington, D.C., 1907.

Whitehouse, Hugh L., ed., *Letters from the Iron Brigade: George W. Partridge, Jr., 1839–1863*, Indianapolis, Guild Press of Indiana, 1994.

Census and Numerical Records

Alphabetical List of Soldiers and Sailors of the Late War Residing in the State of Wisconsin, June 20, 1885, Madison, Secretary of State, 1886.

Busey, John W., and David G. Martin, *Regimental Strengths and Losses at Gettysburg,* Hightstown, N.J., Longstreet House, 1986.

Dyer, F. H., *A Compendium of the War of the Rebellion,* Des Moines, Iowa, 1908; New York, Thomas Yoseloff, 1953.

Fox, William F., *Regimental Losses in the American Civil War,* Albany, N.Y., Albany Publishing Co., 1889.

Roster of Wisconsin Volunteers, War of the Rebellion, 1861–1865, 2 vols., Madison, 1886.

Wisconsin Census Enumeration, 1895; Names of Ex-Soldiers and Sailors Residing in Wisconsin, June 20, 1895, Madison, Democrat Printing Co., 1896.

Wisconsin Census Enumeration, 1905; Names of Ex-Soldiers and Sailors Residing in Wisconsin, June 1, 1905, Madison, Democrat Printing Co., 1896.

Manuscripts and Records

Edward S. Bragg Papers, State Historical Society of Wisconsin.

Edwin A. Brown Papers, private collections.

John H. Cook Papers, State Historical Society of Wisconsin.

Rufus R. Dawes Papers, Newberry Public Library, Chicago.

Rufus R. Dawes Papers, State Historical Society of Wisconsin.

Descriptive Book, Sixth Wisconsin Infantry, U.S. National Archives and Records Service.

George W. Downing Papers, private collection.

Horace Emerson Papers, private collection.

George Fairfield Papers, State Historical Society of Wisconsin.

Andrew Gallup Papers, State Historical Society of Wisconsin.

John C. Hall Papers, Newberry Public Library, Chicago.

Morning Reports, Sixth Wisconsin Infantry, U.S. National Archives and Records Service.

Charles King Papers, Carroll College Library, Waukesha, Wis.

Rufus King Papers, Carroll College Library, Waukesha, Wis.

William Lindwurm Papers, Milwaukee County Historical Society.

Ludolph Longhenry Papers, private collection.

Julius Murray Papers, State Historical Society of Wisconsin.

National Guard, Adjutant General's Office, Regimental Descriptive Rolls, Sixth Infantry, State Historical Society of Wisconsin.

Order Book, First Brigade, First Division, First Army Corps, U.S. National Archives and Records Service.

Order Book, Sixth Wisconsin Infantry, U.S. National Archives and Records Service.

Levi Raymond Papers, private collection.

Earl M. Rogers Papers, Wisconsin Veterans Museum, Madison.

State Militia, Adjutant General's Office, Regimental Muster and Descriptive Rolls, Sixth Infantry, State Historical Society of Wisconsin.

Charles Walker diary, private collection.

Jerome A. Watrous Papers, State Historical Society of Wisconsin.

Cornelius Wheeler Papers, Milwaukee County Historical Society.

Chester A. Wyman Papers, private collection.

U.S. Pension Office, James P. Sullivan file, U.S. National Archives and Record Service.

Newspapers and Periodicals

Appleton Crescent, Appleton, Wis.
Appleton Motor, Appleton, Wis.
Baraboo Republic, Baraboo, Wis.
The Blackhat, Occasional Newsletter of the Sixth Wisconsin Volunteers, Milwaukee.
Blue and Gray Magazine, Columbus, Ohio.
Cashton Record, Cashton, Wis.
Chetek Alert, Chetek, Wis.
Chicago Chronicle.
Chilton Times, Chilton, Wis.
Christian Science Monitor, Boston.
Civil War Times Illustrated.
Columbus Republican, Columbus, Wis.
Gettysburg Magazine, Dayton, Ohio.
Green Bay Advocate, Green Bay, Wis.
La Crosse Chronicle, La Crosse, Wis.
La Crosse Republican and Leader, La Crosse, Wis.
Mauston Star, Mauston, Wis.
Milwaukee Free Press.
Milwaukee History, Milwaukee County Historical Society.
Milwaukee Sentinel.
Milwaukee Sunday Telegraph/Milwaukee Telegraph.
Missouri Republican, St. Louis.
The National Tribune, Washington, D.C.
Portage Register, Portage, Wis.
Prescott Journal, Prescott, Wis.
Sparta Herald, Sparta, Wis.
Vernon County Censor, Viroqua, Wis.
Virginia Country Civil War, Leesburg, Va.
Wisconsin Magazine of History, Madison, Wis.
Wisconsin Newspaper Volumes [clippings from various Civil War Wisconsin newspapers], State Historical Society of Wisconsin.

INDEX

Lance J. Herdegen is director of the Institute for Civil War Studies at Carroll College, Waukesha, Wisconsin. He previously was a reporter, editor, and executive for United Press International (UPI), and covered politics, civil rights, and a variety of events for the international wire service. Herdegen has written for many national publications and is co-author of *An Irishman in the Iron Brigade* and the award-winning *In the Bloody Railroad Cut at Gettysburg.* He is a member of the Civil War Round-table of Milwaukee and the Iron Brigade Association and a former member of the Wisconsin Humanities Council.